OXFORD WORLD'S CLASSICS

# THE ASPERN PAPERS

HENRY JAMES was born in New York in 1843 of ancestry both Irish and Scottish. He received a remarkably cosmopolitan education in New York, London, Paris, and Geneva, and entered law school at Harvard in 1862. After 1866, he lived mostly in Europe, at first writing critical articles, reviews, and short stories for American periodicals. He lived in London for more than twenty years, and in 1898 moved to Rye, where his later novels were written. Under the influence of an ardent sympathy for the British cause in the First World War, Henry James was in 1915 naturalized a British subject. He died in 1916.

In his early novels, which include *Roderick Hudson* (1875) and *The Portrait of a Lady* (1881), he was chiefly concerned with the impact of the older civilization of Europe upon American life. He analysed English character with extreme subtlety in such novels as *What Maisie Knew* (1897) and *The Awkward Age* (1899). In his last three great novels, *The Wings of the Dove* (1902), *The Ambassadors* (1903), and *The Golden Bowl* (1904), he returned to the 'international' theme of the contrast of American and European character.

ADRIAN POOLE is Reader in English and Comparative Literature at the University of Cambridge, and a Fellow of Trinity College, Cambridge. His publications include *Henry James* (Harvester New Readings, 1991), and several articles on James. He has also edited *What Maisie Knew* and *The American* for Oxford World's Classics.

D0191628

## OXFORD WORLD'S CLASSICS

*For over 100 years Oxford World's Classics have brought
readers closer to the world's great literature. Now with over 700
titles—from the 4,000-year-old myths of Mesopotamia to the
twentieth century's greatest novels—the series makes available
lesser-known as well as celebrated writing.*

*The pocket-sized hardbacks of the early years contained
introductions by Virginia Woolf, T. S. Eliot, Graham Greene,
and other literary figures which enriched the experience of reading.
Today the series is recognized for its fine scholarship and
reliability in texts that span world literature, drama and poetry,
religion, philosophy and politics. Each edition includes perceptive
commentary and essential background information to meet the
changing needs of readers.*

OXFORD WORLD'S CLASSICS

═══

HENRY JAMES

# The Aspern Papers
## and Other Stories

═══

*Edited with an Introduction and Notes by*
ADRIAN POOLE

OXFORD
UNIVERSITY PRESS

# OXFORD
UNIVERSITY PRESS

Great Clarendon Street, Oxford OX2 6DP

Oxford University Press is a department of the University of Oxford.
It furthers the University's objective of excellence in research, scholarship,
and education by publishing worldwide in

Oxford New York

Athens Auckland Bangkok Bogotá Buenos Aires Calcutta
Cape Town Chennai Dar es Salaam Delhi Florence Hong Kong Istanbul
Karachi Kuala Lumpur Madrid Melbourne Mexico City Mumbai
Nairobi Paris São Paulo Singapore Taipei Tokyo Toronto Warsaw

with associated companies in Berlin Ibadan

Oxford is a registered trade mark of Oxford University Press
in the UK and in certain other countries

Published in the United States
by Oxford University Press Inc., New York

Introduction, Notes on the texts, Further reading, Notes and list of Variant readings
© Adrian Poole 1983
Chronology © Leon Edel 1963

The moral rights of the author have been asserted

Database right Oxford University Press (maker)

'The Aspern Papers' first published 1888; published in the New York Edition 1908
'The Private Life' first published 1892; published in the New York Edition 1909
'The Middle Years' first published 1893; published in the New York Edition 1909
'The Death of the Lion' first published 1894; published in the New York Edition 1909
First published as a World's Classics paperback 1983
Reissued as an Oxford World's Classics paperback 2000

British Library Cataloguing in Publication Data

Data available

Library of Congress Cataloging in Publication Data
James, Henry, 1843–1916.
The Aspern papers and other stories.  (Oxford world's classics)
Bibliography: p. xxii
Contents: The Aspoern papers  The private life
The middle years  The death of the lion.
I. Poole, Adrian, 1934–  .  II. Title.
PS2112.P6  1983  823'.83  4279

ISBN–13: 978–0–19–283616–8

Printed in Great Britain by
Clays Ltd, St Ives plc

# CONTENTS

# ACKNOWLEDGEMENTS

I WOULD like to acknowledge a debt to Philip Horne's valuable work on James's revisions for the New York Edition, and also to thank both Philip Horne and Robin Kirkpatrick for their helpful suggestions over some of the notes.

Acknowledgement is also due to Messrs Charles Scribner's Sons for the use of the New York Edition texts of Henry James's tales, and his Prefaces.

# INTRODUCTION

## I

WRITING is a risky business. The most confidentially addressed words can be read by the wrong reader, the most scrupulously phrased words misread by the right reader. Of course only writing that tries to be private brings into question such a blunt distinction between right and wrong readers. People who try to make writing their living cannot afford to be too choosy about their readers. Writing is also a rewarding business.

Henry James was intrigued by the risks and rewards of writing and being a writer. What exactly do men and women write for? What kinds of profit do they have in mind and what does it cost them? Reviewing Balzac's *Letters*, James was dismayed by the revelation of that writer's 'consuming money-hunger'. But no less than Balzac or Dickens did James himself as a professional writer have to treat his own 'extraordinary imaginative force as a matter of business'. Freud once infamously observed that artists, like other men, desire to win 'honour, power, wealth, fame and the love of women'; it is just that they go about it, or don't go about it, in their own perverse way. James had a lofty and austere idea of what it might mean to earn the perverse title of 'artist', of what such a commitment might entail in the way of goods given up. But he was never so contemptuous of those worldly goods or his worldly fellows that he did not enjoy the comically promiscuous hospitality with which the term 'writer' could stretch to include Masters and scribblers, Bards and journalists, neglected geniuses and fêted best-sellers, the motley array of men and women who live all heterogeneously by words or make them their pastime.

> As hounds and greyhounds, mungrels, spaniels, curs,
> Shoughs, water-rugs, and demi-wolves are clept
> All by the name of dogs . . .

The four stories collected here are all concerned with writers and writing, and they belong to the critical phase in James's career when he was most urgently reviewing and experimenting with the directions and forms his own artistic energies should take. Not long before the serialisation of 'The Aspern Papers' in the spring of 1888, James confided to his friend W. D. Howells that he had 'entered upon evil days – but this is for your most private ear'. The failure of his last two novels, *The Bostonians* and *The Princess Casamassima* (both 1888), had 'reduced the desire, and the demand, for my productions to zero'. Despite a brave vow that 'some day all my buried prose will kick off its various tombstones at once', his next full-length novel and last for several years, *The Tragic Muse* (1890), seemed to suffer another premature interment; and for five years James devoted himself to the theatre, years which culminated in the deeply wounding and in James's eyes catastrophic first night of his play *Guy Domville* on 5 January 1895.

But there is a quite different way of looking at these critical years. For they are also the years in which, beginning with 'The Aspern Papers' in 1888 and by no means concluding in 1895, James proclaimed his mastery of the forms of short fiction, in such tales as 'The Liar', 'A London Life', 'The Lesson of the Master', 'The Pupil', and the three other tales collected here. Many of the tales of these years are concerned with the life of the artist in general and the writer in particular. They are united by some common preoccupations, above all the ironies of the traffic between the private and public aspects of writing. Writing and reading are in themselves usually solitary and in a sense 'private' activities, but the material production and publication of an object called a book introduces into public circulation the figure of an 'author' who may be bewildered by the lack of correspondence between the way he sees himself and what he does and the way readers do. He enjoys the advantages and liabilities of a kind of ghostly or spectral existence – though of course an author who is literally dead simplifies matters, at least for himself. The author who has not finished with the living is both dangerous and vulnerable. 'You must be as dead as you can', the young admirer in 'The Death of the Lion' perversely urges the ailing author.

But what is a simplification for one person may be a complication for someone else, and these stories are as interested in the people who come into various sorts of contact with fleshly and spectral authors and their works as they are in the writers themselves. In a later story, 'The Birthplace' (1903), James unravels a beautifully extended and pointed joke about the dilemmas of a man committed to administering the sacred shrine of England's supreme poet, a writer too unnameably awesome to be referred to as other than 'He'. 'He' is blessedly safe from the slings and arrows of outrageous tourists and their insatiable hunger for the most trivially 'personal' facts. Morris Gedge, the lugubriously conscientious curator, is increasingly impressed by the insubstantiality of the 'facts', and quietly crucified by the demands of fuelling a legend in which he has an honourably diminishing faith. James was in at the monstrous birth of the modern tourist industry, and he wittily and scornfully records the transformation of art into tourist resort, where posters and T-shirts distract the passionless pilgrim from the ardours of genuine worship. The business of art carries risks and rewards for more than the artist.

Some of the risks and rewards of writing are to do with its peculiarly unstable status as property. Whatever the immaterial meanings and values incorporated in words, writing by definition takes a material form. When he came to revise 'The Aspern Papers' for the New York Edition (1907–9), James enjoyed multiplying the ways in which the narrator refers to the papers as 'material', 'documents', 'literary remains', 'relics and tokens', 'tangible objects', 'mementoes', 'spoils' and so on. This helps call attention to the fact that he never actually sees or touches these things (indeed, some readers have gone so far as to doubt their existence, but this requires an improbably ruthless scepticism); but it also and more importantly stresses that the narrator, let alone the reader, never knows exactly what these things are nor what is in them. The narrator may have his suspicions and desires, but it is sufficient for him to believe in the fact of their existence to justify his plot to turn them into public property. But when exactly and in what sense are words public property? And how and when do they become so? There is of course business for lawyers in these matters, and it is of some interest that the years in which James was writing these stories are those in which the modern laws and agreements governing international copyright got effectively settled. The business of writing was being transformed by the advances of technology and the extensions of markets into a massively organised and global industry. James attended closely to the consequences of an industry so indiscriminately dedicated to publicity and exhibition and celebrification, and its effects on the moral, emotional and aesthetic lives of writers and readers. Needless to say, the attendant risks and rewards were for James more than crudely financial.

The four stories collected here all feature writers and readers, but it is noticeable that the writers are either dead or dying or spectral, and that while the readers seem by comparison to flourish, they do not necessarily do so by virtue of reading. To call them 'readers' in fact begs a question, for it is made ludicrously clear in 'The Death of the Lion' that such people do not need actually to *read* a single word to make some sort of profit out of an author and his works. There is an outrageous comedy, James suggests, in the way people who seem to come into intimate contact with an author and his works can get away without actually reading a line for themselves (editors, reviewers, literary critics), and yet succeed in making money or reputations or hay out of the material fact of someone else's writing. Since reading is usually as solitary and private an act as writing, the opportunities are rife for deceit and subterfuge ('I recently read Proust for the seventh time'), for capitalising on the fact that such words can rarely be proved or disproved ('Oh no you didn't'), but only believed or disbelieved.

James was extremely sensitive to the kinds of trust involved in the acts of writing and reading. To write means if not to be read then certainly to be readable. It commits a writer to a confidence but it also chains him to an anxiety about the believability and worth and use of his words. Before the possibility of these words falling into the wrong hands, of the consequent disbelief, disprizing and abuse to which they are vulnerable, he is helpless. In these stories, the act of writing is itself necessarily a secret, a mystery. And indeed the act of reading, of a real reading that would be as strenuous and creative and responsible as the act of writing, that too is something which necessarily cannot be represented in writing; it can only be *done*. These stories of James's are then only by ironic indirection concerned with the acts of writing and reading. Instead they represent the parodies and substitutes and alternatives that seek to pass for such an intimate and demanding intercourse. We may note how common in these tales is the image of a threshold. Behind the door or window or curtain is the solitary and creative, the 'private' life and work of the writer. At the doorway there cluster and squabble the wardens, guardians, curators, patrons, tourists, disciples, spokesmen, reporters. These tales might be said to represent the drama at his threshold which the writer overhears. Or to look at it from the other side of the threshold – the things you can do with writing, apart from reading it.

## II

James wrote 'The Aspern Papers' in the early summer of 1887 in a villa on Bellosguardo overlooking Florence and tenanted by an American friend, Constance Fenimore Woolson. The delicate importunity of her affection for James may have contributed something to the relationship in the tale between the narrator and Miss Tina. James got the clue for his story earlier that year from an anecdote about a Boston sea-captain with a passion for Shelley, who discovered that 'Claire' Clairmont, once Byron's mistress and mother of his daughter Allegra, was unexpectedly still alive and living in Florence with a younger niece. He laid siege to them in the hope of getting his hands on some letters of Shelley's and Byron's, and when the old lady died, he approached the niece, in James's words, 'on the subject of his desires'. She met him on the subject of her own and told him that he could have them if she could have him. In the Preface to the New York Edition, James looks back at the other most evident source of inspiration behind the tale, the beloved Venice which had harboured the fond tourist on one of his many sojourns between the hearing of the anecdote and the writing of the tale.

But at least initially it was the attraction in the anecdote of a 'picture' and 'a plot' that James recorded in his Notebooks.

the picture of the two faded, queer, poor and discredited old English women – living on into a strange generation, in their musty corner of a foreign town – with these illustrious letters their most precious possession. Then the plot of the Shelley fanatic – his watchings and waitings – the way he *couvers* the treasure.

(*The Notebooks of Henry James*, OUP, 1947, p. 72)

It is typical of James to annex a French word for shades of meaning that cannot be so promptly delivered in English. 'Couver' here has the sense of 'to gaze intently or longingly' at something. It might reasonably be rendered as 'covet' in English, except that this is too limp a word for the broodily possessive impulse which couver implies. There is a fixity and single-mindedness of intent in the French word, which in other contexts is used of the brooding and hatching of hens' eggs and human plots. The Shelley fanatic broods over the treasure, the women's nest-egg, but he broods in frustrated longing and all he can hatch is a plot.

Who is this nameless man who wants to expose Jeffrey Aspern to the light and instead exposes himself? 'For he really would give almost anything.' James had opened his review of Balzac's Letters by saying that a reader's first feeling is that 'he has almost done wrong to read them', and that 'He feels as one who has broken open a cabinet or rummaged an old desk.' But in James's tale the fanatic who 'would give almost anything' never does succeed in breaking anything open or reading the papers. What he does succeed in giving, however, is the story of his failure. He never gets to read the Aspern papers, but he succeeds in writing 'The Aspern Papers'; that is all we and he see of them, but it is enough to make him a kind of (second-best) artist. Towards the end of Chapter IV he recounts the theories which he and his fellow-critic have entertained about Aspern and Juliana, and he says that he 'hatched a little romance'. And it is in this vital and revealing chapter that he confesses most directly to his thoughts and feelings about Jeffrey Aspern, to a sense of 'mystic companionship' and 'moral fraternity'. These and other such confidences suggest a man sufficiently spurred by but insufficiently possessed of his own imaginative powers that he must needs grasp for a source of inspiration outside himself.

He identifies this source as the poet Aspern, but it is important that access to it should take two quite different forms. One is 'the papers', the precious treasure jealously guarded by the 'witch' (or 'witches'), so farcically incompatible with the divinity he is simultaneously forced to acknowledge in the Juliana whom Aspern himself deified. But there is a less direct and less forbidding route to Aspern and the creative source that he represents; it is through the magical form and spirit of Venice itself. Wayne C. Booth has argued, in *The Rhetoric of Fiction* (1961), that the attention which James's Preface pays to the task of evoking through Venice the sense of 'a palpable imaginable *visitable* past' implies a motive that is radically at odds with the plot of the Shelley fanatic, and that the first-person narrator is incapable of fulfilling both functions as plotter and poet. 'This can scarcely be considered as the same person at all,' he says at one point. Well, quite: the identity of this subtly irresolute narrator is far from certain, and he is indeed radically at odds with himself, caught between the fluctuating compulsions to represent a 'poetic' picture and to get on with his 'prosaic' plot.

It is worth observing how frequently words such as 'linger' and 'hesitate' occur in the story. There are different kinds of lingering; there is much room in the word 'almost'. The reader may be interested to consult and compare some of the ways in which James wrote elsewhere about Venice, in particular the three opening chapters of *Italian Hours* (1909), which collect essays usefully written at ten-year intervals (though reprinted in the order 1882, 1892, 1872). In 1882 James wrote that only 'lingering' could reveal the beauties of Venice: 'You desire to embrace it, to caress it; and finally a soft sense of possession grows up and your visit becomes a perpetual love-affair.' The 1892 essay is strikingly more sombre in tone as it laments the flight of the spirit of the past from the brash and greasy clutch of modern tourism. The kind of lingering love in which the 1882 essay confided is now in this 'vast mausoleum' increasingly difficult to entertain.

The 'Aspern' narrator is certainly capable of lingering but less certainly capable of loving. One apparent certainty disappears between the 1888 version and the later New York text. The 1888 narrator describes himself as 'loving' Aspern, but his cooler 1908 avatar speaks only of 'prizing' him. In the bare and spare palazzo that houses the treasure he is after, there seems little encouragement to 'a soft sense of possession'; there may be more in the garden, or beyond and around in Venice's unique ambience – see, he imagines Aspern appealing, 'how the sky and the sea and the rosy air and the marble of the palaces all shimmer and melt together'. But the grip of his plot continually draws his anxious eyes to obstacles and barriers that promise and forbid – walls, doors, windows, the 'horrible green shade', the locked drawer. Money and flowers pass freely across the barriers that separate him from his goal, and there is much reference throughout the tale to gifts and presents and exchanges. But perhaps the only things that are truly and freely given are the 'small presents' the Bordereau women are once supposed to have made, and the glass beads which his servant's girl-friend casually leaves behind her. For the three main characters all presents are now past and everything is to be paid for. 'The interest would be in some price that the man has to pay ...'. What finally stands between him and the papers is Miss Tina. The price – what she asks for them – is love.

The narrator cannot discover or yield to the soft sense of possession; he cannot give up his hunt for love. At one point he says of the two women that he had never met 'so stiff a policy of seclusion' (or in the earlier 1888 text, 'such a violent *parti pris* of seclusion'); 'it was like hunted creatures feigning death'. The image usefully connects with terms which James employed elsewhere to debate the proprieties of making public writing ostensibly private. Of the publication of Flaubert's correspondence he wrote in 1893 that it brought up 'with singular intensity, the whole question of the rights and duties, the decencies and discretions of the insurmountable desire to *know*' (*Selected Literary Criticism*, ed. M. Shapira, 1963, p. 139). A few years later, writing of the publication of George Sand's letters to Alfred de Musset, he produced his most extendedly eloquent representation of what he characterised as 'the greatest of all literary quarrels ... the eternal dispute between the public and the private, between curiosity and delicacy'.

The reporter and the reported have duly and equally to understand that they carry their life in their hands. These are secrets for privacy and silence; let them only be cultivated on the part of the hunted creature with even half the method with which the love of sport – or call it the historic sense – is cultivated on the part of the investigator. They have been left too much to the natural, the instinctive man; but they will be twice as effective after it begins to be observed that they may take their place among the triumphs of civilization. Then at last the game will be fair and the two forces face to face; it will be 'pull devil, pull tailor', and the hardest pull will doubtless provide the happiest result. Then the cunning of the inquirer, envenomed with resistance, will exceed in subtlety and ferocity anything we to-day conceive, and the pale fore-warned victim, with every track covered, every paper burnt and every letter unanswered, will, in the tower of art, the invulnerable granite, stand, without a sally, the siege of all the years.

(*Selected Literary Criticism*, p. 160)

That was one, extraordinary way of imagining the drama. Another was to imagine the anonymous writer of 'The Aspern Papers', the rueful, self-excusing tale of a man who becomes the victim of his own inquiry.

## III

The other three stories collected here illustrate the variety of James's interest in the dilemmas that bring writers and readers together – and keep them apart. Writing makes a difference between a writer and a reader, and in so far as writing also helps them to make their differences up, the understandings and misunderstandings they reach are bound to be blind. There is wry comedy in the way the enthusiastic young reader of 'The Middle Years' unknowingly accosts his admired author as a fellow-reader; there are some more boisterous jokes in 'The Death of the Lion' about the unlikely physical shapes concealed behind the pen-names of 'Guy Walsingham' and 'Dora Forbes'. The benign and withering duplicities in this situation inform all of James's stories of writers and writing; his writers are necessarily two-faced.

'Duplicity' and 'duplication' are important words in the high-spirited comedy of 'The Private Life', the 'rank fantasy' as James called it, inspired by the contrasting images of two eminent Victorians, the painter Lord Leighton and the poet Robert Browning. James found Leighton a supreme type of the artist as social celebrity. On watching Leighton preside over a Royal Academy prize-giving, James wrote: 'Leighton *is* wonderful for such an occasion as that – he *represents* admirably –...'. Elsewhere, on his way to the pantomime with Leighton and perhaps influenced by the occasion, James mischievously called him 'the urbane, the curly, the agreeably artificial'. Leighton turned into the Lord Mellifont of the tale who is all 'representation', though to the too closely inquiring eyes of the narrator and his ally Blanche Adney, what it is that he represents turns out to be only what is expected of him.

The other and contrasting figure of the poet Clare Vawdrey was inspired by Browning, whom on first meeting in London James had described as 'personally, no more like Paracelsus than I to Hercules, but . . . a great gossip and a very "sympathetic" easy creature'. James's first acquaintance with poets receives some fine attention in the third volume of his unfinished autobiography, confusingly but interestingly entitled *The Middle Years*. He wrote: 'The fond prefigurements of youthful piety are predestined more often than not, I think, experience interfering, to strange and violent shocks . . .' (*Autobiography*, ed. F. W. Dupee, 1956, p. 586). It was however Tennyson rather than Browning who administered a 'violent shock' to the eager young James, with 'the full, the monstrous demonstration that Tennyson was not Tennysonian' (ibid. 587); it was, in a delightful phrase, 'like a rap on the knuckles of a sweet superstition'. The Browning he met in the flesh also proved quite unlike the author of *Men and Women* he so much admired, but his disappointment seems always to have been tempered by a sense of a saving awkwardness in Browning, or 'restlessness' as he elsewhere put it – from which it was necessarily the nature of an official Bard such as Tennyson to be conspicuously exempt. The essay he wrote on Browning's burial in Westminster Abbey (reprinted in *English Hours*, 1905) is a moving and perceptive and revealing tribute to an artist who for James successfully claimed the paradoxical role of a modern classic. He had won the public prestige of a classic, while enviably and unrepentantly remaining 'a tremendous and incomparable modern'.

The narrator of 'The Private Life' is a more mildly inquisitive predator on other people's secrets than his nameless-sake in 'The Aspern Papers'. The tale is nicely orchestrated by the device of making the narrator share the role of inquirer with the charming and seductive actress Blanche Adney. As there are two mysteries to be cracked, Lord Mellifont's and Clare Vawdrey's, it seems reasonable to employ two detectives. But the narrator turns out to be another loser. His partner Blanche Adney shows a more vivid determination, as she crudely puts it, to 'get at the one who does it', and succeeds in cornering the 'real'

Vawdrey, while the hapless narrator is like his 'Aspern' confrère caught on the brink of exposing Lord Mellifont by a woman guarding the threshold. Lady Mellifont maintains her hold, such as it is, over her husband's secret, and while Blanche is ecstatically closeted with the 'private' Vawdrey, the narrator finds himself out in the cold in a hut on the hillside, dolefully paired off with the boringly 'public' Vawdrey. The ironic encouragement to dramatic, romantic and erotic climax provided by an Alpine thunderstorm only adds insult to injury.

The cliff and the sea, the late and precious meeting of old and young lend 'The Middle Years' by contrast a grave and tender late-Shakespearean tone. James noted the idea of 'The old artist, or man of letters, who, at the end, feels a kind of anguish of desire for a respite, a prolongation – another period of life to do the *real* thing that he has in him – . . .' (*Notebooks*, p. 121). In the tale the dying writer Dencombe finds this anguish assuaged by the reassurances of a young admirer, Doctor Hugh, who is close to being the ideally selfless and sympathetic 'reader' all his writers are in search of. It is noticeable that in this tale as in 'The Aspern Papers', the relationship between a writer and a reader is threatened by the intervening figures of two women, in this case the Countess and her younger companion Miss Vernham. Here however it is not the writer over whom they mount guard but his mate, the ideal reader. Doctor Hugh cheerfully pays the price of renouncing the worldly temptations the women offer, to prove himself the worthy auditor of the writer's magnificent and moving death-bed speech: 'We work in the dark – we do what we can – we give what we have. Our doubt is our passion and our passion is our task. The rest is the madness of art.'

There is a later story of James's, 'The Great Good Place' (1900), which can profitably be read in close conjunction with 'The Private Life' and 'The Middle Years'. It is a fable about self-division and healing, and it shares with 'The Middle Years' the imagery of water and revival and death. One day the successful writer George Dane finds himself so overwhelmed by the absurd importunities of the social world (more women), that he gratefully accepts the offer of a young admirer to act as his temporary deputy, his front-man. Meanwhile he escapes to 'The Great Good Place', an asylum that is more a state of mind than a place, but is something of a cross between monastery, health-farm and country-club. The balm of this spiritual spa revives the 'inner life', 'and it was the inner life, for people of his generation, victims of the modern madness, mere maniacal extension and motion, that was returning health.' When Dane eventually comes round to the hand-clasp of his servant and the turned back of his young deputy, he is blessed with the sense that the young man is also the good Brother he met in the apparently 'other' world of 'The Great Good Place'. He realises, in a memorable sentence, that 'Everyone was a little someone else.' The self and the world which divided in two have been healed by the discovery of a magical place where other selves can meet up.

In both 'The Middle Years' and 'The Death of the Lion' the writers die in the arms, as it were, of a passionate young disciple. In 'The Death of the Lion' this is some consolation for the writer Neil Paraday, marooned as he is in a country-house that is definitely not a great good place. It is run by a Mrs Weeks Wimbush, 'wife of the boundless brewer and proprietress of the universal menagerie' (her name, like most of the names in the tale, is pointedly satirical, combining both 'whim' and 'ambush'). The streak of savagery in the tone of the tale derives from James's original note about the grotesque irony of a distinguished writer 'in this age of advertisement and newspaperism' whose work no one seems actually to read. 'They must *kill him, hein?* – kill him with the very fury of their selfish exploitation, and then not really have any idea of what they killed him for' (*Notebooks*, p. 148).

But despite the acerbity of the humour surrounding Mrs Weeks Wimbush, the rival novelists 'Guy Walsingham' and 'Dora Forbes', the journalist Mr Morrow and the editor Mr Pinhorn, the tale is a good deal more buoyant than James's original note might suggest. This is partly the effect of putting the story into the pen of another young and nameless aspirant to literary prestige, who tries to alleviate the sense of his own anonymity by wresting some identity from a more successful author. Like the narrator of 'The Aspern Papers', this young acolyte is very much a self-appointed representative. He clutches at the sense of being in 'close correspondence' with the great man, and quickly establishes himself as guardian of the threshold. But he is not particularly successful in this role. He can fend off Mr Morrow but he is powerless before the might of Mrs Weeks Wimbush, of whose mindless patronage the 'Lion' is a more hypnotised but also more amused victim than the young man would wish. He is however compensated for his failures by being possessed of a loyal ally in the shape of the charmingly suggestible Fanny Hurter. She gives a new twist to the role of the younger woman in the pattern sketched by 'The Aspern Papers' and 'The Middle Years'. In those tales, the male disciple had to combat a female duo, of older and younger women. But here, although the narrator is still jousting with the older woman Mrs Weeks Wimbush (who herself has a powerful ally in the Princess), he has managed to secure the younger woman for himself and his cause. The deathbed scene in this tale is markedly less painful than in 'The Middle Years'. For although the writer's precious manuscript is lost, it gives the narrator a purpose in life, the pursuit of this 'lost treasure'. He is more fortunate than the 'Aspern' narrator, being blest in his mission with the writer's approval and the companionship of 'a devoted associate'. He has not done too badly.

These four tales, then, feature in wonderfully varied and intelligent ways some of the kinds of give and take that occur between writers and readers. As the tales wittily and sadly suggest, 'reader' is an optimistic term; there are so many cheaper ways of getting something out of writing than the arduous and inward act such a word should imply. Such afterlife as a writer achieves through his writing is out of his hands, and it will depend as much on what readers will give as on what they will take. Writing hovers between past and future. Something has been done and it is there in words. It lies like buried, human treasure and what others may do with it is anyone's business. James's own writing invites the reader to mind his own business, whatever form it takes of exhumation, salvage or redemption.

ADRIAN POOLE

# NOTE ON THE TEXTS

LIKE almost all of James's 112 tales, these four were first published in magazines and soon afterwards in book form. All four were among the 55 tales revised for inclusion in the 'definitive' New York Edition of 1907–9, and these are the versions reprinted here. In the present edition spaced contractions have been normalised; single quotation marks are substituted for double, and they are positioned according to English conventions instead of American.

'The Aspern Papers' first appeared in the *Atlantic Monthly*, March–May 1888. James had initially suggested to the editor that his tale, which he assured him was 'brilliant, and of a thrilling interest', should appear in two parts, and that it would 'suffer grave injury from being cut otherwise'. But in the event it was published in three parts, of roughly equal length: chapters I–IV (March), chapters V–VII (April), chapters VIII–IX (May). It was then published in September 1888 by Macmillan and Co. in London and New York as a two-volume set entitled *The Aspern Papers*, with the title-story occupying vol. I, and 'Louisa Pallant' and 'The Modern Warning' (originally 'Two Countries') vol. II. It was revised for inclusion in vol. XII of the New York Edition, 1908, heading that volume and accompanied by 'The Turn of the Screw', 'The Liar' and 'The Two Faces'.

'The Private Life' was first published in the *Atlantic Monthly*, April 1892, and then published in book form in *The Private Life* in June 1893 by Osgood, McIlvaine and Co. in the UK, and in August 1893 by Harper and Bros. in the USA. The English edition was in one volume and the American in a two-volume set, but in both cases the accompanying tales were 'The Wheel of Time', 'Lord Beaupré', 'The Visits', 'Collaboration' and 'Owen Wingrave'. 'The Private Life' was revised for vol. XVII of the New York Edition, 1909, which was headed by 'The Altar of the Dead' and included 'The Beast in the Jungle', 'The Birthplace', 'The Private Life', 'Owen Wingrave', 'The Friends of the Friends', 'Sir Edmund Orme', 'The Real Right Thing', 'The Jolly Corner' and 'Julia Bride'.

'The Middle Years' was the sole new tale of James's to appear in his fiftieth year, 1893, in the May issue of *Scribner's Magazine*. It was first published in book form in the grimly entitled *Terminations* in May 1895 by Heinemann in London and June 1895 by Harper and

Bros. in New York. The volume also included 'The Death of the Lion', 'The Coxon Fund' and 'The Altar of the Dead'. The tale was revised for inclusion in vol. XVI of the New York Edition, 1909, of which the contents were 'The Author of Beltraffio', 'The Middle Years', 'Greville Fane', 'Broken Wings', 'The Tree of Knowledge', 'The Abasement of the Northmores', 'The Great Good Place', 'Four Meetings', 'Paste', 'Europe', 'Miss Gunton of Poughkeepsie' and 'Fordham Castle'.

'The Death of the Lion' was the first of three contributions which James made to Henry Harland's *Yellow Book*, the others being 'The Coxon Fund' and 'The Next Time'. James's tale ushered in the first issue in April 1894; James felt it necessary to say in a letter to his elder brother William that although the tale 'appears to have had, for a thing of mine, an unusual success, I hate too much the horrid aspect and company of the whole publication'. It was published along with 'The Middle Years' in *Terminations* in 1895, and revised for vol. XV of the New York Edition, 1909, the volume most pointedly devoted to tales of the literary life and consisting of 'The Lesson of the Master', 'The Death of the Lion', 'The Next Time', 'The Figure in the Carpet' and 'The Coxon Fund'.

# FURTHER READING

### PRIMARY WORKS

SINCE everything that James wrote is concerned in some form or other with the nature and functions of the imagination in the lives of individuals and cultures, his tales about writers, writing and the literary life form a particularly pointed but very far from isolated category in his work as a whole. The following suggestions for further reading are therefore restricted to those writings of James's that centre themselves explicitly on the activities of and complications surrounding writers and other artists. (There are many representatives of the fine arts in James and some of the theatre, but relatively few musicians; Vincent Adney in 'The Private Life' is one of them.)

### i. *Novels*

*Roderick Hudson* (1875). Revised, New York Edition, vol. I.
*The Reverberator* (1888). Revised, New York Editon, vol. XIII.
*The Tragic Muse* (1890). Revised, New York Edition, vol. VII.

### ii. *Tales*

The dates given are those of first publication, which was usually though not always in magazine form. The version of the tales first published in book form may be found in *The Complete Tales of Henry James*, 12 vols., ed. Leon Edel, London: Rupert Hart-Davies, 1962–4; and the earliest serialised versions are being reprinted in *The Tales of Henry James*, ed. Maqbool Aziz, Oxford: Oxford University Press, 1973 –. The revised versions of those tales included in the New York Edition may be found in the relevant volumes as indicated.

'The Madonna of the Future' (1873). Edel, vol. III; N.Y., vol. XIII.
'The Author of Beltraffio' (1884). Edel, vol. V; N.Y., vol. XVL.
'The Liar' (1888). Edel, vol. VI; N. Y., vol. XII.
'The Lesson of the Master' (1888). Edel, vol. VII; N. Y., vol. XV.

'Nona Vincent' (1892). Edel, vol. VIII.

'The Real Thing' (1892). Edel, vol. VIII; N. Y., vol. XVIII.

'Jersey Villas' (1892), later 'Sir Dominick Ferrand'. Edel, vol. VIII.

'Greville Fane' (1892). Edel, vol. VIII; N. Y., vol. XVI.

'The Coxon Fund' (1894). Edel, vol. IX; N. Y., vol XV.

'The Next Time' (1895). Edel, vol. IX; N. Y., vol. XV.

'The Figure in the Carpet' (1896). Edel, vol. IX; N. Y., vol. XV.

'John Delavoy' (1898). Edel, vol. IX.

'The Real Right Thing' (1899). Edel, vol. X; N. Y., vol. XVII.

'The Great Good Place' (1900). Edel, vol. XI; N. Y., vol. XVL.

'The Tree of Knowledge' (1900). Edel, vol. XI; N. Y., vol. XVI.

'The Abasement of the Northmores' (1900). Edel, vol. XI; N. Y., vol. XVI.

'Broken Wings' (1900). Edel, vol. XI; N. Y., vol. VXI.

'The Birthplace' (1903). Edel, vol. XI; N. Y., vol. XVIL.

### iii. *Other Writings*

*Italian Hours*, 1909; repr. New York; Grove Press, 1959, 1979, chs. 1–5.

*Autobiography*, ed. Frederick W. Dupee, London: W. H. Allen, 1956. This comprises *A Small Boy and Others* (1913), *Notes of a Son and Brother* (1914), and *The Middle Years* (1917).

*The Complete Notebooks of Henry James*, ed. Leon Edel and Lyall H. Powers, Oxford and New York: Oxford University Press, 1987.

*Henry James: Literary Criticism*, 2 vols., ed. Leon Edel with the assistance of Mark Wilson, Cambridge and New York: The Library of America, 1984.

*Henry James Letters*, 4 vols., ed. Leon Edel, vols. 1–3, London: Macmillan, 1974–81; vol. 4, Cambridge, Mass. and London: Harvard University Press, 1984.

### SECONDARY WORKS

### i. *Biography*

Edel, Leon, *The Life of Henry James*, 2 vols., London: Peregrine Books, 1977. see especially, vol. I, Book Seven: 'A London Life 1883–9', and vol. II, Book One: 'The Dramatic Years 1890–95'.

Kaplan, Fred, *Henry James: The Imagination of Genius*, London, Sydney, Auckland: Hodder & Stoughton, 1992.

ii. *Criticism*

Baskett, Sam S., 'The Sense of the Present in *The Aspern Papers*', *Papers of the Michigan Academy of Science, Arts and Letters*, XLIV (1959), 381–8.

Beebe, Maurice, 'The Turned Back of Henry James', *South Atlantic Quarterly* (1954); repr. in *Henry James: Modern Judgments*, ed. Tony Turner, London: Macmillan, 1968.

Bell, Millicent, *Meaning in Henry James*, Cambridge, Mass., and London: Harvard University Press, 1991. See ch. 6, '"The Aspern Papers": The Unvisitable Past'.

Booth, Wayne C., *The Rhetoric of Fiction*, Chicago: University of Chicago Press, 1961. See Part III: 'Impersonal Narration', chs. XI and XII.

Holland, Laurence Bedwell, *The Expense of Vision: Essays on the Craft of Henry James*, Princeton: Princeton University Press, 1964. See ch. 3, part 2.

Horne, Philip, *Henry James and Revision: The New York Edition*, Oxford: Clarendon Press, 1990. See ch. 8, 'The Values of *The Aspern Papers*'.

Kappeler, Susanne, *Writing and Reading in Henry James*, London: Macmillan, 1980. See Part I, 'Analysis of Narrative (on 'The Aspern Papers'), and Part II: 'The Guild of Artists and Men of Letters'.

Rivkin, Julie, 'Speaking with the Dead: Ethics and Representation in "The Aspern Papers"', *Henry James Review*, 10.2 (Spring 1989), 135–41.

Rowe, John Carlos, *The Theoretical Dimensions of Henry James*, Madison, Wisconsin and London, 1984. See ch. 3, 'Feminist Issues: Women, Power, and Rebellion in *The Bostonians*, *The Spoils of Poynton*, and *The Aspern Papers*'.

Segal, Ora, *The Lucid Reflector: The Observer in Henry James' Fiction*, New Haven and London: Yale University Press, 1969. See ch. 5, 'The Aspern Papers', and ch. 7, 'Tales of the Literary Life'.

Stein, William Bysshe, '*The Aspern Papers*: A Comedy of Masks', *Nineteenth-Century Fiction*, XIV (Sept. 1959), 172–8.

Tanner, Tony, *Venice Desired*, Oxford and Cambridge, Mass.: Blackwell, 1992. See ch. 4, '*Henry James*: Perpetual Architecture, perpetual fluidity'.

Tintner, Adeline, *Henry James and the Lust of the Eyes: Thirteen Artists in His Work*, Baton Rouge and London: Louisiana State University Press, 1993. See ch. 6 'Lord Leighton and His Paintings in "The Private Life"', and ch. 11, 'Rococo Venice and Longhi'.

Vaid, Krishna Baldev, *Technique in the Tales of Henry James*, Cambridge, Mass.: Harvard University Press, 1964.

# CHRONOLOGY OF HENRY JAMES

## COMPILED BY LEON EDEL

| | |
|---|---|
| 1843 | Born 15 April at No. 21 Washington Place, New York City. |
| 1843–4 | Taken abroad by parents to Paris and London: period of residence at Windsor. |
| 1845–55 | Childhood in Albany and New York. |
| 1855–8 | Attends schools in Geneva, London, Paris and Boulogne-sur-mer and is privately tutored. |
| 1858 | James family settles in Newport, Rhode Island. |
| 1859 | At scientific school in Geneva. Studies German in Bonn. |
| 1860 | At school in Newport. Receives back injury on eve of Civil War while serving as volunteer fireman. Studies art briefly. Friendship with John La Farge. |
| 1862–3 | Spends term in Harvard Law School. |
| 1864 | Family settles in Boston and then in Cambridge. Early anonymous story and unsigned reviews published. |
| 1865 | First signed story published in *Atlantic Monthly*. |
| 1869–70 | Travels in England, France and Italy. Death of his beloved cousin Minny Temple. |
| 1870 | Back in Cambridge, publishes first novel in *Atlantic, Watch and Ward*. |
| 1872–4 | Travels with sister Alice and aunt in Europe; writes impressionistic travel sketches for the *Nation*. Spends autumn in Paris and goes to Italy to write first large novel. |
| 1874–5 | On completion of *Roderick Hudson* tests New York City as residence; writes much literary journalism for *Nation*. First three books published: *Transatlantic Sketches*, *A Passionate Pilgrim* (tales) and *Roderick Hudson*. |
| 1875–6 | Goes to live in Paris. Meets Ivan Turgenev and through him Flaubert, Zola, Daudet, Maupassant and Edmond de Goncourt. Writes *The American*. |
| 1876–7 | Moves to London and settles in 3 Bolton Street, Piccadilly. Revisits Paris, Florence, Rome. |
| 1878 | 'Daisy Miller' published in London establishes fame on both sides of the Atlantic. Publishes first volume of essays, *French Poets and Novelists*. |
| 1879–82 | *The Europeans, Washington Square, Confidence, The Portrait of a Lady*. |
| 1882–3 | Revisits Boston: first visit to Washington. Death of parents. |
| 1884–6 | Returns to London. Sister Alice comes to live near him. Fourteen-volume collection of novels and tales published. |

Writes *The Bostonians* and *The Princess Casamassima*, published in the following year.

1886        Moves to flat at 34 De Vere Gardens West.

1887        Sojourn in Italy, mainly Florence and Venice. 'The Aspern Papers', *The Reverberator*, 'A London Life'. Friendship with grand-niece of Fenimore Cooper – Constance Fenimore Woolson.

1888        *Partial Portraits* and several collections of tales.

1889–90     *The Tragic Muse.*

1890–1      Dramatises *The American*, which has a short run. Writes four comedies, rejected by producers.

1892        Alice James dies in London.

1894        Miss Woolson commits suicide in Venice. James journeys to Italy and visits her grave in Rome.

1895        He is booed at first night of his play *Guy Domville*. Deeply depressed, he abandons the theatre.

1896–7      *The Spoils of Poynton, What Maisie Knew.*

1898        Takes long lease of Lamb House, in Rye, Sussex. 'The Turn of the Screw' published.

1899–1900   *The Awkward Age, The Sacred Fount*. Friendship with Conrad and Wells.

1902–4      *The Ambassadors, The Wings of the Dove* and *The Golden Bowl*. Friendships with H. C. Andersen and Jocelyn Persse.

1905        Revisits USA after 20-year absence, lectures on Balzac and the speech of Americans.

1906–10     *The American Scene*. Edits selective and revised 'New York Edition' of his works in 24 volumes. Friendship with Hugh Walpole.

1910        Death of brother, William James.

1913        Sargent paints his portrait as 70th birthday gift from some 300 friends and admirers. Writes autobiographies, *A Small Boy and Others*, and *Notes of a Son and Brother*.

1914        *Notes on Novelists*. Visits wounded in hospitals.

1915        Becomes a British subject.

1916        Given Order of Merit. Dies 28 February in Chelsea, aged 72. Funeral in Chelsea Old Church. Ashes buried in Cambridge, Mass., family plot.

1976        Commemorative tablet unveiled in Poets' Corner of Westminster Abbey, 17 June.

# PREFACES

THE following extracts are the relevant passages from the Prefaces to vols. XII, XVII, XVI and XV of the New York Edition of *The Novels and Tales of Henry James*, 1907–9.

## I. 'THE ASPERN PAPERS'

I NOT only recover with ease, but I delight to recall, the first impulse given to the idea of 'The Aspern Papers'. It is at the same time true that my present mention of it may perhaps too effectually dispose of any complacent claim to my having 'found' the situation. Not that I quite know indeed what situations the seeking fabulist does 'find'; he seeks them enough assuredly, but his discoveries are, like those of the navigator, the chemist, the biologist, scarce more than alert recognitions. He *comes upon* the interesting thing as Columbus came upon the isle of San Salvador, because he had moved in the right direction for it – also because he knew, with the encounter, what 'making land' then and there represented. Nature had so placed it, to profit – if as profit we may measure the matter! – by his fine unrest, just as history, 'literary history' we in this connexion call it, had in an out-of-the-way corner of the great garden of life thrown off a curious flower that I was to feel worth gathering as soon as I saw it. I got wind of my positive fact, I followed the scent. It was in Florence years ago; which is precisely, of the whole matter, what I like most to remember. The air of the old-time Italy invests it, a mixture that on the faintest invitation I rejoice again to inhale – and this in spite of the mere cold renewal, ever, of the infirm side of that felicity, the sense, in the whole element, of things too numerous, too deep, too obscure, too strange, or even simply too beautiful, for any ease of intellectual relation. One must pay one's self largely with words, I think, one must induce almost any 'Italian subject' to *make believe* it gives up its secret, in order to keep at all on working – or call them perhaps rather playing – terms with the general impression. We entertain it thus, the impression, by the aid of a merciful convention which resembles the fashion of our intercourse with Iberians or Orientals whose form of courtesy places everything they have at our disposal. We thank them and call upon them, but without acting on their professions. The offer has been too large and our assurance is too small; we peep at most into two or three of the chambers of their hospitality, with the rest of the case stretching beyond our ken and escaping our penetration. The pious fiction suffices; we have entered, we have seen, we are charmed. So, right and left, in Italy – before the great historic complexity at least – penetration fails; we scratch at the extensive surface, we meet the perfunctory smile, we hang about in the golden air. But we exaggerate our gathered values only if we are eminently witless. It is fortunately the exhibition in all the world before which, as admirers, we can most remain superficial without feeling silly.

All of which I note, however, perhaps with too scant relevance to the inexhaustible charm of Roman and Florentine memories. Off the ground, at a distance, our fond indifference to being 'silly' grows fonder still; the working convention, as I have called it – the convention of the real revelations and surrenders on one side and the real immersions and appreciations on the other – has not only nothing to keep it down, but every glimpse of contrast, every pang of exile and every nostalgic twinge to keep it up. These latter haunting presences in fact, let me note, almost reduce at first to a mere blurred, sad, scarcely consolable vision this present revisiting, re-appropriating impulse. There are parts of one's past, evidently, that bask consentingly and serenely enough in the light of other days – which is but the intensity of thought; and there are other parts that take it as with agitation and pain, a troubled consciousness that heaves as with the disorder of drinking it deeply in. So it is at any rate, fairly in too thick and rich a retrospect, that I see my old Venice of 'The Aspern Papers', that I see the still earlier one of Jeffrey Aspern himself, and that I see even the comparatively recent Florence that was to drop into my ear the solicitation of these things. I would fain 'lay it on' thick for the very love of them – that at least I may profess; and, with the ground of this desire frankly admitted, something that somehow makes, in the whole story, for a romantic harmony. I have had occasion in the course of these remarks to define my sense of the romantic, and am glad to encounter again here an instance of that virtue as I understand it. I shall presently say why this small case so ranges itself, but must first refer more exactly to the thrill of appreciation it was immediately to excite in me. I saw it somehow at the very first blush as romantic – for the use, of course I mean, I should certainly have had to make of it – that Jane Clairmont, the half-sister of Mary Godwin, Shelley's second wife and for a while the intimate friend of Byron and the mother of his daughter Allegra, should have been living on in Florence, where she had long lived, up to our own day, and that in fact, had I happened to hear of her but a little sooner, I might have seen her in the flesh. The question of whether I should have wished to do so was another matter – the question of whether I shouldn't have preferred to keep her preciously unseen, to run no risk, in other words, by too rude a choice, of depreciating that romance-value which, as I say, it was instantly inevitably to attach (through association above all, with another signal circumstance) to her long survival.

I had luckily not had to deal with the difficult option; difficult in such a case by reason of that odd law which some-how always makes the minimum of valid suggestion serve the man of imagination better than the maximum. The historian, essentially, wants more documents than he can really use; the dramatist only wants more liberties than he can really take. Nothing, fortunately, however, had, as the case stood, depended on my delicacy; I might have 'looked up' Miss Clairmont in previous years had I been earlier informed – the silence about her seemed full of the 'irony of fate'; but I felt myself more concerned with the mere strong fact of her having testified for the reality and the closeness of our relation to the past than with any question of the particular sort of person I might have flattered myself I 'found'. I had certainly at the very least been saved the undue simplicity of pretending to read meanings into things absolutely sealed and beyond test or proof – to tap a fount of waters that couldn't possibly not have run dry. The thrill of learning that she had 'overlapped', and by so much, and the wonder of my having doubtless at several earlier seasons passed again and again, all unknowing, the door of her house, where she sat above, within call and in her habit as she lived, these things gave me all I wanted; I seem to remember in fact that my more or less immediately recognising that I positively oughtn't – 'for anything to come of it' – to have wanted more. I saw, quickly, how something might come of it *thus*; whereas a fine instinct told me that the effect of a nearer view of the case (the case of the overlapping) would probably have had to be quite differently calculable. It was really with another item of knowledge, however, that I measured the mistake I should have made in waking up sooner to the question of opportunity. That item consisted of the action taken on the premises by a person who *had* waked up in time, and the legend of whose consequent adventure, as a few spoken words put it before me, at once kindled a flame. This gentleman, an American of long ago, an ardent Shelleyite, a singularly marked figure and himself in the highest degree a subject for a free sketch – I had known him a little, but there is not a reflected glint of him in 'The Aspern Papers' – was named to me as having made interest with Miss Clairmont to be accepted as a lodger on the calculation that she would have Shelley documents for which, in the possibly not remote event of her death, he would thus enjoy priority of chance to treat with her representatives. He had at any rate, according to the legend, become, on earnest Shelley grounds, her yearning, though also her highly diplomatic, *pensionnaire* – but without gathering, as was to befall, the fruit of his design.

Legend here dropped to another key; it remained in a manner interesting, but became to my ear a trifle coarse, or at least rather vague and obscure. It mentioned a younger female relative of the ancient woman as a person who, for a queer climax, had had to be dealt with; it flickered so for a moment and then, as a light, to my great relief, quite went out. It had flickered indeed but at the best – yet had flickered enough to give me my 'facts', bare facts of intimation; which, scant handful though they were, were more distinct and more numerous than I mostly *like* facts: like them, that is, as we say of an etcher's progressive subject, in an early 'state'. Nine tenths of the artist's interest in them is that of what he shall add to them and how he shall turn them. Mine, however, in the connexion I speak of, had fortunately got away from me, and quite of their own movement, in time not to crush me. So it was, at all events, that my imagination preserved power to react under the mere essential charm – that, I mean, of a final scene of the rich dim Shelley drama played out in the very theatre of our own 'modernity'. This was the beauty that appealed to me; there had been, so to speak, a forward continuity, from the actual man, the divine poet, on; and the curious, the ingenious, the admirable thing would be to throw it backward again, to compress – squeezing it hard! – the connexion that had drawn itself out, and convert so the stretched relation into a value of nearness on our own part. In short I saw my chance as admirable, and one reason, when the direction is right, may serve as well as fifty; but if I 'took over', as I say, everything that was of the essence, I stayed my hand for the rest. The Italian side of the legend closely clung; if only because the so possible terms of my Juliana's life in the Italy of other days could make conceivable for her the fortunate privacy, the long uninvaded and uninterviewed state on which I represent her situation as founded. Yes, a surviving unexploited unparagraphed Juliana was up to a quarter of a century since still supposeable – as much so as any such buried treasure, any such grave unprofaned, would defy probability now. And then the case had the air of the past just in the degree in which that air, I confess, most appeals to me – when the region over which it hangs is far enough away without being too far.

I delight in a palpable imaginable *visitable* past – in the nearer distances and the clearer mysteries, the marks and signs of a world we may reach over to as by making a long arm we grasp an object at the other end of our own table. The table is the one, the common expanse, and where we lean, so stretching, we find it firm and continuous. That, to my imagination, is the past fragrant of all, or of almost all, the poetry of the thing outlived and lost and gone, and yet in which the precious element of closeness, telling so of connexions but tasting so of differences, remains appreciable. With more moves back the element of the appreciable shrinks – just as the charm of looking over a garden-wall into another garden breaks down when successions of walls appear. The other gardens, those still beyond, may be there, but even by use of our longest ladder we are baffled and bewildered – the view is mainly a view of barriers. The one partition makes the place we have wondered about *other*, both richly and recogniseably so; but who shall pretend to impute an effect of composition to the twenty? We are divided of course between liking to feel the past strange and liking to feel it familiar; the difficulty is, for intensity, to catch it at the moment when the scales of the balance hang with the right evenness. I say for intensity, for we may profit by them in other aspects enough if we are content to measure or to feel loosely. It would take me too far, however, to tell why the particular afternoon light that I thus call intense rests clearer to my sense on the Byronic age, as I conveniently name it, than on periods more protected by the 'dignity' of history. With the times beyond, intrinsically more 'strange', the tender grace, for the backward vision, has faded, the afternoon darkened; for any time nearer to us the special effect hasn't begun. So there, to put the matter crudely, is the appeal I fondly recognise, an appeal residing doubtless more in the 'special effect', in some deep associational force, than in a virtue more intrinsic. I am afraid I must add, since I allow myself so much to fantasticate, that the impulse had more than once taken me to project the Byronic age and the afternoon light across the great sea, to see in short whether association would carry so far and what the young century might pass for on that side of the modern world where it was not only itself so irremediably youngest, but was bound up with youth in everything else. There was a refinement of curiosity in this imputation of a golden strangeness to American social facts – though I cannot pretend, I fear, that there was any greater wisdom.

Since what it had come to then was, harmlessly enough, cultivating a sense of the past under that close protection, it was natural, it was fond and filial, to wonder if a few of the distilled drops mightn't be gathered from some vision of, say, 'old' New York. Would that human congeries, to aid obligingly in the production of a fable, be conceivable as 'taking' the afternoon light with the right happy slant? – or could a recogniseable reflexion of the Byronic age, in other words, be picked up on the banks of the Hudson? (Only just there, beyond the great sea, if anywhere: in no other connexion would the question so much as raise its head. I admit that Jeffrey Aspern isn't even feebly localised, but I *thought* New York as I projected him.) It was 'amusing,' in any case, always, to try experiments; and the experiment for the right *transposition* of my Juliana would be to fit her out with an immortalising poet as transposed as herself. Delicacy had demanded, I felt, that my appropriation of the Florentine legend should purge it, first of all, of references too obvious; so that, to begin with, I shifted the scene of the adventure. Juliana, as I saw her, was thinkable only in Byronic and more or less immediately post-Byronic Italy; but there were conditions in which she was ideally arrangeable, as happened, especially in respect to the later time and the long undetected survival; there being absolutely no refinement of the mouldy rococo, in human or whatever other form, that you may not disembark at the dislocated water-steps of almost any decayed monument of Venetian greatness in auspicious quest of. It was a question, in fine, of covering one's tracks – though with no great elaboration I am bound to admit; and I felt I couldn't cover mine more than in postulating a comparative American Byron to match an American Miss Clairmont – she as absolute as she would. I scarce know whether best to say for this device to-day that it cost me little or that it cost me much; it was 'cheap' or expensive according to the degree of verisimilitude artfully obtained. If that degree appears *nil* the 'art', such as it was, is wasted, and my remembrance of the contention, on the part of a highly critical friend who at that time and later on often had my ear, that it had been simply foredoomed to be wasted, puts before me the passage in the private history of 'The Aspern Papers' that I now find, I confess, most interesting. I comfort myself for the needful brevity of a present glance at it by the sense that the general question involved, under criticism, can't but come up for us again at higher pressure.

My friend's argument bore then – at the time and afterward – on my vicious practice, as he maintained, of postulating for the purpose of my fable celebrities who not only *hadn't* existed in the conditions I imputed to them, but who for the most part (and in no case more markedly than in that of Jeffrey Aspern) couldn't possibly have done so. The stricture was to apply itself to a whole group of short fictions in which I had, with whatever ingenuity, assigned to several so-called eminent figures

positions absolutely unthinkable in our actual encompassing
air, an air definitely unfavourable to certain forms of eminence.
It was vicious, my critic contended, to flourish forth on one's
page 'great people', public persons, who shouldn't more or less
square with our quite definite and calculable array of such
notabilities; and by this rule I was heavily incriminated. The
rule demanded that the 'public person' portrayed should be at
least of the tradition, of the general complexion, of the face-
value, exactly, of some past or present producible counterfoil.
Mere private figures, under one's hand, might correspond with
nobody, it being of their essence to be but narrowly known;
the represented state of being conspicuous, on the other hand,
involved before anything else a recognition – and none of my
eminent folk were recogniseable. It was all very well for instance
to have put one's self at such pains for Miriam Rooth in 'The
Tragic Muse'; but *there* was misapplied zeal, there a case of
pitiful waste, crying aloud to be denounced. Miriam is offered
not as a young person passing unnoticed by her age – like the
Biddy Dormers and Julia Dallows, say, of the same book, but
as a high rarity, a time-figure of the scope inevitably attended
by other commemorations. Where on earth would be then
Miriam's inscribed 'counterfoil', and in what conditions of the
contemporary English theatre, in what conditions of criticism,
of appreciation, under what conceivable Anglo-Saxon star,
might we take an artistic value of this order either for produced
or for recognised? We are, as a 'public', chalk-marked by
nothing, more unmistakeably, than by the truth that we know
nothing of such values – any more than, as my friend was to
impress on me, we are susceptible of consciousness of such
others (these in the sphere of literary eminence) as my Neil
Paraday in 'The Death of the Lion', as my Hugh Vereker in
'The Figure in the Carpet', as my Ralph Limbert, above all, in
'The Next Time', as sundry unprecedented and unmatched
heroes and martyrs of the artistic ideal, in short, elsewhere
exemplified in my pages. We shall come to these objects of
animadversion in another hour, when I shall have no difficulty
in producing the defence I found for them – since, obviously,
I hadn't cast them into the world *all* naked and ashamed; and
I deal for the moment but with the stigma in general as Jeffrey
Aspern carries it.

The charge being that I foist upon our early American annals a distinguished presence for which they yield me absolutely no warrant – 'Where, within them, gracious heaven, were we to look for so much as an approach to the social elements of habitat and climate of birds of that note and plumage?' – I find his link with reality then just in the tone of the picture wrought round him. What was that tone but exactly, but exquisitely, calculated, the harmless hocus-pocus under cover of which we might suppose him to have existed? This tone is the tone, artistically speaking, of 'amusement', the current floating that precious influence home quite as one of those high tides watched by the smugglers of old might, in case of their boat's being boarded, be trusted to wash far up the strand the cask of foreign liquor expertly committed to it. If through our lean prime Western period no dim and charming ghost of an adventurous lyric genius might by a stretch of fancy flit, if the time was really too hard to 'take', in the light form proposed, the elegant reflexion, then so much the worse for the time – it was all one could say! The retort to that of course was that such a plea represented no 'link' with reality – which was what was under discussion – but only a link, and flimsy enough too, with the deepest depths of the artificial: the restrictive truth exactly contended for, which may embody my critic's last word rather of course than my own. My own, so far as I shall pretend in that especial connexion to report it, was that one's warrant, in such a case, hangs essentially on the question of whether or no the false element imputed would have borne that test of further development which so exposes the wrong and so consecrates the right. My last word was, heaven forgive me, that, occasion favouring, I could have perfectly 'worked out' Jeffrey Aspern.

## II. 'THE PRIVATE LIFE'

I proceed almost eagerly, in any case, to 'The Private Life' – and at the cost of reaching for a moment over 'The Jolly Corner': I find myself so fondly return to ground on which the history even of small experiments may be more or less written. This mild documentation fairly thickens for me, I confess, the air of the first-mentioned of these tales; the scraps of records flit through that medium, to memory, as with the incalculable brush of wings of the imprisoned bat at eventide. This piece of ingenuity rests for me on such a handful of acute impressions as I may not here tell over at once; so that, to be brief, I select two of the sharpest. Neither of these was, in old London days, I make out, to be resisted even under its single pressure; so that the hour struck with a vengeance for 'Dramatise it, dramatise it!' (dramatise, that is, the combination) from the first glimpse of a good way to work together two cases that happened to have been given me. They were those – as distinct as possible save for belonging alike to the 'world', the London world of a time when Discrimination still a little lifted its head – of a highly distinguished man, constantly to be encountered, whose fortune and whose peculiarity it was to bear out person- ally as little as possible (at least to *my* wondering sense) the high denotements, the rich implications and rare associations, of the genius to which he owed his position and his renown. One may go, naturally, in such a connexion, but by one's own applied measure; and I have never ceased to ask myself, in this particular loud, sound, normal, hearty presence, all so assertive and so whole, all bristling with prompt responses and expected opinions and usual views, radiating all a broad daylight equality of emphasis and impartiality of address (for most relations) – I never ceased, I say, to ask myself what lodgement, on such premises, the rich proud genius one adored could ever have contrived, what domestic commerce the subtlety that was its prime ornament and the world's wonder have enjoyed, under what shelter the obscurity that was its luckless drawback and the world's despair have flourished. The whole aspect and *allure* of the fresh sane man, illustrious and undistinguished – no 'sensitive poor gentleman' he! – was mystifying; they made the question of who then had written the immortal things such a puzzle.

So at least one could but take the case – though one's need for relief depended, no doubt, on what one (so to speak) suffered. The writer of these lines, at any rate, suffered so much – I mean of course but by the unanswered question – that light *had* at last to break under pressure of the whimsical theory of two distinct and alternate presences, the assertion of either of which on any occasion directly involved the entire extinction of the

other. This explained to the imagination the mystery: our
delightful inconceivable celebrity was *double*, constructed in
two quite distinct and 'water-tight' compartments – one of
these figured by the gentleman who sat at a table all alone,
silent and unseen, and wrote admirably deep and brave and
intricate things; while the gentleman who regularly came
forth to sit at a quite different table and substantially and
promiscuously and multitudinously dine stood for its companion.
They had nothing to do, the so dissimilar twins, with each
other; the diner could exist but by the cessation of the writer,
whose emergence, on his side, depended on his – and our! –
ignoring the diner. Thus it was amusing to think of the real
great man as a presence known, in the late London days, all
and only to himself – unseen of other human eye and converted
into his perfectly positive, but quite secondary, *alter ego* by any
approach to a social contact. To the same tune was the social
personage known all and only to society, was he conceivable
but as 'cut dead', on the return home and the threshold of the
closed study, by the waiting spirit who would flash at that
signal into form and possession. Once I had so seen the case
I couldn't see it otherwise; and so to see it moreover was inevitably to feel in it a situation and a motive. The ever-importunate
murmur, 'Dramatise it, dramatise it!' haunted, as I say, one's
perception; yet without giving the idea much support till, by
the happiest turn, the whole possibility was made to glow.

For didn't there immensely flourish in those very days and
exactly in that society the apparition the most qualified to
balance with the odd character I have referred to and to supply
to 'drama,' if 'drama' there was to be, the precious element of
contrast and antithesis? – that most accomplished of artists
and most dazzling of men of the world whose effect on the
mind repeatedly invited to appraise him was to beget in it an
image of representation and figuration so exclusive of any
possible inner self that, so far from there being here a question
of an *alter ego*, a double personality, there seemed scarce a
question of a real and single one, scarce foothold or margin
for any private and domestic *ego* at all. Immense in this case
too, for any analytic witness, the solicitation of wonder – which
struggled all the while, not less amusingly than in the other
example, toward the explanatory secret; a clear view of the

perpetual, essential performer, consummate, infallible, impeccable, and with his high shining elegance, his intensity of presence, on these lines, involving to the imagination an absolutely blank reverse or starved residuum, no *other* power of presence whatever. One said it under one's breath, one really yearned to know: was he, such an embodiment of skill and taste and tone and composition, of every public gloss and grace, thinkable even as occasionally single? – since to be truly single is to be able, under stress, to be separate, to be *solus*, to know at need the interlunar swoon of *some* independent consciousness. Yes, *had* our dazzling friend any such alternative, could he so unattestedly exist, and was the withdrawn, the sequestered, the unobserved and unhonoured condition so much as imputable to him? Wasn't his potentiality of existence public, in fine, to the last squeeze of the golden orange, and when he passed from our admiring sight into the chamber of mystery what, the next minute, was on the other side of the door? It was irresistible to believe at last that there was at such junctures inveterately nothing; and the more so, once I had begun to dramatise, as this supplied the most natural opposition in the world to my fond companion-view – the other side of the door *only* cognisant of the true Robert Browning. One's harmless formula for the poetic employment of this pair of conceits couldn't go much further than 'Play them against each other' – the ingenuity of which small game 'The Private Life' reflects as it can.

### III. 'THE MIDDLE YEARS'

WHAT I had lately and most particularly to say of 'The Coxon Fund' is no less true of 'The Middle Years', first published in *Scribner's Magazine* (1893) – that recollection mainly and most promptly associates with it the number of times I had to do it over to make sure of it. To get it right was to squeeze my subject into the five or six thousand words I had been invited to make it consist of – it consists, in fact, should the curious care to know, of some 5550 – and I scarce perhaps recall another case, with the exception I shall presently name, in which my struggle to keep compression rich, if not, better still, to keep accretions compressed, betrayed for me such community with the anxious effort of some warden of the insane engaged at a

critical moment in making fast a victim's straitjacket. The form
of 'The Middle Years' is not that of the *nouvelle*, but that of
the concise anecdote; whereas the subject treated would perhaps
seem one comparatively demanding 'developments' – if indeed,
amid these mysteries, distinctions were so absolute. (There is of
course neither close nor fixed measure of the reach of a development, which in some connexions seems almost superfluous and
then in others to represent the whole sense of the matter; and
we should doubtless speak more thoroughly by book had we
some secret for exactly tracing deflexions and returns.) However this may be, it was as an anecdote, an anecdote only, that
I was determined my little situation here should figure; to which
end my effort was of course to follow it as much as possible
from its outer edge in, rather than from its centre outward.
That fond formula, I had alas already discovered, may set as
many traps in the garden as its opposite may set in the wood;
so that after boilings and reboilings of the contents of my
small cauldron, after added pounds of salutary sugar, as numerous as those prescribed in the choicest recipe for the thickest jam,
I well remember finding the whole process and act (which, to
the exclusion of everything else, dragged itself out for a month)
one of the most expensive of its sort in which I had ever
engaged.

But I recall, by good luck, no less vividly how much finer a
sweetness than any mere spooned-out saccharine dwelt in the
fascination of the questions involved. Treating a theme that
'gave' much in a form that, at the best, would give little,
might indeed represent a peck of troubles; yet who, none the
less, beforehand, was to pronounce with authority such and
such an idea anecdotic and such and such another develop-
mental? One had, for the vanity of *a priori* wisdom here, only
to be so constituted that to see any form of beauty, for a
particular application, proscribed or even questioned, was forthwith to covet that form more than any other and to desire the
benefit of it exactly there. One had only to be reminded that
for the effect of quick roundness the small smooth situation,
though as intense as one will, is prudently indicated, and
that for a fine complicated entangled air nothing will serve
that doesn't naturally swell and bristle – one had only, I say,
to be so warned off or warned on, to see forthwith no beauty

for the simple thing that shouldn't, and even to perversity,
enrich it, and none for the other, the comparatively intricate,
that shouldn't press it out as a mosaic. After which fashion the
careful craftsman would have prepared himself the special
inviting treat of scarce being able to say, at his highest infatuation, before any series, which might be the light thing weighted
and which the dense thing clarified. The very attempt so to
discriminate leaves him in fact at moments even a little ashamed;
whereby let him shirk here frankly certain of the issues presented by the remainder of our company – there being, independently of these mystic matters, other remarks to make.

## IV. 'THE DEATH OF THE LION'

These pieces have this in common that they deal all with the
literary life, gathering their motive, in each case, from some
noted adventure, some felt embarrassment, some extreme predicament, of the artist enamoured of perfection, ridden by his idea
or paying for his sincerity. They testify indeed, as they thus
stand together, to no general intention – they minister only, I
think, to an emphasised effect. The particular case, in respect to
each situation depicted, appealed to me but on its merits;
though I was to note with interest, as my sense more and more
opened itself, that situations of the order I speak of might again
and again be conceived. They rose before me, in fine, as numerous, and thus, here, even with everything not included, they
have added themselves up. I must further mention that if they
enjoy in common their reference to the troubled artistic consciousness, they make together, by the same stroke, this other
rather blank profession, that few of them recall to me, however
dimly, any scant pre-natal phase.

In putting them sundry such critical questions so much after
the fact I find it interesting to make out – critically interesting
of course, which is all our interest here pretends to be – that
whereas any anecdote about life pure and simple, as it were,
proceeds almost as a matter of course from some good jog of
fond fancy's elbow, some pencilled note on somebody else's case,
so the material for any picture of personal states so specifically
complicated as those of my hapless friends in the present volume
will have been drawn preponderantly from the depths of the

designer's own mind. This, amusingly enough, is what, on the evidence before us, I seem critically, as I say, to gather – that the states represented, the embarrassments and predicaments studied, the tragedies and comedies recorded, can be intelligibly fathered but on his own intimate experience. I have already mentioned the particular rebuke once addressed me on all this ground, the question of where on earth, where roundabout us at this hour, I had 'found' my Neil Paradays, my Ralph Limberts, my Hugh Verekers and other such supersubtle fry. I was reminded then, as I have said, that these represented eminent cases fell to the ground, as by their foolish weight, unless I could give chapter and verse for the eminence. I was reduced to confessing I couldn't, and yet must repeat again here how little I was so abashed. On going over these things I see, to our critical edification, exactly why – which was because I was able to plead that my postulates, my animating presences, were all, to their great enrichment, their intensification of value, ironic; the strength of applied irony being surely in the sincerities, the lucidities, the utilities that stand behind it. When it's not a campaign, of a sort, on behalf of the something better (better than the obnoxious, the provoking object) that blessedly, as is assumed, *might* be, it's not worth speaking of. But this is exactly what we mean by operative irony. It implies and projects the possible other case, the case rich and edifying where the actuality is pretentious and vain. So it plays its lamp; so, essentially, it carries that smokeless flame, which makes clear, with all the rest, the good cause that guides it. My application of which remarks is that the studies here collected have their justification in the ironic spirit, the spirit expressed by my being able to reply promptly enough to my friend: 'If the life about us for the last thirty years refuses warrant for these examples, then so much the worse for that life. The *constatation* would be so deplorable that instead of making it we must dodge it: there are decencies that in the name of the general self-respect we must take for granted, there's a kind of rudimentary intellectual honour to which we must, in the interest of civilisation, at least pretend.' But I must really reproduce the whole passion of my retort.

'What does your contention of non-existent conscious *exposures*, in the midst of all the stupidity and vulgarity and hypocrisy, imply but that we have been, nationally, so to speak, graced with no instance of recorded sensibility fine enough to react against these things? – an admission too distressing. What one would accordingly fain do is to baffle any such calamity, to *create* the record, in default of any other enjoyment of it; to imagine, in a word, the honourable, the producible case. What better example than this of the high and helpful public and, as it were, civic use of the imagination? – a faculty for the possible fine employments of which in the interest of morality my esteem grows every hour I live. How can one consent to make a picture of the preponderant futilities and vulgarities and miseries of life without the impulse to exhibit as well from time to time, in its place, some fine example of the reaction, the opposition or the escape? One does, thank heaven, encounter here and there symptoms of immunity from the general infection; one recognises with rapture, on occasion, signs of a protest against the rule of the cheap and easy; and one sees thus that the tradition of a high aesthetic temper needn't, after all, helplessly and ignobly perish. These reassurances are one's warrant, accordingly, for so many recognitions of the apparent doom and the exasperated temper – whether with the spirit and the career fatally bruised and finally broken in the fray, or privileged but to gain from it a finer and more militant edge. I have had, I admit, to project *signal* specimens – have had, naturally, to make and to keep my cases interesting; the only way to achieve which was to suppose and represent them eminent. In other words I was inevitably committed, always, to the superior case; so that if this is what you reprehensively mean, that I have been thus beguiled into citing celebrities without analogues and painting portraits without models, I plead guilty to the critical charge. Only what I myself mean is that I carry my guilt lightly and have really in face of each perpetrated licence scarce patience to defend myself.' So I made my point ...

# THE ASPERN PAPERS

# THE ASPERN PAPERS

## I

I HAD taken Mrs Prest into my confidence; without her in truth I should have made but little advance, for the fruitful idea in the whole business dropped from her friendly lips. It was she who found the short cut and loosed the Gordian knot. It is not supposed easy for women to rise to the large free view of anything, anything to be done; but they sometimes throw off a bold conception – such as a man wouldn't have risen to – with singular serenity. 'Simply make them take you in on the footing of a lodger' – I don't think that unaided I should have risen to that. I was beating about the bush, trying to be ingenious, wondering by what combination of arts I might become an acquaintance, when she offered this happy suggestion that the way to become an acquaintance was first to become an intimate. Her actual knowledge of the Misses Bordereau was scarcely larger than mine, and indeed I had brought with me from England some definite facts that were new to her. Their name had been mixed up ages before with one of the greatest names of the century, and they now lived obscurely in Venice, lived on very small means, unvisited, unapproachable, in a sequestered and dilapidated old palace: this was the substance of my friend's impression of them. She herself had been established in Venice some fifteen years and had done a great deal of good there; but the circle of her benevolence had never embraced the two shy, mysterious and, as was somehow supposed, scarcely respectable Americans – they were believed to have lost in their long exile all national quality, besides being as their name implied of some remoter French affiliation – who asked no favours and desired no attention. In the early years of her residence she had made an attempt to see them, but this had been successful only as regards the little one, as Mrs Prest called the niece; though in fact I afterwards found her the bigger of the two in inches. She had heard Miss Bordereau was

ill and had a suspicion she was in want, and had gone to the
house to offer aid, so that if there were suffering, American
suffering in particular, she shouldn't have it on her conscience.
The 'little one' had received her in the great cold tarnished
Venetian *sala*, the central hall of the house, paved with marble
and roofed with dim cross-beams, and hadn't even asked her to
sit down. This was not encouraging for me, who wished to sit
so fast, and I remarked as much to Mrs Prest. She replied however with profundity 'Ah, but there's all the difference: I went
to confer a favour and you'll go to ask one. If they're proud
you'll be on the right side.' And she offered to show me their
house to begin with – to row me thither in her gondola. I
let her know I had already been to look at it half a dozen times;
but I accepted her invitation, for it charmed me to hover about
the place. I had made my way to it the day after my arrival in
Venice – it had been described to me in advance by the friend
in England to whom I owed definite information as to their
possession of the papers – laying siege to it with my eyes while
I considered my plan of campaign. Jeffrey Aspern had never
been in it that I knew of, but some note of his voice seemed to
abide there by a roundabout implication and in a 'dying fall'.

Mrs Prest knew nothing about the papers, but was interested
in my curiosity, as always in the joys and sorrows of her
friends. As we went, however, in her gondola, gliding there
under the sociable hood with the bright Venetian picture
framed on either side by the movable window, I saw how my
eagerness amused her and that she found my interest in my
possible spoil a fine case of monomania. 'One would think you
expected from it the answer to the riddle of the universe,' she
said; and I denied the impeachment only by replying that if I
had to choose between that precious solution and a bundle of
Jeffrey Aspern's letters I knew indeed which would appear to
me the greater boon. She pretended to make light of his genius
and I took no pains to defend him. One doesn't defend one's
god: one's god is in himself a defence. Besides, today, after his
long comparative obscuration, he hangs high in the heaven of
our literature for all the world to see; he's a part of the light
by which we walk. The most I said was that he was no doubt
not a woman's poet; to which she rejoined aptly enough that he
had been at least Miss Bordereau's. The strange thing had been

for me to discover in England that she was still alive: it was as if I had been told Mrs Siddons was, or Queen Caroline, or the famous Lady Hamilton, for it seemed to me that she belonged to a generation as extinct. 'Why she must be tremendously old – at least a hundred,' I had said; but on coming to consider dates I saw it not strictly involved that she should have far exceeded the common span. None the less she was of venerable age and her relations with Jeffrey Aspern had occurred in her early womanhood. 'That's her excuse,' said Mrs Prest half-sententiously and yet also somewhat as if she were ashamed of making a speech so little in the real tone of Venice. As if a woman needed an excuse for having loved the divine poet! He had been not only one of the most brilliant minds of his day – and in those years, when the century was young, there were, as everyone knows, many – but one of the most genial men and one of the handsomest.

The niece, according to Mrs Prest, was of minor antiquity, and the conjecture was risked that she was only a grand-niece. This was possible; I had nothing but my share in the very limited knowledge of my English fellow worshipper John Cumnor, who had never seen the couple. The world, as I say, had recognised Jeffrey Aspern, but Cumnor and I had recognised him most. The multitude today flocked to his temple, but of that temple he and I regarded ourselves as the appointed ministers. We held, justly, as I think, that we had done more for his memory than anyone else, and had done it simply by opening lights into his life. He had nothing to fear from us because he had nothing to fear from the truth, which alone at such a distance of time we could be interested in establishing. His early death had been the only dark spot, as it were, on his fame, unless the papers in Miss Bordereau's hands should perversely bring out others. There had been an impression about 1825 that he had 'treated her badly', just as there had been an impression that he had 'served', as the London populace says, several other ladies in the same masterful way. Each of these cases Cumnor and I had been able to investigate, and we had never failed to acquit him conscientiously of any grossness. I judged him perhaps more indulgently than my friend; certainly, at any rate, it appeared to me that no man could have walked straighter in the given circumstances. These had been almost always difficult and dangerous. Half the women of his time, to speak liberally, had flung themselves at his head, and while the fury raged – the more that it was very catching – accidents, some of them grave, had not failed to occur. He was not a woman's poet, as I had said to Mrs Prest, in the modern phase of his reputation; but the situation had been different when the man's own voice was mingled with his song. That voice, by every testimony, was one of the most charming ever heard. 'Orpheus and the Mænads!' had been of course my foreseen judgement when first I turned over his correspondence. Almost all the Mænads were unreasonable and many of them unbearable; it struck me that he had been kinder and more considerate than in his place – if I could imagine myself in any such box – I should have found the trick of.

It was certainly strange beyond all strangeness, and I shall not take up space with attempting to explain it, that whereas among all these other relations and in these other directions of research we had to deal with phantoms and dust, the mere echoes of echoes, the one living source of information that had lingered on into our time had been unheeded by us. Every one of Aspern's contemporaries had, according to our belief, passed away; we had not been able to look into a single pair of eyes into which his had looked or to feel a transmitted contact in any aged hand that his had touched. Most dead of all did poor Miss Bordereau appear, and yet she alone had survived. We exhausted in the course of months our wonder that we had not found her out sooner, and the substance of our explanation was that she had kept so quiet. The poor lady on the whole had had reason for doing so. But it was a revelation to us that self-effacement on such a scale had been possible in the latter half of the nineteenth century – the age of newspapers and telegrams and photographs and interviewers. She had taken no great trouble for it either – hadn't hidden herself away in an undiscoverable hole, had boldly settled down in a city of exhibition. The one apparent secret of her safety had been that Venice contained so many much greater curiosities. And then accident had somehow favoured her, as was shown for example in the fact that Mrs Prest had never happened to name her to me, though I had spent three weeks in Venice – under her nose, as it were – five years before. My friend indeed had not named her much to anyone; she appeared almost to have forgotten the fact of her continuance. Of course Mrs Prest hadn't the nerves of an editor. It was meanwhile no explanation of the old woman's having eluded us to say that she lived abroad, for our researches had again and again taken us – not only by correspondence but by personal enquiry – to France, to Germany, to Italy, in which countries, not counting his important stay in England, so many of the too few years of Aspern's career had been spent. We were glad to think at least that in all our promulgations – some people now consider I believe that we have overdone them – we had only touched in passing and in the most discreet manner on Miss Bordereau's connexion. Oddly enough, even if we had had the material – and we had often wondered what could have become of it – this would have been the most difficult episode to handle.

The gondola stopped, the old palace was there; it was a house of the class which in Venice carries even in extreme dilapidation the dignified name. 'How charming! It's grey and pink!' my companion exclaimed; and that is the most comprehensive description of it. It was not particularly old, only two or three centuries; and it had an air not so much of decay as of quiet discouragement, as if it had rather missed its career. But its wide front, with a stone balcony from end to end of the *piano nobile* or most important floor, was architectural enough, with the aid of various pilasters and arches; and the stucco with which in the intervals it had long ago been endued was rosy in the April afternoon. It overlooked a clean melancholy rather lonely canal, which had a narrow *riva* or convenient footway on either side. 'I don't know why – there are no brick gables,' said Mrs Prest, 'but this corner has seemed to me before more Dutch than Italian, more like Amsterdam than like Venice. It's eccentrically neat, for reasons of its own; and though you may pass on foot scarcely anyone ever thinks of doing so. It's as negative – considering *where* it is – as a Protestant Sunday. Perhaps the people are afraid of the Misses Bordereau. I dare say they have the reputation of witches.'

I forget what answer I made to this – I was given up to two other reflexions. The first of these was that if the old lady lived in such a big and imposing house she couldn't be in any sort of misery and therefore wouldn't be tempted by a chance to let a couple of rooms. I expressed this fear to Mrs. Prest, who gave me a very straight answer. 'If she didn't live in a big house how could it be a question of her having rooms to spare? If she were not amply lodged you'd lack ground to approach her. Besides, a big house here, and especially in this *quartier perdu*, proves nothing at all: it's perfectly consistent with a state of penury. Dilapidated old palazzi, if you'll go out of the way for them, are to be had for five shillings a year. And as for the people who live in them – no, until you've explored Venice socially as much as I have, you can form no idea of their domestic desolation. They live on nothing, for they've nothing to live on.' The other idea that had come into my head was connected with a high blank wall which appeared to confine an expanse of ground on one side of the house. Blank I call it, but it was figured over with the patches that please a painter, repaired breaches, crumblings of plaster, extrusions of brick that had turned pink with time; while a few thin trees, with the poles of certain rickety trellises, were visible over the top. The place was a garden and apparently attached to the house. I suddenly felt that so attached it gave me my pretext.

I sat looking out on all this with Mrs Prest (it was covered with the golden glow of Venice) from the shade of our *felze*, and she asked me if I would go in then, while she waited for me, or come back another time. At first I couldn't decide – it was doubtless very weak of me. I wanted still to think I *might* get a footing, and was afraid to meet failure, for it would leave me, as I remarked to my companion, without another arrow for my bow. 'Why not another?' she enquired as I sat there hesitating and thinking it over; and she wished to know why even now and before taking the trouble of becoming an inmate – which might be wretchedly uncomfortable after all, even if it succeeded – I hadn't the resource of simply offering them a sum of money down. In that way I might get what I wanted without bad nights.

'Dearest lady,' I exclaimed, 'excuse the impatience of my tone when I suggest that you must have forgotten the very fact – surely I communicated it to you – which threw me on your ingenuity. The old woman won't have her relics and tokens so much as spoken of; they're personal, delicate, intimate, and she hasn't the feelings of the day, God bless her! If I should

sound that note first I should certainly spoil the game. I
arrive at my spoils only by putting her off her guard, and I
can put her off her guard only by ingratiating diplomatic arts.
Hypocrisy, duplicity are my only chance. I'm sorry for it, but
there's no baseness I wouldn't commit for Jeffrey Aspern's sake.
First I must take tea with her – then tackle the main job.'
And I told over what had happened to John Cumnor on his
respectfully writing to her. No notice whatever had been taken
of his first letter, and the second had been answered very
sharply, in six lines, by the niece. 'Miss Bordereau requested
her to say that she couldn't imagine what he meant by troubling
them. They had none of Mr Aspern's "literary remains", and
if they *had* had wouldn't have dreamed of showing them to
anyone on any account whatever. She couldn't imagine what
he was talking about and begged he would let her alone.' I
certainly didn't want to be met that way.

'Well,' said Mrs Prest after a moment and all provokingly,
'perhaps they really haven't anything. If they deny it flat how
are you sure?'

'John Cumnor's sure, and it would take me long to tell you
how his conviction, or his very strong presumption – strong
enough to stand against the old lady's not unnatural fib – has
built itself up. Besides, he makes much of the internal evidence
of the niece's letter.'

'The internal evidence?'

'Her calling him "Mr Aspern".'

'I don't see what that proves.'

'It proves familiarity, and familiarity implies the possession
of mementoes, of tangible objects. I can't tell you how that
"Mr" affects me – how it bridges over the gulf of time and
brings our hero near to me – nor what an edge it gives to my
desire to see Juliana. You don't say "Mr" Shakespeare.'

'Would I, any more, if I had a box full of his letters?'

'Yes, if he had been your lover and someone wanted them.'
And I added that John Cumnor was so convinced, and so all
the more convinced by Miss Bordereau's tone, that he would
have come himself to Venice on the undertaking were it not
for the obstacle of his having, for any confidence, to disprove
his identity with the person who had written to them, which
the old ladies would be sure to suspect in spite of dissimulation

e of name. If they were to ask him point-blank if
ot their snubbed correspondent it would be too
or him to lie; whereas I was fortunately not tied in
. I was a fresh hand – I could protest without lying.

you'll have to take a false name,' said Mrs Prest. 'Juliana
at of the world as much as it is possible to live, but she
has none the less probably heard of Mr Aspern's editors. She
perhaps possesses what you've published.'

'I've thought of that,' I returned; and I drew out of my
pocket-book a visiting-card neatly engraved with a well-chosen
nom de guerre.

'You're very extravagant – it adds to your immorality. You
might have done it in pencil or ink,' said my companion.

'This looks more genuine.'

'Certainly you've the courage of your curiosity. But it will
be awkward about your letters; they won't come to you in that
mask.'

'My banker will take them in and I shall go every day to
get them. It will give me a little walk.'

'Shall you depend all on that?' asked Mrs Prest. 'Aren't you
coming to see me?'

'Oh you'll have left Venice for the hot months long before
there are any results. I'm prepared to roast all summer – as
well as through the long hereafter perhaps you'll say! Meanwhile John Cumnor will bombard me with letters addressed, in
my feigned name, to the care of the padrona.'

'She'll recognise his hand,' my companion suggested.

'On the envelope he can disguise it.'

'Well, you're a precious pair! Doesn't it occur to you that
even if you're able to say you're not Mr Cumnor in person
they may still suspect you of being his emissary?'

'Certainly, and I see only one way to parry that.'

'And what may that be?'

I hesitated a moment. 'To make love to the niece.'

'Ah,' cried my friend, 'wait till you see her!'

## II

'I MUST work the garden – I must work the garden,' I said to myself five minutes later and while I waited, upstairs, in the long, dusky sala, where the bare scagliola floor gleamed vaguely in a chink of the closed shutters. The place was impressive, yet looked somehow cold and cautious. Mrs Prest had floated away, giving me a rendezvous at the end of half an hour by some neighbouring water-steps; and I had been let into the house, after pulling the rusty bell-wire, by a small red-headed and white-faced maid-servant, who was very young and not ugly and wore clicking pattens and a shawl in the fashion of a hood. She had not contented herself with opening the door from above by the usual arrangement of a creaking pulley, though she had looked down at me first from an upper window, dropping the cautious challenge which in Italy precedes the act of admission. I was irritated as a general thing by this survival of mediaeval manners, though as so fond, if yet so special, an antiquarian I suppose I ought to have liked it; but, with my resolve to be genial from the threshold at any price, I took my false card out of my pocket and held it up to her, smiling as if it were a magic token. It had the effect of one indeed, for it brought her, as I say, all the way down. I begged her to hand it to her mistress, having first written on it in Italian the words: 'Could you very kindly see a gentleman, a travelling American, for a moment?' The little maid wasn't hostile – even that was perhaps something gained. She coloured, she smiled and looked both frightened and pleased. I could see that my arrival was a great affair, that visits in such a house were rare and that she was a person who would have liked a bustling place. When she pushed forward the heavy door behind me I felt my foot in the citadel and promised myself ever so firmly to keep it there. She pattered across the damp stony lower hall and I followed her up the high staircase – stonier still, as it seemed – without an invitation. I think she had meant I should wait for her below, but such was not my idea, and I took up my station in the sala. She flitted, at the far end of it, into impenetrable regions, and I looked at the place with my heart beating as I had known it to do in dentists' parlours. It had a gloomy grandeur, but owed its character almost all to its noble shape and to the fine architectural doors, as high as those of grand frontages, which, leading into the various rooms, repeated themselves on either side at intervals. They were surmounted with old faded painted escutcheons, and here and there in the spaces between them hung brown pictures, which I noted as speciously bad, in battered and tarnished frames that were yet more desirable than the canvases themselves. With the exception of several straw-bottomed chairs that kept their backs to the wall the grand obscure vista contained little else to minister to effect. It was evidently never used save as a passage, and scantly even as that. I may add that by the time the door through which the maid-servant had escaped opened again my eyes had grown used to the want of light.

I hadn't meanwhile meant by my private ejaculation that I must myself cultivate the soil of the tangled enclosure which lay beneath the windows, but the lady who came toward me from the distance over the hard shining floor might have supposed as much from the way in which, as I went rapidly to meet her, I exclaimed, taking care to speak Italian: 'The garden, the garden – do me the pleasure to tell me if it's yours!'

She stopped short, looking at me with wonder; and then, 'Nothing here is mine,' she answered in English, coldly and sadly.

'Oh you're English; how delightful!' I ingenuously cried. 'But surely the garden belongs to the house?'

'Yes, but the house doesn't belong to me.' She was a long lean pale person, habited apparently in a dull-coloured dressing-gown, and she spoke very simply and mildly. She didn't ask me to sit down, any more than years before – if she were the niece – she had asked Mrs Prest, and we stood face to face in the empty pompous hall.

'Well then, would you kindly tell me to whom I must address myself? I'm afraid you'll think me horribly intrusive, but you know I *must* have a garden – upon my honour I must!'

Her face was not young, but it was candid; it was not fresh, but it was clear. She had large eyes which were not bright, and a great deal of hair which was not 'dressed,' and long fine hands which were – possibly – not clean. She clasped these members almost convulsively as, with a confused alarmed look, she broke out: 'Oh don't take it away from us; we like it ourselves!'

'You have the use of it then?'

'Oh yes. If it wasn't for that – !' And she gave a wan vague smile.

'Isn't it a luxury, precisely? That's why, intending to be in Venice some weeks, possibly all summer, and having some literary work, some reading and writing to do, so that I must be quiet and yet if possible a great deal in the open air – that's why I've felt a garden to be really indispensable. I appeal to your own experience,' I went on with as sociable a smile as I could risk. 'Now can't I look at yours?'

'I don't know, I don't understand,' the poor woman murmured, planted there and letting her weak wonder deal – helplessly enough, as I felt – with my strangeness.

'I mean only from one of those windows – such grand ones as you have here – if you'll let me open the shutters.' And I walked toward the back of the house. When I had advanced halfway I stopped and waited as in the belief she would accompany me. I had been of necessity quite abrupt, but I strove at the same time to give her the impression of extreme courtesy. 'I've looked at furnished rooms all over the place, and it seems impossible to find any with a garden attached. Naturally in a place like Venice gardens are rare. It's absurd if you like, for a man, but I can't live without flowers.'

'There are none to speak of down there.' She came nearer, as if, though she mistrusted me, I had drawn her by an invisible thread. I went on again, and she continued as she followed me: 'We've a few, but they're very common. It costs too much to cultivate them; one has to have a man.'

'Why shouldn't I be the man?' I asked. 'I'll work without wages; or rather I'll put in a gardener. You shall have the sweetest flowers in Venice.'

She protested against this with a small quaver of sound that might have been at the same time a gush of rapture for my free sketch. Then she gasped: 'We don't know you – we don't know you.'

'You know me as much as I know you; or rather much

more, because you know my name. And if you're English I'm almost a countryman.'

'We're not English,' said my companion, watching me in practical submission while I threw open the shutters of one of the divisions of the wide high window.

'You speak the language so beautifully: might I ask what you are?' Seen from above the garden was in truth shabby, yet I felt at a glance that it had great capabilities. She made no rejoinder, she was so lost in her blankness and gentleness, and I exclaimed: 'You don't mean to say you're also by chance American?'

'I don't know. We used to be.'

'Used to be? Surely you haven't changed?'

'It's so many years ago. We don't seem to be anything now.'

'So many years that you've been living here? Well, I don't wonder at that; it's a grand old house. I suppose you all use the garden,' I went on, 'but I assure you I shouldn't be in your way. I'd be very quiet and stay quite in one corner.'

'We all use it?' she repeated after me vaguely, not coming close to the window but looking at my shoes. She appeared to think me capable of throwing her out.

'I mean all your family — as many as you are.'

'There's only one other than me. She's very old. She never goes down.'

I feel again my thrill at this close identification of Juliana; in spite of which, however, I kept my head. 'Only one other in all this great house!' I feigned to be not only amazed but almost scandalised. 'Dear lady, you must have space then to spare!'

'To spare?' she repeated — almost as for the rich unwonted joy to her of spoken words.

'Why you surely don't live (two quiet women — I see *you* are quiet, at any rate) in fifty rooms!' Then with a burst of hope and cheer I put the question straight. 'Couldn't you for a good rent *let* me two or three? That would set me up!'

I had now struck the note that translated my purpose, and I needn't reproduce the whole of the tune I played. I ended by making my entertainer believe me an undesigning person, though of course I didn't even attempt to persuade her I was not an eccentric one. I repeated that I had studies to pursue; that I wanted quiet; that I delighted in a garden and had vainly sought one up and down the city: that I would undertake that before another month was over the dear old house should be smothered in flowers. I think it was the flowers that won my suit, for I afterwards found that Miss Tina – for such the name of this high tremulous spinster proved somewhat incongruously to be – had an insatiable appetite for them. When I speak of my suit as won I mean that before I left her she had promised me she would refer the question to her aunt. I invited information as to who her aunt might be and she answered 'Why Miss Bordereau!' with an air of surprise, as if I might have been expected to know. There were contradictions like this in Miss Tina which, as I observed later, contributed to make her rather pleasingly incalculable and interesting. It was the study of the two ladies to live so that the world shouldn't talk of them or touch them, and yet they had never altogether accepted the idea that it didn't hear of them. In Miss Tina at any rate a grateful susceptibility to human contact had not died out, and contact of a limited order there would be if I should come to live in the house.

'We've never done anything of the sort; we've never had a lodger or any kind of inmate.' So much as this she made a point of saying to me. 'We're very poor, we live very badly – almost on nothing. The rooms are very bare – those you might take; they've nothing at all in them. I don't know how you'd sleep, how you'd eat.'

'With your permission I could easily put in a bed and a few tables and chairs. C'est la moindre des choses and the affair of an hour or two. I know a little man from whom I can hire for a trifle what I should so briefly want, what I should use; my gondolier can bring the things round in his boat. Of course in this great house you must have a second kitchen, and my servant, who's a wonderfully handy fellow' – this personage was an evocation of the moment – 'can easily cook me a chop there. My tastes and habits are of the simplest: I live on flowers!' And then I ventured to add that if they were very poor it was all the more reason they should let their rooms. They were bad economists – I had never heard of such a waste of material.

I saw in a moment my good lady had never before been spoken to in any such fashion – with a humorous firmness that didn't exclude sympathy, that was quite founded on it.

She might easily have told me that my sympathy was impertinent, but this by good fortune didn't occur to her. I left her
with the understanding that she would submit the question to
her aunt and that I might come back the next day for their
decision.

'The aunt will refuse; she'll think the whole proceeding very
*louche!*' Mrs Prest declared shortly after this, when I had
resumed my place in her gondola. She had put the idea into my
head and now – so little are women to be counted on – she
appeared to take a despondent view of it. Her pessimism pro-
voked me and I pretended to have the best hopes; I went so far
as to boast of a distinct prevision of success. Upon this Mrs
Prest broke out: 'Oh I see what's in your head! You fancy
you've made such an impression in five minutes that she's dying
for you to come and can be depended on to bring the old one
round. If you do get in you'll count it as a triumph.'

I did count it as a triumph, but only for the commentator –
in the last analysis – not for the man, who had not the tradition
of personal conquest. When I went back on the morrow the
little maid-servant conducted me straight through the long sala
– it opened there as before in large perspective and was lighter
now, which I thought a good omen – into the apartment from
which the recipient of my former visit had emerged on that
occasion. It was a spacious shabby parlour with a fine old
painted ceiling under which a strange figure sat alone at one
of the windows. They come back to me now almost with the
palpitation they caused, the successive states marking my consciousness that as the door of the room closed behind me I was
really face to face with the Juliana of some of Aspern's most
exquisite and most renowned lyrics. I grew used to her afterwards, though never completely; but as she sat there before
me my heart beat as fast as if the miracle of resurrection had
taken place for my benefit. Her presence seemed somehow to
contain and express his own, and I felt nearer to him at that
first moment of seeing her than I ever had been before or ever
have been since. Yes, I remember my emotions in their order,
even including a curious little tremor that took me when I
saw the niece not to be there. With her, the day before, I had
become sufficiently familiar, but it almost exceeded my courage
– much as I had longed for the event – to be left alone with

so terrible a relic as the aunt. She was too strange, too literally resurgent. Then came a check from the perception that we weren't really face to face, inasmuch as she had over her eyes a horrible green shade which served for her almost as a mask. I believed for the instant that she had put it on expressly, so that from underneath it she might take me all in without my getting at herself. At the same time it created a presumption of some ghastly death's-head lurking behind it. The divine Juliana as a grinning skull – the vision hung there until it passed. Then it came to me that she *was* tremendously old – so old that death might take her at any moment, before I should have time to compass my end. The next thought was a correction to that; it lighted up the situation. She would die next week, she would die tomorrow – then I could pounce on her possessions and ransack her drawers. Meanwhile she sat there neither moving nor speaking. She was very small and shrunken, bent forward with her hands in her lap. She was dressed in black and her head was wrapped in a piece of old black lace which showed no hair.

My emotion keeping me silent she spoke first, and the remark she made was exactly the most unexpected.

# III

'OUR house is very far from the centre, but the little canal is very *comme il faut*.'

'It's the sweetest corner of Venice and I can imagine nothing more charming,' I hastened to reply. The old lady's voice was very thin and weak, but it had an agreeable, cultivated murmur and there was wonder in the thought that that individual note had been in Jeffrey Aspern's ear.

'Please to sit down there. I hear very well,' she said quietly, as if perhaps I had been shouting; and the chair she pointed to was at a certain distance. I took possession of it, assuring her I was perfectly aware of my intrusion and of my not having been properly introduced, and that I could but throw myself on her indulgence. Perhaps the other lady, the one I had had the honour of seeing the day before, would have explained to her about the garden. That was literally what had given me courage to take a step so unconventional. I had fallen in love at sight with the whole place – she herself was probably so used to it that she didn't know the impression it was capable of making on a stranger – and I had felt it really a case to risk something. Was her own kindness in receiving me a sign that I was not wholly out in my calculation? It would make me extremely happy to think so. I could give her my word of honour that I was a most respectable inoffensive person and that as a co-tenant of the palace, so to speak, they would be barely conscious of my existence. I would conform to any regulations, any restrictions, if they would only let me enjoy the garden. Moreover I should be delighted to give her references, guarantees; they would be of the very best, both in Venice and in England, as well as in America.

She listened to me in perfect stillness and I felt her look at me with great penetration, though I could see only the lower part of her bleached and shrivelled face. Independently of the refining process of old age it had a delicacy which once must have been great. She had been very fair, she had had a wonderful complexion. She was silent a little after I had ceased speaking; then she began: 'If you're so fond of a garden why don't you go to *terra firma*, where there are so many far better than this?'

'Oh it's the combination!' I answered, smiling; and then with rather a flight of fancy: 'It's the idea of a garden in the middle of the sea.'

'This isn't the middle of the sea; you can't so much as see the water.'

I stared a moment, wondering if she wished to convict me of fraud. 'Can't see the water? Why, dear madam, I can come up to the very gate in my boat.'

She appeared inconsequent, for she said vaguely in reply to this: 'Yes, if you've got a boat. I haven't any; it's many years since I've been in one of the *gondole*.' She uttered these words as if they designed a curious far-away craft known to her only by hearsay.

'Let me assure you of the pleasure with which I would put mine at your service!' I returned. I had scarcely said this however before I became aware that the speech was in questionable taste and might also do me the injury of making me appear too eager, too possessed of a hidden motive. But the old woman remained impenetrable and her attitude worried me by suggesting that she had a fuller vision of me than I had of her. She gave me no thanks for my somewhat extravagant offer, but remarked that the lady I had seen the day before was her niece; she would presently come in. She had asked her to stay away a little on purpose – had had her reasons for seeing me first alone. She relapsed into silence and I turned over the fact of these unmentioned reasons and the question of what might come yet; also that of whether I might venture on some judicious remark in praise of her companion. I went so far as to say I should be delighted to see our absent friend again: she had been so very patient with me, considering how odd she must have thought me – a declaration which drew from Miss Bordereau another of her whimsical speeches.

'She has very good manners; I bred her up myself!' I was on the point of saying that that accounted for the easy grace of the niece, but I arrested myself in time, and the next moment the old woman went on: 'I don't care who you may be – I don't want to know: it signifies very little today.' This had all the air of being a formula of dismissal, as if her next words would be that I might take myself off now that she had had the amusement of looking on the face of such a monster of indiscretion. Therefore I was all the more surprised when she added in her soft venerable quaver: 'You may have as many rooms as you like – if you'll pay me a good deal of money.'

I hesitated but an instant, long enough to measure what she meant in particular by this condition. First it struck me that she must have really a large sum in her mind; then I reasoned quickly that her idea of a large sum would probably not correspond to my own. My deliberation, I think, was not so visible as to diminish the promptitude with which I replied: 'I will pay with pleasure and of course in advance whatever you may think it proper to ask me.'

'Well then, a thousand francs a month,' she said instantly, while her baffling green shade continued to cover her attitude.

The figure, as they say, was startling and my logic had been at fault. The sum she had mentioned was, by the Venetian measure of such matters, exceedingly large; there was many an old palace in an out-of-the-way corner that I might on such terms have enjoyed the whole of by the year. But so far as my resources allowed I was prepared to spend money, and my decision was quickly taken. I would pay her with a smiling face what she asked, but in that case I would make it up by getting hold of my 'spoils' for nothing. Moreover if she had asked five times as much I should have risen to the occasion, so odious would it have seemed to me to stand chaffering with Aspern's Juliana. It was queer enough to have a question of money with her at all. I assured her that her views perfectly met my own and that on the morrow I should have the pleasure of putting three months' rent into her hand. She received this announcement with apparent complacency and with no discoverable sense that after all it would become her to say that I ought to see the rooms first. This didn't occur to her, and indeed her serenity was mainly what I wanted. Our little agreement was just concluded when the door opened and the younger lady appeared on the threshold. As soon as Miss Bordereau saw her niece she cried out almost gaily: 'He'll give three thousand – three thousand tomorrow!'

Miss Tina stood still, her patient eyes turning from one of us to the other; then she brought out, scarcely above her breath: 'Do you mean francs?'

'Did you mean francs or dollars?' the old woman asked of me at this.

'I think francs were what you said,' I sturdily smiled.

'That's very good,' said Miss Tina, as if she had felt how overreaching her own question might have looked.

'What do *you* know? You're ignorant,' Miss Bordereau remarked; not with acerbity but with a strange soft coldness.

'Yes, of money – certainly of money!' Miss Tina hastened to concede.

'I'm sure you've your own fine branches of knowledge,' I took the liberty of saying genially. There was something painful to me, somehow, in the turn the conversation had taken, in the discussion of dollars and francs.

'She had a very good education when she was young. I looked into that myself,' said Miss Bordereau. Then she added: 'But she has learned nothing since.'

'I've always been with *you*,' Miss Tina rejoined very mildly, and of a certainty with no intention of an epigram.

'Yes, but for that – !' her aunt declared with more satirical force. She evidently meant that but for this her niece would never have got on at all; the point of the observation however being lost on Miss Tina, though she blushed at hearing her history revealed to a stranger. Miss Bordereau went on, addressing herself to me: 'And what time will you come tomorrow with the money?'

'The sooner the better. If it suits you I'll come at noon.'

'I'm always here, but I have my hours,' said the old woman as if her convenience were not to be taken for granted.

'You mean the times when you receive?'

'I never receive. But I'll see you at noon, when you come with the money.'

'Very good, I shall be punctual.' To which I added: 'May I shake hands with you on our contract?' I thought there ought to be some little form; it would make me really feel easier, for I was sure there would be no other. Besides, though Miss Bordereau couldn't today be called personally attractive and there was something even in her wasted antiquity that bade one stand at one's distance, I felt an irresistible desire to hold in my own for a moment the hand Jeffrey Aspern had pressed.

For a minute she made no answer, and I saw that my proposal

failed to meet with her approbation. She indulged in no movement of withdrawal, which I half-expected; she only said
coldly: 'I belong to a time when that was not the custom.'

I felt rather snubbed but I exclaimed good-humouredly to
Miss Tina 'Oh you'll do as well!' I shook hands with her while
she assented with a small flutter. 'Yes, yes, to show it's all
arranged!'

'Shall you bring the money in gold?' Miss Bordereau demanded as I was turning to the door.

I looked at her a moment. 'Aren't you a little afraid, after
all, of keeping such a sum as that in the house?' It was not that
I was annoyed at her avidity, but was truly struck with the
disparity between such a treasure and such scanty means of
guarding it.

'Whom should I be afraid of if I'm not afraid of you?' she
asked with her shrunken grimness.

'Ah well,' I laughed, 'I shall be in point of fact a protector
and I'll bring gold if you prefer.'

'Thank you,' the old woman returned with dignity and with
an inclination of her head which evidently signified my dismissal. I passed out of the room, thinking how hard it would
be to circumvent her. As I stood in the sala again I saw that
Miss Tina had followed me, and I supposed that as her aunt
had neglected to suggest I should take a look at my quarters it
was her purpose to repair the omission. But she made no such
overture; she only stood there with a dim, though not a languid
smile, and with an effect of irresponsible incompetent youth
almost comically at variance with the faded facts of her person.
She was not infirm, like her aunt, but she struck me as more
deeply futile, because her inefficiency was inward, which was
not the case with Miss Bordereau's. I waited to see if she would
offer to show me the rest of the house, but I didn't precipitate
the question, inasmuch as my plan was from this moment to
spend as much of my time as possible in her society. A minute
indeed elapsed before I committed myself.

'I've had better fortune than I hoped. It was very kind of
her to see me. Perhaps you said a good word for me.'

'It was the idea of the money,' said Miss Tina.

'And did you suggest that?'

'I told her you'd perhaps pay largely.'

'What made you think that?'

'I told her I thought you were rich.'

'And what put that into your head?'

'I don't know; the way you talked.'

'Dear me, I must talk differently now,' I returned. 'I'm sorry to say it's not the case.'

'Well,' said Miss Tina, 'I think that in Venice the *forestieri* in general often give a great deal for something that after all isn't much.' She appeared to make this remark with a comforting intention, to wish to remind me that if I had been extravagant I wasn't foolishly singular. We walked together along the sala, and as I took its magnificent measure I observed that I was afraid it wouldn't form a part of my *quartiere*. Were my rooms by chance to be among those that opened into it? 'Not if you go above – to the second floor,' she answered as if she had rather taken for granted I would know my proper place.

'And I infer that that's where your aunt would like me to be.'

'She said your apartments ought to be very distinct.'

'That certainly would be best.' And I listened with respect while she told me that above I should be free to take whatever I might like; that there was another staircase, but only from the floor on which we stood, and that to pass from it to the garden-level or to come up to my lodging I should have in effect to cross the great hall. This was an immense point gained; I foresaw that it would constitute my whole leverage in my relations with the two ladies. When I asked Miss Tina how I was to manage at present to find my way up she replied with an access of that sociable shyness which constantly marked her manner:

'Perhaps you can't. I don't see – unless I should go with you.' She evidently hadn't thought of this before.

We ascended to the upper floor and visited a long succession of empty rooms. The best of them looked over the garden; some of the others had above the opposite rough-tiled house-tops a view of the blue lagoon. They were all dusty and even a little disfigured with long neglect, but I saw that by spending a few hundred francs I should be able to make three or four of them habitable enough. My experiment was turning out costly, yet now that I had all but taken possession I ceased to allow this to trouble me. I mentioned to my companion a few of the things I should put in, but she replied rather more precipitately than usual that I might do exactly what I liked: she seemed to wish to notify me that the Misses Bordereau would take none but the most veiled interest in my proceedings. I guessed that her aunt had instructed her to adopt this tone, and I may as well say now that I came afterwards to distinguish perfectly (as I believed) between the speeches she made on her own responsibility and those the old woman imposed upon her. She took no notice of the unswept condition of the rooms and indulged neither in explanations nor in apologies. I said to myself that this was a sign Juliana and her niece – disenchanting idea! – were untidy persons with a low Italian standard; but I afterwards recognised that a lodger who had forced an entrance had no *locus standi* as a critic. We looked out of a good many windows, for there was nothing within the rooms to look at, and still I wanted to linger. I asked her what several different objects in the prospect might be, but in no case did she appear to know. She was evidently not familiar with the view – it was as if she had not looked at it for years – and I presently saw that she was too preoccupied with something else to pretend to care for it. Suddenly she said – the remark was not suggested:

'I don't know whether it will make any difference to you, but the money is for me.'

'The money—?'

'The money you're going to bring.'

'Why you'll make me wish to stay here two or three years!' I spoke as benevolently as possible, though it had begun to act on my nerves that these women so associated with Aspern should so constantly bring the pecuniary question back.

'That would be very good for me,' she answered almost gaily.

'You put me on my honour!'

She looked as if she failed to understand this, but went on: 'She wants me to have more. She thinks she's going to die.'

'Ah not soon I hope!' I cried with genuine feeling. I had perfectly considered the possibility of her destroying her documents on the day she should feel her end at hand. I believed that she would cling to them till then, and I was as convinced of her reading Aspern's letters over every night or at least pressing them to her withered lips. I would have given a good deal for some view of those solemnities. I asked Miss Tina if her venerable relative were seriously ill, and she replied that she was only very tired – she had lived so extraordinarily long. That was what she said herself – she wanted to die for a change. Besides, all her friends had been dead for ages; either they ought to have remained or she ought to have gone. That was another thing her aunt often said: she was not at all resigned – resigned, that is, to life.

'But people don't die when they like, do they?' Miss Tina enquired. I took the liberty of asking why, if there was actually enough money to maintain both of them, there would not be more than enough in case of her being left alone. She considered this difficult problem a moment and then said: 'Oh well, you know, she takes care of me. She thinks that when I'm alone I shall be a great fool and shan't know how to manage.'

'I should have supposed rather that you took care of *her*. I'm afraid she's very proud.'

'Why, have you discovered that already?' Miss Tina cried with a dimness of glad surprise.

'I was shut up with her there for a considerable time and she struck me, she interested me extremely. It didn't take me long to make my discovery. She won't have much to say to me while I'm here.'

'No, I don't think she will,' my companion averred.

'Do you suppose she has some suspicion of me?'

Miss Tina's honest eyes gave me no sign I had touched a mark. 'I shouldn't think so – letting you in after all so easily.'

'You call it easily? She has covered her risk,' I said. 'But where is it one could take an advantage of her?'

'I oughtn't to tell you if I knew, ought I?' And Miss Tina added, before I had time to reply to this, smiling dolefully: 'Do you think we've any weak points?'

'That's exactly what I'm asking. You'd only have to mention them for me to respect them religiously.'

She looked at me hereupon with that air of timid but candid and even gratified curiosity with which she had confronted me from the first; after which she said: 'There's nothing to tell. We're terribly quiet. I don't know how the days pass. We've no life.'

'I wish I might think I should bring you a little.'

'Oh we know what we want,' she went on. 'It's all right.'

There were twenty things I desired to ask her: how in the world they did live; whether they had any friends or visitors, any relations in America or in other countries. But I judged such probings premature; I must leave it to a later chance. 'Well, don't *you* be proud,' I contented myself with saying. 'Don't hide from me altogether.'

'Oh I must stay with my aunt,' she returned without looking at me. And at the same moment, abruptly, without any ceremony of parting, she quitted me and disappeared, leaving me to make my own way downstairs. I stayed a while longer, wandering about the bright desert – the sun was pouring in – of the old house, thinking the situation over on the spot. Not even the pattering little *serva* came to look after me, and I reflected that after all this treatment showed confidence.

# IV

PERHAPS it did, but all the same, six weeks later, towards the middle of June, the moment when Mrs Prest undertook her annual migration, I had made no measurable advance. I was obliged to confess to her that I had no results to speak of. My first step had been unexpectedly rapid, but there was no appearance it would be followed by a second. I was a thousand miles from taking tea with my hostesses – that privilege of which, as I reminded my good friend, we both had had a vision. She reproached me with lacking boldness and I answered that even to be bold you must have an opportunity: you may push on through a breach, but you can't batter down a dead wall. She returned that the breach I had already made was big enough to admit an army and accused me of wasting precious hours in whimpering in her salon when I ought to have been carrying on the struggle in the field. It is true that I went to see her very often – all on the theory that it would console me (I freely expressed my discouragement) for my want of success on my own premises. But I began to feel that it didn't console me to be perpetually chaffed for my scruples, especially since I was really so vigilant; and I was rather glad when my ironic friend closed her house for the summer. She had expected to draw amusement from the drama of my intercourse with the Misses Bordereau, and was disappointed that the intercourse, and consequently the drama, had not come off. 'They'll lead you on to your ruin,' she said before she left Venice. 'They'll get all your money without showing you a scrap.' I think I settled down to my business with more concentration after her departure.

It was a fact that up to that time I had not, save on a single brief occasion, had even a moment's contact with my queer hostesses. The exception had occurred when I carried them according to my promise the terrible three thousand francs. Then I found Miss Tina awaiting me in the hall, and she took the money from my hand with a promptitude that prevented my seeing her aunt. The old lady had promised to receive me, yet apparently thought nothing of breaking that vow. The money was contained in a bag of chamois leather, of respectable

dimensions, which my banker had given me, and Miss Tina
had to make a big fist to receive it. This she did with extreme
solemnity, though I tried to treat the affair a little as a joke.
It was in no jocular strain, yet it was with a clearness akin to a
brightness that she enquired, weighing the money in her two
palms: 'Don't you think it's too much?' To which I replied that
this would depend on the amount of pleasure I should get for it.
Hereupon she turned away from me quickly, as she had done
the day before, murmuring in a tone different from any she
had used hitherto: 'Oh pleasure, pleasure – there's no pleasure
in this house!'

After that, for a long time, I never saw her, and I wondered
the common chances of the day shouldn't have helped us to
meet. It could only be evident that she was immensely on her
guard against them; and in addition to this the house was so big
that for each other we were lost in it. I used to look out for
her hopefully as I crossed the sala in my comings and goings,
but I was not rewarded with a glimpse of the tail of her dress.
It was as if she never peeped out of her aunt's apartment. I
used to wonder what she did there week after week and year
after year. I had never met so stiff a policy of seclusion; it was
more than keeping quiet – it was like hunted creatures feigning
death. The two ladies appeared to have no visitors whatever
and no sort of contact with the world. I judged at least that
people couldn't have come to the house and that Miss Tina
couldn't have gone out without my catching some view of it.
I did what I disliked myself for doing – considering it but as
once in a way: I questioned my servant about their habits and
let him infer that I should be interested in any information he
might glean. But he gleaned amazingly little for a knowing
Venetian: it must be added that where there is a perpetual fast
there are very few crumbs on the floor. His ability in other
ways was sufficient, if not quite all I had attributed to him on
the occasion of my first interview with Miss Tina. He had
helped my gondolier to bring me round a boat-load of furniture;
and when these articles had been carried to the top of the
palace and distributed according to our associated wisdom he
organised my household with such dignity as answered to its
being composed exclusively of himself. He made me in short as
comfortable as I could be with my indifferent prospects. I should

have been glad if he had fallen in love with Miss Bordereau's maid or, failing this, had taken her in aversion: either event might have brought about some catastrophe, and a catastrophe might have led to some parley. It was my idea that she would have been sociable, and I myself on various occasions saw her flit to and fro on domestic errands, so that I was sure she was accessible. But I tasted of no gossip from that fountain, and I afterwards learned that Pasquale's affections were fixed upon an object that made him heedless of other women. This was a young lady with a powdered face, a yellow cotton gown and much leisure, who used often to come to see him. She practised, at her convenience, the art of a stringer of beads – these ornaments are made in Venice to profusion; she had her pocket full of them and I used to find them on the floor of my apartment – and kept an eye on the possible rival in the house. It was not for me of course to make the domestics tattle, and I never said a word to Miss Bordereau's cook.

It struck me as a proof of the old woman's resolve to have nothing to do with me that she should never have sent me a receipt for my three months' rent. For some days I looked out for it and then, when I had given it up, wasted a good deal of time in wondering what her reason had been for neglecting so indispensable and familiar a form. At first I was tempted to send her a reminder; after which I put by the idea – against my judgement as to what was right in the particular case – on the general ground of wishing to keep quiet. If Miss Bordereau suspected me of ulterior aims she would suspect me less if I should be businesslike, and yet I consented not to be. It was possible she intended her omission as an impertinence, a visible irony, to show how she could overreach people who attempted to overreach her. On that hypothesis it was well to let her see that one didn't notice her little tricks. The real reading of the matter, I afterwards gathered, was simply the poor lady's desire to emphasise the fact that I was in the enjoyment of a favour as rigidly limited as it had been liberally bestowed. She had given me part of her house, but she wouldn't add to that so much as a morsel of paper with her name on it. Let me say that even at first this didn't make me too miserable, for the whole situation had the charm of its oddity. I foresaw that I should have a summer after my own literary heart, and the sense of playing with my opportunity was much greater after all than any sense of being played with. There could be no Venetian business without patience, and since I adored the place I was much more in the spirit of it for having laid in a large provision. That spirit kept me perpetual company and seemed to look out at me from the revived immortal face – in which all his genius shone – of the great poet who was my prompter. I had invoked him and he had come; he hovered before me half the time; it was as if his bright ghost had returned to earth to assure me he regarded the affair as his own no less than as mine and that we should see it fraternally and fondly to a conclusion. It was as if he had said: 'Poor dear, be easy with her; she has some natural prejudices; only give her time. Strange as it may appear to you she was very attractive in 1820. Meanwhile aren't we in Venice together, and what better place is there for the meeting of dear friends? See how it glows with the advancing summer; how the sky and the sea and the rosy air and the marble of the palaces all shimmer and melt together.' My eccentric private errand became a part of the general romance and the general glory – I felt even a mystic companionship, a moral fraternity with all those who in the past had been in the service of art. They had worked for beauty, for a devotion; and what else was I doing? That element was in everything that Jeffrey Aspern had written, and I was only bringing it to light.

I lingered in the sala when I went to and fro; I used to watch – as long as I thought decent – the door that led to Miss Bordereau's part of the house. A person observing me might have supposed I was trying to cast a spell on it or attempting some odd experiment in hypnotism. But I was only praying it might open or thinking what treasure probably lurked behind it. I hold it singular, as I look back, that I should never have doubted for a moment that the sacred relics were there; never have failed to know the joy of being beneath the same roof with them. After all they were under my hand – they had not escaped me yet; and they made my life continuous, in a fashion, with the illustrious life they had touched at the other end. I lost myself in this satisfaction to the point of assuming – in my quiet extravagance – that poor Miss Tina also went back, and still went back, as I used to phrase it. She did indeed, the gentle spinster, but not quite so far as Jeffrey Aspern, who was simple hearsay to her quite as he was to me. Only she had lived for years, with Juliana, she had seen and handled all mementoes and – even though she was stupid – some esoteric knowledge had rubbed off on her. That was what the old woman represented – esoteric knowledge; and this was the idea with which my critical heart used to thrill. It literally beat faster often, of an evening when I had been out, as I stopped with my candle in the re-echoing hall on my way up to bed. It was as if at such a moment as that, in the stillness and after the long contradiction of the day, Miss Bordereau's secrets were in the air, the wonder of her survival more vivid. These were the acute impressions. I had them in another form, with more of a certain shade of reciprocity, during the hours I sat in the garden looking up over the top of my book at the closed windows of my hostess. In these windows no sign of life ever appeared; it was as if, for fear of my catching a glimpse of them, the two ladies passed their days in the dark. But this only emphasised their having matters to conceal; which was what I had wished to prove. Their motionless shutters became as expressive as eyes consciously closed, and I took comfort in the probability that, though invisible themselves, they kept me in view between the lashes.

I made a point of spending as much time as possible in the garden, to justify the picture I had originally given of my horticultural passion. And I not only spent time, but (hang it! as I said) spent precious money. As soon as I had got my rooms arranged and could give the question proper thought I surveyed the place with a clever expert and made terms for having it put in order. I was sorry to do this, for personally I liked it better as it was, with its weeds and its wild rich tangle, its sweet characteristic Venetian shabbiness. I had to be consistent, to keep my promise that I would smother the house in flowers. Moreover I clung to the fond fancy that by flowers I should make my way – I should succeed by big nosegays. I would batter the old women with lilies – I would bombard their citadel with roses. Their door would have to yield to the pressure when a mound of fragrance should be heaped against it. The place in truth had been brutally neglected. The Venetian capacity for dawdling is of the largest, and for a good many days

unlimited litter was all my gardener had to show for his min-
istrations. There was a great digging of holes and carting about
of earth, and after a while I grew so impatient that I had
thoughts of sending for my 'results' to the nearest stand. But
I felt sure my friends would see through the chinks of their
shutters where such tribute *couldn't* have been gathered, and
might so make up their minds against my veracity. I possessed
my soul and finally, though the delay was long, perceived some
appearances of bloom. This encouraged me and I waited serenely
enough till they multiplied. Meanwhile the real summer days
arrived and began to pass, and as I look back upon them they
seem to me almost the happiest of my life. I took more and
more care to be in the garden whenever it was not too hot. I had
an arbour arranged and a low table and an armchair put into
it; and I carried out books and portfolios – I had always some
business of writing in hand – and worked and waited and
mused and hoped, while the golden hours elapsed and the plants
drank in the light and the inscrutable old palace turned pale
and then, as the day waned, began to recover and flush and my
papers rustled in the wandering breeze of the Adriatic.

Considering how little satisfaction I got from it at first it is
wonderful I shouldn't have grown more tired of trying to guess
what mystic rites of ennui the Misses Bordereau celebrated in
their darkened rooms; whether this had always been the tenor
of their life and how in previous years they had escaped elbow-
ing their neighbours. It was supposable they had then had other
habits, forms and resources; that they must once have been
young or at least middle-aged. There was no end to the questions
it was possible to ask about them and no end to the answers
it was not possible to frame. I had known many of my country-
people in Europe and was familiar with the strange ways they
were liable to take up there; but the Misses Bordereau formed
altogether a new type of the American absentee. Indeed it was
clear the American name had ceased to have any application to
them – I had seen this in the ten minutes I spent in the old
woman's room. You could never have said whence they came
from the appearance of either of them; wherever it was they
had long ago shed and unlearned all native marks and notes.
There was nothing in them one recognised or fitted, and, putting
the question of speech aside, they might have been Norwegians

or Spaniards. Miss Bordereau, after all, had been in Europe
nearly three quarters of a century; it appeared by some verses
addressed to her by Aspern on the occasion of his own second
absence from America – verses of which Cumnor and I had
after infinite conjecture established solidly enough the date –
that she was even then, as a girl of twenty, on the foreign side
of the sea. There was a profession in the poem – I hope not
just for the phrase – that he had come back for her sake. We
had no real light on her circumstances at that moment, any
more than we had upon her origin, which we believed to be of
the sort usually spoken of as modest. Cumnor had a theory
that she had been a governess in some family in which the poet
visited and that, in consequence of her position, there was from
the first something unavowed, or rather something quite clan-
destine, in their relations. I on the other hand had hatched a
little romance according to which she was the daughter of an
artist, a painter or a sculptor, who had left the Western world,
when the century was fresh, to study in the ancient schools.
It was essential to my hypothesis that this amiable man should
have lost his wife, should have been poor and unsuccessful and
should have had a second daughter of a disposition quite different from Juliana's. It was also indispensable that he should
have been accompanied to Europe by these young ladies and
should have established himself there for the remainder of a
struggling saddened life. There was a further implication that
Miss Bordereau had had in her youth a perverse and reckless,
albeit a generous and fascinating character, and that she had
braved some wondrous chances. By what passions had she been
ravaged, by what adventures and sufferings had she been
blanched, what store of memories had she laid away for the
monotonous future?

I asked myself these things as I sat spinning theories about
her in my arbour and the bees droned in the flowers. It was
incontestable that, whether for right or for wrong, most readers
of certain of Aspern's poems (poems not as ambiguous as the
sonnets – scarcely more divine, I think – of Shakespeare) had
taken for granted that Juliana had not always adhered to the
steep footway of renunciation. There hovered about her name a
perfume of impenitent passion, an intimation that she had not
been exactly as the respectable young person in general. Was

this a sign that her singer had betrayed her, had given her
away, as we say nowadays, to posterity? Certain it is that it would
have been difficult to put one's finger on the passage in which
her fair fame suffered injury. Moreover was not any fame
fair enough that was so sure of duration and was associated
with works immortal through their beauty? It was a part of my
idea that the young lady had had a foreign lover – and say
an unedifying tragical rupture – before her meeting with Jeffrey
Aspern. She had lived with her father and sister in a queer old-
fashioned expatriated artistic Bohemia of the days when the
aesthetic was only the academic and the painters who knew
the best models for *contadina* and *pifferaro* wore peaked hats
and long hair. It was a society less awake than the coteries of
today – in its ignorance of the wonderful chances, the opportunities of the early bird, with which its path was strewn – to
tatters of old stuff and fragments of old crockery; so that Miss
Bordereau appeared not to have picked up or have inherited
many objects of importance. There was no enviable *bric-à-brac*,
with its provoking legend of cheapness, in the room in which I
had seen her. Such a fact as that suggested bareness, but none
the less it worked happily into the sentimental interest I had
always taken in the early movements of my countrymen as
visitors to Europe. When Americans went abroad in 1820 there
was something romantic, almost heroic in it, as compared with
the perpetual ferryings of the present hour, the hour at which
photography and other conveniences have annihilated surprise.
Miss Bordereau had sailed with her family on a tossing brig
in the days of long voyages and sharp differences; she had had
her emotions on the top of yellow diligences, passed the night
at inns where she dreamed of travellers' tales, and was most
struck, on reaching the Eternal City, with the elegance of
Roman pearls and scarfs and mosaic brooches. There was something touching to me in all that, and my imagination frequently
went back to the period. If Miss Bordereau carried it there of
course Jeffrey Aspern had at other times done so with greater
force. It was a much more important fact, if one was looking at
¹⋯ genius critically, that he had lived in the days before the
⋯al transfusion. It had happened to me to regret that he had
⋯ Europe at all; I should have lived to see what he would
⋯itten without that experience, by which he had in-

contestably been enriched. But as his fate had ruled otherwise I went with him – I tried to judge how the general old order would have struck him. It was not only there, however, I watched him; the relations he had entertained with the special new had even a livelier interest. His own country after all had had most of his life, and his muse, as they said at that time, was essentially American. That was originally what I had prized him for: that at a period when our native land was nude and crude and provincial, when the famous 'atmosphere' it is supposed to lack was not even missed, when literature was lonely there and art and form almost impossible, he had found means to live and write like one of the first; to be free and general and not at all afraid; to feel, understand and express everything.

# V

I WAS seldom at home in the evening, for when I attempted to occupy myself in my apartments the lamplight brought in a swarm of noxious insects, and it was too hot for closed windows. Accordingly I spent the late hours either on the water – the moonlights of Venice are famous – or in the splendid square which serves as a vast forecourt to the strange old church of Saint Mark. I sat in front of Florian's café eating ices, listening to music, talking with acquaintances: the traveller will remember how the immense cluster of tables and little chairs stretches like a promontory into the smooth lake of the Piazza. The whole place, of a summer's evening, under the stars and with all the lamps, all the voices and light footsteps on marble – the only sounds of the immense arcade that encloses it – is an open-air saloon dedicated to cooling drinks and to a still finer degustation, that of the splendid impressions received during the day. When I didn't prefer to keep mine to myself there was always a stray tourist, disencumbered of his Baedeker, to discuss them with, or some domesticated painter rejoicing in the return of the season of strong effects. The great basilica, with its low domes and bristling embroideries, the mystery of its mosaic and sculpture, looked ghostly in the tempered gloom, and the sea-breeze passed between the twin columns of the Piazzetta, the lintels of a door no longer guarded, as gently as if a rich curtain swayed there. I used sometimes on these occasions to think of the Misses Bordereau and of the pity of their being shut up in apartments which in the Venetian July even Venetian vastness couldn't relieve of some stuffiness. Their life seemed miles away from the life of the Piazza, and no doubt it was really too late to make the austere Juliana change her habits. But poor Miss Tina would have enjoyed one of Florian's ices, I was sure; sometimes I even had thoughts of carrying one home to her. Fortunately my patience bore fruit and I was not obliged to do anything so ridiculous.

One evening about the middle of July I came in earlier than usual – I forget what chance had led to this – and instead of going up to my quarters made my way into the garden. The temperature was very high; it was such a night as one would gladly have spent in the open air, and I was in no hurry to go to bed. I had floated home in my gondola, listening to the slow splash of the oar in the dark narrow canals, and now the only thought that occupied me was that it would be good to recline at one's length in the fragrant darkness on a garden-bench. The odour of the canal was doubtless at the bottom of that aspiration, and the breath of the garden, as I entered it, gave consistency to my purpose. It was delicious – just such an air as must have trembled with Romeo's vows when he stood among the thick flowers and raised his arms to his mistress's balcony. I looked at the windows of the palace to see if by chance the example of Verona – Verona being not far off – had been followed; but everything was dim, as usual, and everything was still. Juliana might on the summer nights of her youth have murmured down from open windows at Jeffrey Aspern, but Miss Tina was not a poet's mistress any more than I was a poet. This however didn't prevent my gratification from being great as I became aware on reaching the end of the garden that my younger padrona was seated in one of the bowers. At first I made out but an indistinct figure, not in the least counting on such an overture from one of my hostesses; it even occurred to me that some enamoured maid-servant had stolen in to keep a tryst with her sweetheart. I was going to turn away, not to frighten her, when the figure rose to its height and I recognised Miss Bordereau's niece. I must do myself the justice that I didn't wish to frighten her either, and much as I had longed for some such accident I should have been capable of retreating. It was as if I had laid a trap for her by coming home earlier than usual and by adding to that oddity my invasion of the garden. As she rose she spoke to me, and then I guessed that perhaps, secure in my almost inveterate absence, it was her nightly practice to take a lonely airing. There was no trap in truth, because I had had no suspicion. At first I took the words she uttered for an impatience of my arrival; but as she repeated them – I hadn't caught them clearly – I had the surprise of hearing her say: 'Oh dear, I'm so glad you've come!' She and her aunt had in common the property of unexpected speeches. She came out of the arbour almost as if to throw herself in my arms.

I hasten to add that I escaped this ordeal and that she didn't even then shake hands with me. It was an ease to her to see me and presently she told me why – because she was nervous when out-of-doors at night alone. The plants and shrubs looked so strange in the dark, and there were all sorts of queer sounds – she couldn't tell what they were – like the noises of animals. She stood close to me, looking about her with an air of greater security but without any demonstration of interest in me as an individual. Then I felt how little nocturnal prowlings could have been her habit, and I was also reminded – I had been afflicted by the same in talking with her before I took possession – that it was impossible to allow too much for her simplicity.

'You speak as if you were lost in the backwoods,' I cheeringly laughed. 'How you manage to keep out of this charming place when you've only three steps to take to get into it is more than I've yet been able to discover. You hide away amazingly so long as I'm on the premises, I know; but I had a hope you peeped out a little at other times. You and your poor aunt are worse off than Carmelite nuns in their cells. Should you mind telling me how you exist without air, without exercise, without any sort of human contact? I don't see how you carry on the common business of life.'

She looked at me as if I had spoken a strange tongue, and her answer was so little of one that I felt it make for irritation. 'We go to bed very early – earlier than you'd believe.' I was on the point of saying that this only deepened the mystery, but she gave me some relief by adding: 'Before you came we weren't so private. But I've never been out at night.'

'Never in these fragrant alleys, blooming here under your nose?'

'Ah,' said Miss Tina, 'they were never nice till now!' There was a finer sense in this and a flattering comparison, so that it seemed to me I had gained some advantage. As I might follow that further by establishing a good grievance I asked her why, since she thought my garden nice, she had never thanked me in any way for the flowers I had been sending up in such quantities for the previous three weeks. I had not been discouraged – there had been, as she would have observed, a daily armful; but I had been brought up in the common forms and a word of recognition now and then would have touched me in the right place.

'Why I didn't know they were for me!'

'They were for both of you. Why should I make a difference?'

Miss Tina reflected as if she might be thinking of a reason for that, but she failed to produce one. Instead of this she asked abruptly: 'Why in the world do you want so much to know us?'

'I ought after all to make a difference,' I replied. 'That question's your aunt's; it isn't yours. You wouldn't ask it if you hadn't been put up to it.'

'She didn't tell me to ask you,' Miss Tina replied without confusion. She was indeed the oddest mixture of shyness and straightness.

'Well, she has often wondered about it herself and expressed her wonder to you. She has insisted on it, so that she has put the idea into your head that I'm insufferably pushing. Upon my word I think I've been very. discreet. And how completely your aunt must have lost every tradition of sociability, to see anything out of the way in the idea that respectable intelligent people, living as we do under the same roof, should occasionally exchange a remark! What could be more natural? We're of the same country and have at least some of the same tastes, since, like you, I'm intensely fond of Venice.'

My friend seemed incapable of grasping more than one clause in any proposition, and she now spoke quickly, eagerly, as if she were answering my whole speech. 'I'm not in the least fond of Venice. I should like to go far away!'

'Has she always kept you back so?' I went on, to show her I could be as irrelevant as herself.

'She told me to come out tonight; she has told me very often,' said Miss Tina. 'It is I who wouldn't come. I don't like to leave her.'

'Is she too weak, is she really failing?' I demanded, with more emotion, I think, than I meant to betray. I measured this by the way her eyes rested on me in the darkness. It embarrassed me a little, and to turn the matter off I continued genially: 'Do let us sit down together comfortably somewhere – while you tell me all about her.'

Miss Tina made no resistance to this. We found a bench less secluded, less confidential, as it were, than the one in the arbour; and we were still sitting there when I heard midnight ring out from those clear bells of Venice which vibrate with a solemnity of their own over the lagoon and hold the air so much more than the chimes of other places. We were together more than an hour, and our interview gave, as it struck me, a great lift to my undertaking. Miss Tina accepted the situation without a protest; she had avoided me for three months, yet now she treated me almost as if these three months had made me an old friend. If I had chosen I might have gathered from this that though she had avoided me she had given a good deal of consideration to doing so. She paid no attention to the flight of time – never worried at my keeping her so long away from her aunt. She talked freely, answering questions and asking them and not even taking advantage of certain longish pauses by which they were naturally broken to say she thought she had better go in. It was almost as if she were waiting for something – something I might say to her – and intended to give me my opportunity. I was the more struck by this as she told me how much less well her aunt had been for a good many days, and in a way that was rather new. She was markedly weaker; at moments she showed no strength at all; yet more than ever before she wished to be left alone. That was why she had told her to come out – not even to remain in her own room, which was alongside; she pronounced poor Miss Tina 'a worry, a bore and a source of aggravation'. She sat still for hours together, as if for long sleep; she had always done that, musing and dozing; but at such times formerly she gave, in breaks, some small sign of life, of interest, liking her companion to be near her with her work. This sad personage confided to me that at present her aunt was so motionless as to create the fear she was dead; moreover she scarce ate or drank – one couldn't see what she lived on. The great thing was that she still on most days got up; the serious job was to dress her, to wheel her out of her bedroom. She clung to as many of her old habits as possible and had always, little company as they had received for years, made a point of sitting in the great parlour.

I scarce knew what to think of all this – of Miss Tina's sudden conversion to sociability and of the strange fact that the more the old woman appeared to decline to her end the less she should desire to be looked after. The story hung in-

differently together, and I even asked myself if it mightn't be a
trap laid for me, the result of a design to make me show my
hand. I couldn't have told why my companions (as they could
only by courtesy be called) should have this purpose – why they
should try to trip up so lucrative a lodger. But at any hazard
I kept on my guard, so that Miss Tina shouldn't have occasion
again to ask me what I might really be 'up to'. Poor woman,
before we parted for the night my mind was at rest as to what
*she* might be. She was up to nothing at all.

She told me more about their affairs than I had hoped; there
was no need to be prying, for it evidently drew her out simply
to feel me listen and care. She ceased wondering why I *should*,
and at last, while describing the brilliant life they had led years
before, she almost chattered. It was Miss Tina who judged it
brilliant; she said that when they first came to live in Venice,
years and years back – I found her essentially vague about
dates and the order in which events had occurred – there was
never a week they hadn't some visitor or didn't make some
pleasant *passeggio* in the town. They had seen all the curiosities;
they had even been to the Lido in a boat – she spoke as if I
might think there was a way on foot; they had had a collation
there, brought in three baskets and spread out on the grass.
I asked her what people they had known and she said Oh very
nice ones – the Cavaliere Bombicci and the Contessa Altemura,
with whom they had had a great friendship! Also English people
– the Churtons and the Goldies and Mrs Stock-Stock, whom
they had loved dearly; she was dead and gone, poor dear. That
was the case with most of their kind circle – this expression was
Miss Tina's own; though a few were left, which was a wonder
considering how they had neglected them. She mentioned the
names of two or three Venetian old women; of a certain doctor,
very clever, who was so attentive – he came as a friend, he had
really given up practice; of the *avvocato* Pochintesta, who wrote
beautiful poems and had addressed one to her aunt. These people
came to see them without fail every year, usually at the *capo
d'anno*, and of old her aunt used to make them some little
present – her aunt and she together: small things that she, Miss
Tina, turned out with her own hand, paper lamp-shades, or
mats for the decanters of wine at dinner, or those woollen things
that in cold weather are worn on the wrists. The last few years

there hadn't been many presents; she couldn't think what to make and her aunt had lost interest and never suggested. But the people came all the same; if the good Venetians liked you once they liked you for ever.

There was affecting matter enough in the good faith of this sketch of former social glories; the picnic at the Lido had remained vivid through the ages and poor Miss Tina evidently was of the impression that she had had a dashing youth. She had in fact had a glimpse of the Venetian world in its gossiping home-keeping parsimonious professional walks; for I noted for the first time how nearly she had acquired by contact the trick of the familiar soft-sounding almost infantile prattle of the place. I judged her to have imbibed this invertebrate dialect from the natural way the names of things and people – mostly purely local – rose to her lips. If she knew little of what they represented she knew still less of anything else. Her aunt had drawn in – the failure of interest in the table-mats and lamp-shades was a sign of that – and she hadn't been able to mingle in society or to entertain it alone; so that her range of reminiscence struck one as an old world altogether. Her tone, hadn't it been so decent, would have seemed to carry one back to the queer rococo Venice of Goldoni and Casanova. I found myself mistakenly think of her too as one of Jeffrey Aspern's contemporaries; this came from her having so little in common with my own. It was possible, I indeed reasoned, that she hadn't even heard of him; it might very well be that Juliana had forborne to lift for innocent eyes the veil that covered the temple of her glory. In this case she perhaps wouldn't know of the existence of the papers, and I welcomed that presumption – it made me feel more safe with her – till I remembered we had believed the letter of disavowal received by Cumnor to be in the hand-writing of the niece. If it had been dictated to her she had of course to know what it was about; though the effect of it withal was to repudiate the idea of any connexion with the poet. I held it probable at all events that Miss Tina hadn't read a word of his poetry. Moreover if, with her companion, she had always escaped invasion and research, there was little occasion for her having got it into her head that people were 'after' the letters. People had not been after them, for people hadn't heard of them. Cumnor's fruitless feeler would have been a solitary accident.

When midnight sounded Miss Tina got up; but she stopped at the door of the house only after she had wandered two or three times with me round the garden. 'When shall I see you again?' I asked before she went in; to which she replied with promptness that she should like to come out the next night. She added however that she shouldn't come – she was so far from doing everything she liked.

'You might do a few things I like,' I quite sincerely sighed.

'Oh you – I don't believe you!' she murmured at this, facing me with her simple solemnity.

'Why don't you believe me?'

'Because I don't understand you.'

'That's just the sort of occasion to have faith.' I couldn't say more, though I should have liked to, as I saw I only mystified her; for I had no wish to have it on my conscience that I might pass for having made love to her. Nothing less should I have seemed to do had I continued to beg a lady to 'believe in me' in an Italian garden on a midsummer night. There was some merit in my scruples, for Miss Tina lingered and lingered: I made out in her the conviction that she shouldn't really soon come down again and the wish therefore to protract the present. She insisted too on making the talk between us personal to ourselves; and altogether her behaviour was such as would have been possible only to a perfectly artless and a considerably witless woman.

'I shall like the flowers better now that I know them also meant for me.'

'How could you have doubted it? If you'll tell me the kind you like best I'll send a double lot.'

'Oh I like them all best!' Then she went on familiarly: 'Shall you study – shall you read and write – when you go up to your rooms?'

'I don't do that at night – at this season. The lamplight brings in the animals.'

'You might have known that when you came.'

'I did know it!'

'And in winter do you work at night?'

'I read a good deal, but I don't often write.' She listened as if these details had a rare interest, and suddenly a temptation quite at odds with all the prudence I had been teaching myself glimmered at me in her plain mild face. Ah yes, she was safe and I could make her safer! It seemed to me from one moment to another that I couldn't wait longer – that I really must take a sounding. So I went on: 'In general before I go to sleep (very often in bed; it's a bad habit, but I confess to it) I read some great poet. In nine cases out of ten it's a volume of Jeffrey Aspern.'

I watched her well as I pronounced that name, but I saw nothing wonderful. Why should I indeed? Wasn't Jeffrey Aspern the property of the human race?

'Oh *we* read him – we *have* read him,' she quietly replied.

'He's my poet of poets – I know him almost by heart.'

For an instant Miss Tina hesitated; then her sociability was too much for her. 'Oh by heart – that's nothing;' and, though dimly, she quite lighted. 'My aunt used to know him, to know him' – she paused an instant and I wondered what she was going to say – 'to know him as a visitor.'

'As a visitor?' I guarded my tone.

'He used to call on her and take her out.'

I continued to stare. 'My dear lady, he died a hundred years ago!'

'Well,' she said amusingly, 'my aunt's a hundred and fifty.'

'Mercy on us!' I cried; 'why didn't you tell me before? I should like so to ask her about him.'

'She wouldn't care for that – she wouldn't tell you,' Miss Tina returned.

'I don't care what she cares for! She *must* tell me – it's not a chance to be lost.'

'Oh you should have come twenty years ago. Then she still talked about him.'

'And what did she say?' I eagerly asked.

'I don't know – that he liked her immensely.'

'And she – didn't she like *him*?'

'She said he was a god.' Miss Tina gave me this information flatly, without expression; her tone might have made it a piece of trivial gossip. But it stirred me deeply as she dropped the words into the summer night; their sound might have been the light rustle of an old unfolded love-letter.

'Fancy, fancy!' I murmured. And then: 'Tell me this, please – has she got a portrait of him? They're distressingly rare.'

'A portrait? I don't know,' said Miss Tina; and now there was discomfiture in her face. 'Well, good-night!' she added; and she turned into the house.

I accompanied her into the wide dusky stone-paved passage that corresponded on the ground floor with our great sala. It opened at one end into the garden, at the other upon the canal, and was lighted now only by the small lamp always left for me to take up as I went to bed. An extinguished candle which Miss Tina apparently had brought down with her stood on the same table with it. 'Good-night, good-night!' I replied, keeping beside her as she went to get her light. 'Surely you'd know, shouldn't you, if she had one?'

'If she had what?' the poor lady asked, looking at me queerly over the flame of her candle.

'A portrait of the god. I don't know what I wouldn't give to see it.'

'I don't know what she has got. She keeps her things locked up.' And Miss Tina went away toward the staircase with the sense evidently of having said too much.

I let her go – I wished not to frighten her – and I contented myself with remarking that Miss Bordereau wouldn't have locked up such a glorious possession as that: a thing a person would be proud of and hang up in a prominent place on the parlour-wall. Therefore of course she hadn't any portrait. Miss Tina made no direct answer to this and, candle in hand, with her back to me, mounted two or three degrees. Then she stopped short and turned round, looking at me across the dusky space.

'Do you write – do you write?' There was a shake in her voice – she could scarcely bring it out.

'Do I write? Oh don't speak of my writing on the same day with Aspern's!'

'Do you write about *him* – do you pry into his life?'

'Ah that's your aunt's question; it can't be yours!' I said in a tone of slightly wounded sensibility.

'All the more reason then that you should answer it. Do you, please?'

I thought I had allowed for the falsehoods I should have to tell, but I found that in fact when it came to the point I hadn't. Besides, now that I had an opening there was a kind of relief in being frank. Lastly – it was perhaps fanciful, even fatuous –

I guessed that Miss Tina personally wouldn't in the last resort be less my friend. So after a moment's hesitation I answered: 'Yes, I've written about him and I'm looking for more material. In heaven's name have you got any?'

'*Santo Dio!*' she exclaimed without heeding my question; and she hurried upstairs and out of sight. I might count upon her in the last resort, but for the present she was visibly alarmed. The proof of it was that she began to hide again, so that for a fortnight I kept missing her. I found my patience ebbing and after four or five days of this I told the gardener to stop the 'floral tributes'.

# VI

ONE afternoon, at last, however, as I came down from my quarters to go out, I found her in the sala: it was our first encounter on that ground since I had come to the house. She put on no air of being there by accident; there was an ignorance of such arts in her honest angular diffidence. That I might be quite sure she was waiting for me she mentioned it at once, but telling me with it that Miss Bordereau wished to see me: she would take me into the room at that moment if I had time. If I had been late for a love-tryst I would have stayed for this, and I quickly signified that I should be delighted to wait on my benefactress. 'She wants to talk with you – to know you,' Miss Tina said, smiling as if she herself appreciated that idea; and she led me to the door of her aunt's apartment. I stopped her a moment before she had opened it, looking at her with some curiosity. I told her that this was a great satisfaction to me and a great honour; but all the same I should like to ask what had made Miss Bordereau so markedly and suddenly change. It had been only the other day that she wouldn't suffer me near her. Miss Tina was not embarrassed by my question; she had as many little unexpected serenities, plausibilities almost, as if she told fibs, but the odd part of them was that they had on the contrary their source in her truthfulness. 'Oh my aunt varies,' she answered; 'it's so terribly dull – I suppose she's tired.'

'But you told me she wanted more and more to be alone.'

Poor Miss Tina coloured as if she found me too pushing. 'Well, if you don't believe she wants to see you, I haven't invented it! I think people often are capricious when they're very old.'

'That's perfectly true. I only wanted to be clear as to whether you've repeated to her what I told you the other night.'

'What you told me?'

'About Jeffrey Aspern – that I'm looking for materials.'

'If I had told her do you think she'd have sent for you?'

'That's exactly what I want to know. If she wants to keep him to herself she might have sent for me to tell me so.'

'She won't speak of him,' said Miss Tina. Then as she opened the door she added in a lower tone: 'I told her nothing.'

The old woman was sitting in the same place in which I had seen her last, in the same position, with the same mystifying bandage over her eyes. Her welcome was to turn her almost invisible face to me and show me that while she sat silent she saw me clearly. I made no motion to shake hands with her; I now felt too well that this was out of place for ever. It had been sufficiently enjoined on me that she was too sacred for trivial modernisms – too venerable to touch. There was something so grim in her aspect – it was partly the accident of her green shade – as I stood there to be measured, that I ceased on the spot to doubt her suspecting me, though I didn't in the least myself suspect that Miss Tina hadn't just spoken the truth. She hadn't betrayed me, but the old woman's brooding instinct had served her; she had turned me over and over in the long still hours and had guessed. The worst of it was that she looked terribly like an old woman who at a pinch would, even like Sardanapalus, burn her treasure. Miss Tina pushed a chair forward, saying to me 'This will be a good place for you to sit.' As I took possession of it I asked after Miss Bordereau's health; expressed the hope that in spite of the very hot weather it was satisfactory. She answered that it was good enough – good enough; that it was a great thing to be alive.

'Oh as to that, it depends upon what you compare it with!' I returned with a laugh.

'I don't compare – I don't compare. If I did that I should have given everything up long ago.'

I liked to take this for a subtle allusion to the rapture she had known in the society of Jeffrey Aspern – though it was true that such an allusion would have accorded ill with the wish I imputed to her to keep him buried in her soul. What it accorded with was my constant conviction that no human being had ever had a happier social gift than his, and what it seemed to convey was that nothing in the world was worth speaking of if one pretended to speak of that. But one didn't pretend! Miss Tina sat down beside her aunt, looking as if she had reason to believe some wonderful talk would come off between us.

'It's about the beautiful flowers,' said the old lady; 'you sent us so many – I ought to have thanked you for them before. But I don't write letters and I receive company but at long intervals.'

She hadn't thanked me while the flowers continued to come, but she departed from her custom so far as to send for me as soon as she began to fear they wouldn't come any more. I noted this; I remembered what an acquisitive propensity she had shown when it was a question of extracting gold from me, and I privately rejoiced at the happy thought I had had in suspending my tribute. She had missed it and was willing to make a concession to bring it back. At the first sign of this concession I could only go to meet her. 'I'm afraid you haven't had many, of late, but they shall begin again immediately – tomorrow, tonight.'

'Oh do send us some tonight!' Miss Tina cried as if it were a great affair.

'What else should you do with them? It isn't a manly taste to make a bower of your room,' the old woman remarked.

'I don't make a bower of my room, but I'm exceedingly fond of growing flowers, of watching their ways. There's nothing unmanly in that; it has been the amusement of philosophers, of statesmen in retirement; even I think of great captains.'

'I suppose you know you can sell them – those you don't use,' Miss Bordereau went on. 'I dare say they wouldn't give you much for them; still, you could make a bargain.'

'Oh I've never in my life made a bargain, as you ought pretty well to have gathered. My gardener disposes of them and I ask no questions.'

'I'd ask a few, I can promise you!' said Miss Bordereau; and it was so I first heard the strange sound of her laugh, which was as if the faint 'walking' ghost of her old-time tone had suddenly cut a caper. I couldn't get used to the idea that this vision of pecuniary profit was most what drew out the divine Juliana.

'Come into the garden yourself and pick them; come as often as you like; come every day. The flowers are all for you,' I pursued, addressing Miss Tina and carrying off this veracious statement by treating it as an innocent joke. 'I can't imagine why she doesn't come down,' I added for Miss Bordereau's benefit.

'You must make her come; you must come up and fetch her,'

the old woman said to my stupefaction. 'That odd thing you've made in the corner will do very well for her to sit in.'

The allusion to the most elaborate of my shady coverts, a sketchy 'summer-house,' was irreverent; it confirmed the impression I had already received that there was a flicker of impertinence in Miss Bordereau's talk, a vague echo of the boldness or the archness of her adventurous youth and which had somehow automatically outlived passions and faculties. None the less I asked: 'Wouldn't it be possible for you to come down there yourself? Wouldn't it do you good to sit there in the shade and the sweet air?'

'Oh sir, when I move out of this it won't be to sit in the air, and I'm afraid that any that may be stirring around me won't be particularly sweet! It will be a very dark shade indeed. But that won't be just yet,' Miss Bordereau continued cannily, as if to correct any hopes this free glance at the last receptacle of her mortality might lead me to entertain. 'I've sat here many a day and have had enough of arbours in my time. But I'm not afraid to wait till I'm called.'

Miss Tina had expected, as I felt, rare conversation, but perhaps she found it less gracious on her aunt's side – considering I had been sent for with a civil intention – than she had hoped. As to give the position a turn that would put our companion in a light more favourable she said to me: 'Didn't I tell you the other night that she had sent me out? You see I can do what I like!'

'Do you pity her – do you teach her to pity herself?' Miss Bordereau demanded, before I had time to answer this appeal. 'She has a much easier life than I had at her age.'

'You must remember it has been quite open to me,' I said, 'to think you rather inhuman.'

'Inhuman? That's what the poets used to call the women a hundred years ago. Don't try that; you won't do as well as they!' Juliana went on. 'There's no more poetry in the world – that I know of at least. But I won't bandy words with you,' she said, and I well remember the old-fashioned artificial sound she gave the speech. 'You make me talk, talk, talk! It isn't good for me at all.' I got up at this and told her I would take no more of her time; but she detained me to put a question. 'Do you remember, the day I saw you about the rooms, that you offered us the use of your gondola?' And when I assented promptly, struck again with her disposition to make a 'good thing' of my being there and wondering what she now had in her eye, she produced: 'Why don't you take that girl out in it and show her the place?'

'Oh dear aunt, what do you want to do with me?' cried the 'girl' with a piteous quaver. 'I know all about the place!'

'Well then go with him and explain!' said Miss Bordereau, who gave an effect of cruelty to her implacable power of retort. This showed her as a sarcastic profane cynical old woman. 'Haven't we heard that there have been all sorts of changes in all these years? You ought to see them, and at your age – I don't mean because you're so young – you ought to take the chances that come. You're old enough, my dear, and this gentleman won't hurt you. He'll show you the famous sunsets, if they still go on – *do* they go on? The sun set for me so long ago. But that's not a reason. Besides, I shall never miss you; you think you're too important. Take her to the Piazza; it used to be very pretty,' Miss Bordereau continued, addressing herself to me. 'What have they done with the funny old church? I hope it hasn't tumbled down. Let her look at the shops; she may take some money, she may buy what she likes.'

Poor Miss Tina had got up, discountenanced and helpless, and as we stood there before her aunt it would certainly have struck a spectator of the scene that our venerable friend was making rare sport of us. Miss Tina protested in a confusion of exclamations and murmurs; but I lost no time in saying that if she would do me the honour to accept the hospitality of my boat I would engage she really shouldn't be bored. Or if she didn't want so much of my company the boat itself, with the gondolier, was at her service; he was a capital oar and she might have every confidence. Miss Tina, without definitely answering this speech, looked away from me and out of the window, quite as if about to weep, and I remarked that once we had Miss Bordereau's approval we could easily come to an understanding. We would take an hour, whichever she liked, one of the very next days. As I made my obeisance to the old lady I asked her if she would kindly permit me to see her again.

For a moment she kept me; then she said: 'Is it very necessary to your happiness?'

'It diverts me more than I can say.'

'You're wonderfully civil. Don't you know it almost kills me?'

'How can I believe that when I see you more animated, more brilliant than when I came in?'

'That's very true, aunt,' said Miss Tina. 'I think it does you good.'

'Isn't it touching, the solicitude we each have that the other shall enjoy herself?' sneered Miss Bordereau. 'If you think me brilliant today you don't know what you're talking about; you've never seen an agreeable woman. What do you people know about good society?' she cried; but before I could tell her, 'Don't try to pay me a compliment; I've been spoiled,' she went on. 'My door's shut, but you may sometimes knock.'

With this she dismissed me and I left the room. The latch closed behind me, but Miss Tina, contrary to my hope, had remained within. I passed slowly across the hall and before taking my way downstairs waited a little. My hope was answered; after a minute my conductress followed me. 'That's a delightful idea about the Piazza,' I said. 'When will you go – tonight, tomorrow?'

She had been disconcerted, as I have mentioned, but I had already perceived, and I was to observe again, that when Miss Tina was embarrassed she didn't – as most women would have in like case – turn away, floundering and hedging, but came closer, as it were, with a deprecating, a clinging appeal to be spared, to be protected. Her attitude was a constant prayer for aid and explanation, and yet no woman in the world could have been less of a comedian. From the moment you were kind to her she depended on you absolutely; her self-consciousness dropped and she took the greatest intimacy, the innocent intimacy that was all she could conceive, for granted. She didn't know, she now declared, what possessed her aunt, who had changed so quickly, who had got some idea. I replied that she must catch the idea and let me have it: we would go and take an ice together at Florian's and she should report while we listened to the band.

'Oh it will take me a long time to be able to "report"!' she said rather ruefully; and she could promise me this satisfaction neither for that night nor for the next. I was patient now, however, for I felt I had only to wait; and in fact at the end of the week, one lovely evening after dinner, she stepped into my gondola, to which in honour of the occasion I had attached a second oar.

We swept in the course of five minutes into the Grand Canal; whereupon she uttered a murmur of ecstasy as fresh as if she had been a tourist just arrived. She had forgotten the splendour of the great water-way on a clear summer evening, and how the sense of floating between marble palaces and reflected lights disposed the mind to freedom and ease. We floated long and far, and though my friend gave no high-pitched voice to her glee I was sure of her full surrender. She was more than pleased, she was transported; the whole thing was an immense liberation. The gondola moved with slow strokes, to give her time to enjoy it, and she listened to the plash of the oars, which grew louder and more musically liquid as we passed into narrow canals, as if it were a revelation of Venice. When I asked her how long it was since she had thus floated she answered: 'Oh I don't know; a long time – not since my aunt began to be ill.' This was not the only show of her extreme vagueness about the previous years and the line marking off the period of Miss Bordereau's eminence. I was not at liberty to keep her out long, but we took a considerable *giro* before going to the Piazza. I asked her no questions, holding off by design from her life at home and the things I wanted to know; I poured, rather, treasures of information about the objects before and around us into her ears, describing also Florence and Rome, discoursing on the charms and advantages of travel. She reclined, receptive, on the deep leather cushions, turned her eyes conscientiously to everything I noted and never mentioned to me till some time afterwards that she might be supposed to know Florence better than I, as she had lived there for years with her kinswoman. At last she said with the shy impatience of a child. 'Are we not really going to the Piazza? That's what I want to see!' I immediately gave the order that we should go straight, after which we sat silent with the expectation of arrival. As some time still passed, however, she broke out of her own movement: 'I've found out what's the matter with my aunt: she's afraid you'll go!'

I quite gasped. 'What has put that into her head?'

'She has had an idea you've not been happy. That's why she's different now.'

'You mean she wants to make me happier?'

'Well, she wants you not to go. She wants you to stay.'

'I suppose you mean on account of the rent,' I remarked candidly.

Miss Tina's candour but profited. 'Yes, you know; so that I shall have more.'

'How much does she want you to have?' I asked with all the gaiety I now felt. 'She ought to fix the sum, so that I may stay till it's made up.'

'Oh that wouldn't please me,' said Miss Tina. 'It would be unheard of, your taking that trouble.'

'But suppose I should have my own reasons for staying in Venice?'

'Then it would be better for you to stay in some other house.'

'And what would your aunt say to that?'

'She wouldn't like it at all. But I should think you'd do well to give up your reasons and go away altogether.'

'Dear Miss Tina,' I said, 'it's not so easy to give up my reasons!'

She made no immediate answer to this, but after a moment broke out afresh: 'I think I know what your reasons are!'

'I dare say, because the other night I almost told you how I wished you'd help me to make them good.'

'I can't do that without being false to my aunt.'

'What do you mean by being false to her?'

'Why she would never consent to what you want. She has been asked, she has been written to. It makes her fearfully angry.'

'Then she *has* papers of value?' I precipitately cried.

'Oh she has everything!' sighed Miss Tina with a curious weariness, a sudden lapse into gloom.

These words caused all my pulses to throb, for I regarded them as precious evidence. I felt them too deeply to speak, and in the interval the gondola approached the Piazzetta. After we had disembarked I asked my companion if she would rather walk round the square or go and sit before the great café; to which she replied that she would do whichever I liked best –

I must only remember again how little time she had. I assured her there was plenty to do both, and we made the circuit of the long arcades. Her spirits revived at the sight of the bright shop-windows, and she lingered and stopped, admiring or disapproving of their contents, asking me what I thought of things, theorising about prices. My attention wandered from her; her words of a while before 'Oh she has everything!' echoed so in my consciousness. We sat down at last in the crowded circle at Florian's, finding an unoccupied table among those that were ranged in the square. It was a splendid night and all the world out-of-doors; Miss Tina couldn't have wished the elements more auspicious for her return to society. I saw she felt it all even more than she told, but her impressions were well-nigh too many for her. She had forgotten the attraction of the world and was learning that she had for the best years of her life been rather mercilessly cheated of it. This didn't make her angry; but as she took in the charming scene her face had, in spite of its smile of appreciation, the flush of a wounded surprise. She didn't speak, sunk in the sense of opportunities, for ever lost, that ought to have been easy; and this gave me a chance to say to her: 'Did you mean a while ago that your aunt has a plan of keeping me on by admitting me occasionally to her presence?'

'She thinks it will make a difference with you if you sometimes see her. She wants you so much to stay that she's willing to make that concession.'

'And what good does she consider I think it will do me to see her?'

'I don't know; it must be interesting,' said Miss Tina simply. 'You told her you found it so.'

'So I did; but everyone doesn't think that.'

'No, of course not, or more people would try.'

'Well, if she's capable of making that reflexion she's capable also of making this further one,' I went on: 'that I must have a particular reason for not doing as others do, in spite of the interest she offers – for not leaving her alone.' Miss Tina looked as if she failed to grasp this rather complicated proposition; so I continued: 'If you've not told her what I said to you the other night may she not at least have guessed it?'

'I don't know – she's very suspicious.'

'But she hasn't been made so by indiscreet curiosity, by persecution?'

'No, no; it isn't that,' said Miss Tina, turning on me a troubled face. 'I don't know how to say it: it's on account of something – ages ago, before I was born – in her life.'

'Something? What sort of thing?' – and I asked it as if I could have no idea.

'Oh she has never told me.' And I was sure my friend spoke the truth.

Her extreme limpidity was almost provoking, and I felt for the moment that she would have been more satisfactory if she had been less ingenuous. 'Do you suppose it's something to which Jeffrey Aspern's letters and papers – I mean the things in her possession – have reference?'

'I dare say it is!' my companion exclaimed as if this were a very happy suggestion. 'I've never looked at any of those things.'

'None of them? Then how do you know what they are?'

'I don't,' said Miss Tina placidly. 'I've never had them in my hands. But I've seen them when she has had them out.'

'Does she have them out often?'

'Not now, but she used to. She's very fond of them.'

'In spite of their being compromising?'

'Compromising?' Miss Tina repeated as if vague as to what that meant. I felt almost as one who corrupts the innocence of youth.

'I allude to their containing painful memories.'

'Oh I don't think anything's painful.'

'You mean there's nothing to affect her reputation?'

An odder look even than usual came at this into the face of Miss Bordereau's niece – a confession, it seemed, of helplessness, an appeal to me to deal fairly, generously with her. I had brought her to the Piazza, placed her among charming influences, paid her an attention she appreciated, and now I appeared to show it all as a bribe – a bribe to make her turn in some way against her aunt. She was of a yielding nature and capable of doing almost anything to please a person markedly kind to her; but the greatest kindness of all would be not to presume too much on this. It was strange enough, as I afterwards thought, that she had not the least air of resenting my want of consideration for her aunt's character, which would have been in the worst possible taste if anything less vital – from my point of view – had been at stake. I don't think she really measured it. 'Do you mean she ever did something bad?' she asked in a moment.

'Heaven forbid I should say so, and it's none of my business. Besides, if she did,' I agreeably put it, 'that was in other ages, in another world. But why shouldn't she destroy her papers?'

'Oh she loves them too much.'

'Even now, when she may be near her end?'

'Perhaps when she's sure of that she will.'

'Well, Miss Tina,' I said, 'that's just what I should like you to prevent.'

'How can I prevent it?'

'Couldn't you get them away from her?'

'And give them to you?'

This put the case, superficially, with sharp irony, but I was sure of her not intending that. 'Oh I mean that you might let me see them and look them over. It isn't for myself, or that I should want them at any cost to any one else. It's simply that they would be of such immense interest to the public, such immeasurable importance as a contribution to Jeffrey Aspern's history.'

She listened to me in her usual way, as if I abounded in matters she had never heard of, and I felt almost as base as the reporter of a newspaper who forces his way into a house of mourning. This was marked when she presently said: 'There was a gentleman who some time ago wrote to her in very much those words. He also wanted her papers.'

'And did she answer him?' I asked, rather ashamed of not having my friend's rectitude.

'Only when he had written two or three times. He made her very angry.'

'And what did she say?'

'She said he was a devil,' Miss Tina replied categorically.

'She used that expression in her letter?'

'Oh no; she said it to me. She made me write to him.'

'And what did you say?'

'I told him there were no papers at all.'

'Ah poor gentleman!' I groaned.

'I knew there were, but I wrote what she bade me.'

'Of course you had to do that. But I hope I shan't pass for a devil.'

'It will depend upon what you ask me to do for you,' my companion smiled.

'Oh if there's a chance of *your* thinking so my affairs in a bad way! I shan't ask you to steal for me, nor even to fib – for you *can't* fib, unless on paper. But the principal thing is this – to prevent her destroying the papers.'

'Why I've no control of her,' said Miss Tina. 'It's she who controls me.'

'But she doesn't control her own arms and legs, does she? The way she would naturally destroy her letters would be to burn them. Now she can't burn them without fire, and she can't get fire unless you give it her.'

'I've always done everything she has asked,' my poor friend pleaded. 'Besides, there's Olimpia.'

I was on the point of saying that Olimpia was probably corruptible, but I thought it best not to sound that note. So I simply put it that this frail creature might perhaps be managed.

'Everyone can be managed by my aunt,' said Miss Tina. And then she remembered that her holiday was over; she must go home.

I laid my hand on her arm, across the table, to stay her a moment. 'What I want of you is a general promise to help me.'

'Oh how *can* I, how *can* I?' she asked, wondering and troubled. She was half-surprised, half-frightened at my attaching that importance to her, at my calling on her for action.

'This is the main thing: to watch our friend carefully and warn me in time, before she commits that dreadful sacrilege.'

'I can't watch her when she makes me go out.'

'That's very true.'

'And when you do too.'

'Mercy on us – do you think she'll have done anything tonight?'

'I don't know. She's very cunning.'

'Are you trying to frighten me?' I asked.

I felt this question sufficiently answered when my companion murmured in a musing, almost envious way: 'Oh but she loves them – she loves them!'

This reflexion, repeated with such emphasis, gave me great

comfort; but to obtain more of that balm I said: 'If she shouldn't intend to destroy the objects we speak of before her death she'll probably have made some disposition by will.'

'By will?'

'Hasn't she made a will for your benefit?'

'Ah she has so little to leave. That's why she likes money,' said Miss Tina.

'Might I ask, since we're really talking things over, what you and she live on?'

'On some money that comes from America, from a gentleman – I think a lawyer – in New York. He sends it every quarter. It isn't much!'

'And won't she have disposed of that?'

My companion hesitated – I saw she was blushing. 'I believe it's mine,' she said; and the look and tone which accompanied these words betrayed so the absence of the habit of thinking of herself that I almost thought her charming. The next instant she added: 'But she had in an *avvocato* here once, ever so long ago. And some people came and signed something.'

'They were probably witnesses. And you weren't asked to sign? Well then,' I argued, rapidly and hopefully, 'it's because you're the legatee. She must have left all her documents to you!'

'If she has it's with very strict conditions,' Miss Tina responded, rising quickly, while the movement gave the words a small character of decision. They seemed to imply that the bequest would be accompanied with a proviso that the articles bequeathed should remain concealed from every inquisitive eye, and that I was very much mistaken if I thought her the person to depart from an injunction so absolute.

'Oh of course you'll have to abide by the terms,' I said; and she uttered nothing to mitigate the rigour of this conclusion. None the less, later on, just before we disembarked at her own door after a return which had taken place almost in silence, she said to me abruptly: 'I'll do what I can to help you.' I was grateful for this – it was very well so far as it went; but it didn't keep me from remembering that night in a worried waking hour that I now had her word for it to re-enforce my own impression that the old woman was full of craft.

# VII

THE fear of what this side of her character might have led her to do made me nervous for days afterwards. I waited for an intimation from Miss Tina; I almost read it as her duty to keep me informed, to let me know definitely whether or no Miss Bordereau had sacrificed her treasures. But as she gave no sign I lost patience and determined to put the case to the very touch of my own senses. I sent late one afternoon to ask if I might pay the ladies a visit, and my servant came back with surprising news. Miss Bordereau could be approached without the least difficulty; she had been moved out into the sala and was sitting by the window that overlooked the garden. I descended and found this picture correct; the old lady had been wheeled forth into the world and had a certain air, which came mainly perhaps from some brighter element in her dress, of being prepared again to have converse with it. It had not yet, however, begun to flock about her; she was perfectly alone and, though the door leading to her own quarters stood open, I had at first no glimpse of Miss Tina. The window at which she sat had the afternoon shade and, one of the shutters having been pushed back, she could see the pleasant garden, where the summer sun had by this time dried up too many of the plants – she could see the yellow light and the long shadows.

'Have you come to tell me you'll take the rooms for six months more?' she asked as I approached her, startling me by something coarse in her cupidity almost as much as if she hadn't already given me a specimen of it. Juliana's desire to make our acquaintance lucrative had been, as I have sufficiently indicated, a false note in my image of the woman who had inspired a great poet with immortal lines; but I may say here definitely that I after all recognised large allowance to be made for her. It was I who had kindled the unholy flame; it was I who had put into her head that she had the means of making money. S'  ppeared never to have thought of that; she had been living         lly for years, in a house five times too big for her, on a           that I could explain only by the presumption that,             as it was, the space she enjoyed cost her next to nothing and that, small as were her revenues, they left her, for Venice, an appreciable margin. I had descended on her one day and taught her to calculate, and my almost extravagant comedy on the subject of the garden had presented me irresistibly in the light of a victim. Like all persons who achieve the miracle of changing their point of view late in life, she had been intensely converted: she had seized my hint with a desperate tremulous clutch.

I invited myself to go and get one of the chairs that stood, at a distance, against the wall – she had given herself no concern as to whether I should sit or stand; and while I placed it near her I began gaily: 'Oh dear madam, what an imagination you have, what an intellectual sweep! I'm a poor devil of a man of letters who lives from day to day. How can I take palaces by the year? My existence is precarious. I don't know whether six months hence I shall have bread to put in my mouth. I've treated myself for once; it has been an immense luxury. But when it comes to going on—!'

'Are your rooms too dear? if they are you can have more for the same money,' Juliana responded. 'We can arrange, we can *combinare*, as they say here.'

'Well yes, since you ask me, they're too dear, much too dear,' I said. 'Evidently you suppose me richer than I am.'

She looked at me as from the mouth of her cave. 'If you write books don't you sell them?'

'Do you mean don't people buy them? A little, a very little – not so much as I could wish. Writing books, unless one be a great genius – and even then! – is the last road to fortune. I think there's no more money to be made by good letters.'

'Perhaps you don't choose nice subjects. What do you write about?' Miss Bordereau implacably pursued.

'About the books of other people. I'm a critic, a commentator, an historian, in a small way.' I wondered what she was coming to.

'And what other people now?'

'Oh better ones than myself: the great writers mainly – the great philosophers and poets of the past; those who are dead and gone and can't, poor darlings, speak for themselves.'

'And what do you say about them?'

'I say they sometimes attached themselves to very clever

women!' I replied as for pleasantness. I had measured, as I thought, my risk, but as my words fell upon the air they were to strike me as imprudent. However, I had launched them and I wasn't sorry, for perhaps after all the old woman would be willing to treat. It seemed tolerably obvious that she knew my secret: why therefore drag the process out? But she didn't take what I had said as a confession; she only asked:

'Do you think it's right to rake up the past?'

'I don't feel that I know what you mean by raking it up. How can we get at it unless we dig a little? The present has such a rough way of treading it down.'

'Oh I like the past, but I don't like critics,' my hostess declared with her hard complacency.

'Neither do I, but I like their discoveries.'

'Aren't they mostly lies?'

'The lies are what they sometimes discover,' I said, smiling at the quiet impertinence of this. 'They often lay bare the truth.'

'The truth is God's, it isn't man's: we had better leave it alone. Who can judge of it? – who can say?'

'We're terribly in the dark, I know,' I admitted; 'but if we give up trying what becomes of all the fine things? What becomes of the work I just mentioned, that of the great philosophers and poets? It's all vain words if there's nothing to measure it by.'

'You talk as if you were a tailor,' said Miss Bordereau whimsically; and then she added quickly and in a different manner: 'This house is very fine; the proportions are magnificent. Today I wanted to look at this part again. I made them bring me out here. When your man came just now to learn if I would see you I was on the point of sending for you to ask if you didn't mean to go on. I wanted to judge what I'm letting you have. This sala is very grand,' she pursued like an auctioneer, moving a little, as I guessed, her invisible eyes. 'I don't believe you often have lived in such a house, eh?'

'I can't often afford to!' I said.

'Well then how much will you give me for six months?'

I was on the point of exclaiming – and the air of excruciation in my face would have denoted a moral fact – 'Don't, Juliana; for his sake, don't!' But I controlled myself and asked less passionately: 'Why should I remain so long as that?'

'I thought you liked it,' said Miss Bordereau with her shrivelled dignity.

'So I thought I should.'

For a moment she said nothing more, and I left my own words to suggest to her what they might. I half-expected her to say, coldly enough, that if I had been disappointed we needn't continue the discussion, and this in spite of the fact that I believed her now to have in her mind – however it had come there – what would have told her that my disappointment was natural. But to my extreme surprise she ended by observing: 'If you don't think we've treated you well enough perhaps we can discover some way of treating you better.' This speech was somehow so incongruous that it made me laugh again, and I excused myself by saying that she talked as if I were a sulky boy pouting in the corner and having to be 'brought round'. I hadn't a grain of complaint to make; and could anything have exceeded Miss Tina's graciousness in accompanying me a few nights before to the Piazza? At this the old woman went on: 'Well, you brought it on yourself!' And then in a different tone: 'She's a very fine girl.' I assented cordially to this pro- position, and she expressed the hope that I did so not merely to be obliging, but that I really liked her. Meanwhile I wondered still more what Miss Bordereau was coming to. 'Except for me, today,' she said, 'she hasn't a relation in the world.' Did she by describing her niece as amiable and unencumbered wish to represent her as a *parti*?

It was perfectly true that I couldn't afford to go on with my rooms at a fancy price and that I had already devoted to my undertaking almost all the hard cash I had set apart for it. My patience and my time were by no means exhausted, but I should be able to draw upon them only on a more usual Venetian basis. I was willing to pay the precious personage with whom my pecuniary dealings were such a discord twice as much as any other *padrona di casa* would have asked, but I wasn't willing to pay her twenty times as much. I told her so plainly, and my plainness appeared to have some success, for she exclaimed: 'Very good; you've done what I asked – you've made an offer!'

'Yes, but not for half a year. Only by the month.'

'Oh I must think of that then.' She seemed disappointed that

I wouldn't tie myself to a period, and I guessed that she wished both to secure me and to discourage me; to say severely: 'Do you dream that you can get off with less than six months? Do you dream that even by the end of that time you'll be appreciably nearer your victory?' What was most in my mind was that she had a fancy to play me the trick of making me engage myself when in fact she had sacrificed her treasure. There was a moment when my suspense on this point was so acute that I all but broke out with the question, and what kept it back was but an instinctive recoil – lest it should be a mistake – from the last violence of self-exposure. She was such a subtle old witch that one could never tell where one stood with her. You may imagine whether it cleared up the puzzle when, just after she had said she would think of my proposal and without any formal transition, she drew out of her pocket with an embarrassed hand a small object wrapped in crumpled white paper. She held it there a moment and then resumed: 'Do you know much about curiosities?'

'About curiosities?'

'About antiquities, the old gimcracks that people pay so much for today. Do you know the kind of price they bring?'

I thought I saw what was coming, but I said ingenuously: 'Do you want to buy something?'

'No, I want to sell. What would an amateur give me for that?' She unfolded the white paper and made a motion for me to take from her a small oval portrait. I possessed myself of it with fingers of which I could only hope that they didn't betray the intensity of their clutch, and she added: 'I would part with it only for a good price.'

At the first glance I recognised Jeffrey Aspern, and was well aware that I flushed with the act. As she was watching me however I had the consistency to exclaim: 'What a striking face! Do tell me who he is.'

'He's an old friend of mine, a very distinguished man in his day. He gave it me himself, but I'm afraid to mention his name, lest you never should have heard of him, critic and historian as you are. I know the world goes fast and one generation forgets another. He was all the fashion when I was young.'

She was perhaps amazed at my assurance, but I was surprised at hers; at her having the energy, in her state of health and at her time of life, to wish to sport with me to that tune simply for her private entertainment – the humour to test me and practise on me and befool me. This at least was the interpretation that I put upon her production of the relic, for I couldn't believe she really desired to sell it or cared for any information I might give her. What she wished was to dangle it before my eyes and put a prohibitive price on it. 'The face comes back to me, it torments me,' I said, turning the object this way and that and looking at it very critically. It was a careful but not a supreme work of art, larger than the ordinary miniature and representing a young man with a remarkably handsome face, in a high-collared green coat and a buff waistcoat. I felt in the little work a virtue of likeness and judged it to have been painted when the model was about twenty-five. There are, as all the world knows, three other portraits of the poet in existence, but none of so early a date as this elegant image. 'I've never seen the original, clearly a man of a past age, but I've seen other reproductions of this face,' I went on. 'You expressed doubt of this generation's having heard of the gentleman, but he strikes me for all the world as a celebrity. Now who is he? I can't put my finger on him – I can't give him a label. Wasn't he a writer? Surely he's a poet.' I was determined that it should be she, not I, who should first pronounce Jeffrey Aspern's name.

My resolution was taken in ignorance of Miss Bordereau's extremely resolute character, and her lips never formed in my hearing the syllables that meant so much for her. She neglected to answer my question, but raised her hand to take back the picture, using a gesture which though impotent was in a high degree peremptory. 'It's only a person who should know for himself that would give me my price,' she said with a certain dryness.

'Oh then you have a price?' I didn't restore the charming thing; not from any vindictive purpose, but because I instinctively clung to it. We looked at each other hard while I retained it.

'I know the least I would take. What it occurred to me to ask you about is the most I shall be able to get.'

She made a movement, drawing herself together as if, in a spasm of dread at having lost her prize, she had been impelled to the immense effort of rising to snatch it from me. I instantly placed it in her hand again, saying as I did so: 'I should like to have it myself, but with your ideas it would be quite beyond my mark.'

She turned the small oval plate over in her lap, with its face down, and I heard her catch her breath as after a strain or an escape. This however did not prevent her saying in a moment: 'You'd buy a likeness of a person you don't know by an artist who has no reputation?'

'The artist may have no reputation, but that thing's wonderfully well painted,' I replied, to give myself a reason.

'It's lucky you thought of saying that, because the painter was my father.'

'That makes the picture indeed precious!' I returned with gaiety; and I may add that a part of my cheer came from this proof I had been right in my theory of Miss Bordereau's origin. Aspern had of course met the young lady on his going to her father's studio as a sitter. I observed to Miss Bordereau that if she would entrust me with her property for twenty-four hours I should be happy to take advice on it; but she made no other reply than to slip it in silence into her pocket. This convinced me still more that she had no sincere intention of selling it during her lifetime, though she may have desired to satisfy herself as to the sum her niece, should she leave it to her, might expect eventually to obtain for it. 'Well, at any rate, I hope you won't offer it without giving me notice,' I said as she remained irresponsive. 'Remember me as a possible purchaser.'

'I should want your money first!' she returned with unexpected rudeness; and then, as if she bethought herself that I might well complain of such a tone and wished to turn the matter off, asked abruptly what I talked about with her niece when I went out with her that way of an evening.

'You speak as if we had set up the habit,' I replied. 'Certainly I should be very glad if it were to become our pleasant custom. But in that case I should feel a still greater scruple at betraying a lady's confidence.'

'Her confidence? Has my niece confidence?'

'Here she is – she can tell you herself,' I said; for Miss Tina now appeared on the threshold of the old woman's parlour. 'Have you confidence, Miss Tina? Your aunt wants very much to know.'

'Not in her, not in her!' the younger lady declared, shaking her head with a dolefulness that was neither jocular nor affected. 'I don't know what to do with her; she has fits of horrid imprudence. She's so easily tired – and yet she has begun to roam, to drag herself about the house.' And she looked down at her yoke-fellow of long years with a vacancy of wonder, as if all their contact and custom hadn't made her perversities, on occasion, any more easy to follow.

'I know what I'm about. I'm not losing my mind. I dare say you'd like to think so,' said Miss Bordereau with a crudity of cynicism.

'I don't suppose you came out here yourself. Miss Tina must have had to lend you a hand,' I interposed for conciliation.

'Oh she insisted we should push her; and when she insists!' said Miss Tina, in the same tone of apprehension: as if there were no knowing what service she disapproved of her aunt might force her next to render.

'I've always got most things done I wanted, thank God! The people I've lived with have humoured me,' the old woman continued, speaking out of the white ashes of her vanity.

I took it pleasantly up. 'I suppose you mean they've obeyed you.'

'Well, whatever it is – when they like one.'

'It's just because I like you that I want to resist,' said Miss Tina with a nervous laugh.

'Oh I suspect you'll bring Miss Bordereau upstairs next to pay me a visit,' I went on: to which the old lady replied:

'Oh no; I can keep an eye on you from here!'

'You're very tired; you'll certainly be ill tonight!' cried Miss Tina.

'Nonsense, dear; I feel better at this moment than I've done for a month. Tomorrow I shall come out again. I want to be where I can see this clever gentleman.'

'Shouldn't you perhaps see me better in your sitting-room?' I asked.

'Don't you mean shouldn't you have a better chance at *me*?' she returned, fixing me a moment with her green shade.

'Ah I haven't that anywhere! I look at you but don't see you.'

'You agitate her dreadfully – and that's not good,' said Miss Tina, giving me a reproachful deterrent headshake.

'I want to watch you – I want to watch you!' Miss Bordereau went on.

'Well then let us spend as much of our time together as possible – I don't care where. That will give you every facility.'

'Oh I've seen you enough for today. I'm satisfied. Now I'll go home,' Juliana said. Miss Tina laid her hands on the back of the wheeled chair and began to push, but I begged her to let me take her place. 'Oh yes, you may move me this way – you shan't in any other!' the old woman cried as she felt herself propelled firmly and easily over the smooth hard floor. Before we reached the door of her own apartment she bade me stop, and she took a long last look up and down the noble sala. 'Oh it's a prodigious house!' she murmured; after which I pushed her forward. When we had entered the parlour Miss Tina let me know she should now be able to manage, and at the same moment the little red-haired *donna* came to meet her mistress. Miss Tina's idea was evidently to get her aunt immediately back to bed. I confess that in spite of this urgency I was guilty of the indiscretion of lingering; it held me there to feel myself so close to the objects I coveted – which would be probably put away somewhere in the faded unsociable room. The place had indeed a bareness that suggested no hidden values; there were neither dusky nooks nor curtained corners, neither massive cabinets nor chests with iron bands. Moreover it was possible, it was perhaps even likely, that the old lady had consigned her relics to her bedroom, to some battered box that was shoved under the bed, to the drawer of some lame dressing-table, where they would be in the range of vision by the dim night-lamp. None the less I turned an eye on every article of furniture, on every conceivable cover for a hoard, and noticed that there were half a dozen things with drawers, and in particular a tall old secretary with brass ornaments of the style of the Empire – a receptacle somewhat infirm but still capable of keeping rare secrets. I don't know why this article so engaged me, small purpose as I had of breaking into it; but I stared at it so hard that Miss Tina noticed me and changed colour. Her doing this made me think I was right and that, wherever they might have been before, the Aspern papers at that moment languished behind the peevish little lock of the secretary. It was hard to turn my attention from the dull mahogany front when I reflected that a plain panel divided me from the goal of my hopes; but I gathered up my slightly scattered prudence and with an effort took leave of my hostess. To make the effort graceful I said to her that I should certainly bring her an opinion about the little picture.

'The little picture?' Miss Tina asked in surprise.

'What do *you* know about it, my dear?' the old woman demanded. 'You needn't mind. I've fixed my price.'

'And what may that be?'

'A thousand pounds.'

'Oh Lord!' cried poor Miss Tina irrepressibly.

'Is that what she talks to you about?' said Miss Bordereau.

'Imagine your aunt's wanting to know!' I had to separate from my younger friend with only those words, though I should have liked immensely to add: 'For heaven's sake meet me tonight in the garden!'

# VIII

As it turned out the precaution had not been needed, for three hours later, just as I had finished my dinner, Miss Tina appeared, unannounced, in the open doorway of the room in which my simple repasts were served. I remember well that I felt no surprise at seeing her; which is not a proof of my not believing in her timidity. It was immense, but in a case in which there was a particular reason for boldness it never would have prevented her from running up to my floor. I saw that she was now quite full of a particular reason; it threw her forward – made her seize me, as I rose to meet her, by the arm.

'My aunt's very ill; I think she's dying!'

'Never in the world,' I answered bitterly. 'Don't you be afraid!'

'Do go for a doctor – do, do! Olimpia's gone for the one we always have, but she doesn't come back; I don't know what has happened to her. I told her that if he wasn't at home she was to follow him where he had gone; but apparently she's following him all over Venice. I don't know what to do – she looks so as if she were sinking.'

'May I see her, may I judge?' I asked. 'Of course I shall be delighted to bring some one; but hadn't we better send my man instead, so that I may stay with you?'

Miss Tina assented to this and I dispatched my servant for the best doctor in the neighbourhood. I hurried downstairs with her, and on the way she told me that an hour after I quitted them in the afternoon Miss Bordereau had had an attack of 'oppression', a terrible difficulty in breathing. This had subsided, but had left her so exhausted that she didn't come up; she seemed all spent and gone. I repeated that she wasn't gone, that she wouldn't go yet; whereupon Miss Tina gave me a sharper sidelong glance than she had ever favoured me withal and said: 'Really, what do you mean? I suppose you don't accuse her of making-believe!' I forget what reply I made to this, but I fear that in my heart I thought the old woman capable of any weird manœuvre. Miss Tina wanted to know what I had done to her; her aunt had told her I had made her so angry. I declared

I had done nothing whatever – I had been exceedingly careful; to which my companion rejoined that our friend had assured her she had had a scene with me – a scene that had upset her. I answered with some resentment that the scene had been of *her* making – that I couldn't think what she was angry with me for unless for not seeing my way to give a thousand pounds for the portrait of Jeffrey Aspern. 'And did she show you that? Oh gracious – oh deary me!' groaned Miss Tina, who seemed to feel the situation pass out of her control and the elements of her fate thicken round her. I answered her I'd give anything to possess it, yet that I had no thousand pounds; but I stopped when we came to the door of Miss Bordereau's room. I had an immense curiosity to pass it, but I thought it my duty to represent to Miss Tina that if I made the invalid angry she ought perhaps to be spared the sight of me. 'The sight of you? Do you think she can *see*?' my companion demanded almost with indignation. I did think so but forbore to say it, and I softly followed my conductress.

I remember that what I said to her as I stood for a moment beside the old woman's bed was: 'Does she never show you her eyes then? Have you never seen them?' Miss Bordereau had been divested of her green shade, but – it was not my fortune to behold Juliana in her nightcap – the upper half of her face was covered by the fall of a piece of dingy lacelike muslin, a sort of extemporised hood which, wound round her head, descended to the end of her nose, leaving nothing visible but her white withered cheeks and puckered mouth, closed tightly and, as it were, consciously. Miss Tina gave me a glance of surprise, evidently not seeing a reason for my impatience. 'You mean she always wears something? She does it to preserve them.'

'Because they're so fine?'

'Oh today, today!' And Miss Tina shook her head speaking very low. 'But they used to be magnificent!'

'Yes indeed, – we've Aspern's word for that.' And as I looked again at the old woman's wrappings I could imagine her not having wished to allow any supposition that the great poet had overdone it. But I didn't waste my time in considering Juliana, in whom the appearance of respiration was so slight as to suggest that no human attention could ever help her more.

I turned my eyes once more all over the room, rummaging with them the closets, the chests of drawers, the tables. Miss Tina at once noted their direction and read, I think, what was in them; but she didn't answer it, turning away restlessly, anxiously, so that I felt rebuked, with reason, for an appetite well-nigh indecent in the presence of our dying companion. All the same I took another view, endeavouring to pick out mentally the receptacle to try first, for a person who should wish to put his hand on Miss Bordereau's papers directly after her death. The place was a dire confusion; it looked like the dressing-room of an old actress. There were clothes hanging over chairs, odd-looking shabby bundles here and there, and various pasteboard boxes piled together, battered, bulging and discoloured, which might have been fifty years old. Miss Tina after a moment noticed the direction of my eyes again, and, as if she guessed how I judged such appearances – forgetting I had no business to judge them at all – said, perhaps to defend herself from the imputation of complicity in the disorder:

'She likes it this way; we can't move things. There are old bandboxes she has had most of her life.' Then she added, half-taking pity on my real thought: 'Those things were *there*.' And she pointed to a small low trunk which stood under a sofa that just allowed room for it. It struck me as a queer super-annuated coffer, of painted wood, with elaborate handles and shrivelled straps and with the colour – it had last been endued with a coat of light green – much rubbed off. It evidently had travelled with Juliana in the olden time – in the days of her adventures, which it had shared. It would have made a strange figure arriving at a modern hotel.

'*Were* there – they aren't now?' I asked, startled by Miss Tina's implication.

She was going to answer, but at that moment the doctor came in – the doctor whom the little maid had been sent to fetch and whom she had at last overtaken. My servant, going on his own errand, had met her with her companion in tow, and in the sociable Venetian spirit, retracing his steps with them, had also come up to the threshold of the padrona's room, where I saw him peep over the doctor's shoulder. I motioned him away the more instantly that the sight of his prying face reminded me how little I myself had to do there – an admonition confirmed by the sharp way the little doctor eyed me, his air of taking me for a rival who had the field before him. He was a short fat brisk gentleman who wore the tall hat of his profession and seemed to look at everything but his patient. He kept me still in range, as if it struck him I too should be better for a dose, so that I bowed to him and left him with the women, going down to smoke a cigar in the garden. I was nervous; I couldn't go further; I couldn't leave the place. I don't know exactly what I thought might happen, but I felt it important to be there. I wandered about the alleys – the warm night had come on – smoking cigar after cigar and studying the light in Miss Bordereau's windows. They were open now, I could see; the situation was different. Sometimes the light moved, but not quickly; it didn't suggest the hurry of a crisis. Was the old woman dying or was she already dead? Had the doctor said that there was nothing to be done at her tremendous age but to let her quietly pass away? or had he simply announced with a look a little more conventional that the end of the end had come? Were the other two women just going and coming over the offices that follow in such a case? It made me uneasy not to be nearer, as if I thought the doctor himself might carry away the papers with him. I bit my cigar hard while it assailed me again that perhaps there were now no papers to carry!

I wandered about an hour and more. I looked out for Miss Tina at one of the windows, having a vague idea that she might come there to give me some sign. Wouldn't she see the red tip of my cigar in the dark and feel sure I was hanging on to know what the doctor had said? I'm afraid it's a proof of the grossness of my anxieties that I should have taken in some degree for granted at such an hour, in the midst of the greatest change that could fall on her, poor Miss Tina's having also a free mind for them. My servant came down and spoke to me; he knew nothing save that the doctor had gone after a visit of half an hour. If he had stayed half an hour then Miss Bordereau was still alive: it couldn't have taken so long to attest her decease. I sent the man out of the house; there were moments when the sense of his curiosity annoyed me, and this was one of them. He had been watching my cigar-tip from an upper window, if Miss Tina hadn't; he couldn't know what I was after and I couldn't tell him, though I suspected in him fantastic private theories about me which he thought fine and which, had I more exactly known them, I should have thought offensive.

I went upstairs at last, but I mounted no higher than the sala. The door of Miss Bordereau's apartment was open, showing from the parlour the dimness of a poor candle. I went toward it with a light tread, and at the same moment Miss Tina appeared and stood looking at me as I approached. 'She's better, she's better,' she said even before I had asked. 'The doctor has given her something; she woke up, came back to life while he was there. He says there's no immediate danger.'

'No immediate danger? Surely he thinks her condition serious.'

'Yes, because she had been excited. That affects her dreadfully.'

'It will do so again then, because she works herself up. She did so this afternoon.'

'Yes, she mustn't come out any more,' said Miss Tina with one of her lapses into a deeper detachment.

'What's the use of making such a remark as that,' I permitted myself to ask, 'if you begin to rattle her about again the first time she bids you?'

'I won't – I won't do it any more.'

'You must learn to resist her,' I went on.

'Oh yes, I shall; I shall do so better if you tell me it's right.'

'You mustn't do it for me – you must do it for yourself. It all comes back to you, if you're scared and upset.'

'Well, I'm not upset now,' said Miss Tina placidly enough. 'She's very quiet.'

'Is she conscious again – does she speak?'

'No, she doesn't speak but she takes my hand. She holds it fast.'

'Yes,' I returned, 'I can see what force she still has by the way she grabbed that picture this afternoon. But if she holds you fast how comes it that you're here?'

Miss Tina waited a little; though her face was in deep shadow – she had her back to the light in the parlour and I had put down my own candle far off, near the door of the sala – I thought I saw her smile ingenuously. 'I came on purpose – I had heard your step.'

'Why I came on tiptoe, as soundlessly as possible.'

'Well, I had heard you,' said Miss Tina.

'And is your aunt alone now?'

'Oh no – Olimpia sits there.'

On my side I debated. 'Shall we then pass in there?' And I nodded at the parlour; I wanted more and more to be on the spot.

'We can't talk there – she'll hear us.'

I was on the point of replying that in that case we'd sit silent, but I felt too much this wouldn't do, there was something I desired so immensely to ask her. Thus I hinted we might walk a little in the sala, keeping more at the other end, where we shouldn't disturb our friend. Miss Tina assented unconditionally; the doctor was coming again, she said, and she would be there to meet him at the door. We strolled through the fine superfluous hall, where on the marble floor – particularly as at first we said nothing – our footsteps were more audible than I had expected. When we reached the other end – the wide window, inveterately closed, connecting with the balcony that overhung the canal – I submitted that we had best remain there, as she would see the doctor arrive the sooner. I opened the window and we passed out on the balcony. The air of the canal seemed even heavier, hotter than that of the sala. The place was hushed and void; the quiet neighbourhood had gone to sleep. A lamp, here and there, over the narrow black water, glimmered in double; the voice of a man going homeward singing, his jacket on his shoulder and his hat on his ear, came to us from a distance. This didn't prevent the scene from being very *comme il faut*, as Miss Bordereau had called it the first time I saw her. Presently a gondola passed along the canal with its slow rhythmical plash, and as we listened we watched it in silence. It didn't stop, it didn't carry the doctor; and after it had gone on I said to Miss Tina:

'And where are they now – the things that were in the trunk?'

'In the trunk!'

'That green box you pointed out to me in her room. You said her papers had been there; you seemed to mean she had transferred them.'

'Oh yes; they're not in the trunk,' said Miss Tina.

'May I ask if you've looked?'

'Yes, I've looked – for you.'

'How for me, dear Miss Tina? Do you mean you'd have given them to me if you had found them?' – and I fairly trembled with the question.

She delayed to reply and I waited. Suddenly she broke out: 'I don't know what I'd do – what I wouldn't!'

'Would you look again – somewhere else?'

She had spoken with a strange unexpected emotion, and she went on in the same tone: 'I can't – I can't – while she lies there. It isn't decent.'

'No, it isn't decent,' I replied gravely. 'Let the poor lady rest in peace.' And the words, on my lips, were not hypocritical, for I felt reprimanded and shamed.

Miss Tina added in a moment, as if she had guessed this and were sorry for me, but at the same time wished to explain that I did push her, or at least harp on the chord, too much: 'I can't deceive her that way. I can't deceive her – perhaps on her deathbed.'

'Heaven forbid I should ask you, though I've been guilty myself!'

'You've been guilty?'

'I've sailed under false colours.' I felt now I must make a clean breast of it, must tell her I had given her an invented name on account of my fear her aunt would have heard of me and so refuse to take me in. I explained this as well as that I had really been a party to the letter addressed them by John Cumnor months before.

She listened with great attention, almost in fact gaping for wonder, and when I had made my confession she said: 'Then your real name – what is it?' She repeated it over twice when I had told her, accompanying it with the exclamation 'Gracious, gracious!' Then she added: 'I like your own best.'

'So do I' – and I felt my laugh rueful. 'Ouf! it's a relief to get rid of the other.'

'So it was a regular plot – a kind of conspiracy?'

'Oh a conspiracy – we were only two,' I replied, leaving out of course Mrs Prest.

She considered; I thought she was perhaps going to pronounce us very base. But this was not her way, and she remarked after a moment, as in candid impartial contemplation: 'How much you must want them!'

'Oh I do, passionately!' I grinned, I fear, to admit. And this chance made me go on, forgetting my compunction of a moment before. 'How can she possibly have changed their place herself? How can she walk? How can she arrive at that sort of muscular exertion? How can she lift and carry things?'

'Oh when one wants and when one has so much will!' said Miss Tina as if she had thought over my question already herself and had simply had no choice but that answer – the idea that in the dead of night, or at some moment when the coast was clear, the old woman had been capable of a miraculous effort.

'Have you questioned Olimpia? Hasn't she helped her – hasn't she done it for her?' I asked; to which my friend replied promptly and positively that their servant had had nothing to do with the matter, though without admitting definitely that she had spoken to her. It was as if she were a little shy, a little ashamed now, of letting me see how much she had entered into my uneasiness and had me on her mind. Suddenly she said to me without any immediate relevance:

'I rather feel you a new person, you know, now that you've a new name.'

'It isn't a new one; it's a very good old one, thank fortune!'

She looked at me a moment. 'Well, I do like it better.

'Oh if you didn't I would almost go on with the other!'

'Would you really?'

I laughed again, but I returned for all answer: 'Of course if she can rummage about that way she can perfectly have burnt them.'

'You must wait – you must wait,' Miss Tina mournfully moralised; and her tone ministered little to my patience, for it seemed after all to accept that wretched possibility. I would teach myself to wait, I declared nevertheless; because in the first place I couldn't do otherwise and in the second I had her promise, given me the other night, that she would help me.

'Of course if the papers are gone that's no use,' she said; not as if she wished to recede, but only to be conscientious.

'Naturally. But if you could only find out!' I groaned, quivering again.

'I thought you promised you'd wait.'

'Oh you mean wait even for that?'

'For what then?'

'Ah nothing,' I answered rather foolishly, being ashamed to tell her what had been implied in my acceptance of delay – the idea that she would perhaps do more for me than merely find out.

I know not if she guessed this; at all events she seemed to bethink herself of some propriety of showing me more rigour. 'I didn't promise to deceive, did I? I don't think I did.'

'It doesn't much matter whether you did or not, for you couldn't!'

Nothing is more possible than that she wouldn't have contested this even hadn't she been diverted by our seeing the doctor's gondola shoot into the little canal and approach the house. I noted that he came as fast as if he believed our proprietress still in danger. We looked down at him while he disembarked and then went back into the sala to meet him. When he came up, however, I naturally left Miss Tina to go off with him alone, only asking her leave to come back later for news.

I went out of the house and walked far, as far as the Piazza, where my restlessness declined to quit me. I was unable to sit down; it was very late now though there were people still at the little tables in front of the cafés: I could but uneasily revolve, and I did so half a dozen times. The only comfort, none the less, was in my having told Miss Tina who I really was. At last I took my way home again, getting gradually and all but inextricably lost, as I did whenever I went out in Venice: so that it was considerably past midnight when I reached my door. The sala, upstairs, was as dark as usual and my lamp as I crossed it found nothing satisfactory to show me. I was disappointed, for I had notified Miss Tina that I would come back for a report, and I thought she might have left a light there as a sign. The door of the ladies' apartment was closed; which seemed a hint that my faltering friend had gone to bed in impatience of waiting for me. I stood in the middle of the place, considering, hoping she would hear me and perhaps peep out, saying to myself too that she would never go to bed with her aunt in a state so critical; she would sit up and watch – she would be in a chair, in her dressing-gown. I went nearer the door; I stopped there and listened. I heard nothing at all and at last I tapped gently. No answer came and after another minute I turned the handle. There was no light in the room; this ought to have prevented my entrance, but it had no such effect. If I have frankly stated the importunities, the indelicacies, of which my desire to possess myself of Jeffrey Aspern's papers had made me capable I needn't shrink, it seems to me, from confessing this last indiscretion. I regard it as the worst thing I did, yet there were extenuating circumstances. I was deeply though doubtless not disinterestedly anxious for more news of Juliana, and Miss Tina had accepted from me, as it were, a rendezvous which it might have been a point of honour with me to keep. It may be objected that her leaving the place dark was a positive sign that she released me, and to this I can only reply that I wished not to be released.

The door of Miss Bordereau's room was open and I could see beyond it the faintness of a taper. There was no sound – my footstep caused no one to stir. I came further into the room; I lingered there lamp in hand. I wanted to give Miss Tina a chance to come to me if, as I couldn't doubt, she were still with her aunt. I made no noise to call her; I only waited to see if she wouldn't notice my light. She didn't, and I explained this – I found afterwards I was right – by the idea that she had fallen asleep. If she had fallen asleep her aunt was not on her mind, and my explanation ought to have led me to go out as I had come. I must repeat again that it didn't, for I found myself at the same moment given up to something else. I had no definite purpose, no bad intention, but felt myself held to the spot by an acute, though absurd, sense of opportunity. Opportunity for what I couldn't have said, inasmuch as it wasn't in my mind that I might proceed to thievery. Even had this tempted me I was confronted with the evident fact that Miss Bordereau didn't leave her secretary, her cupboard and the drawers of her tables gaping. I had no keys, no tools and no ambition to smash her furniture. None the less it came to me that I was now, perhaps alone, unmolested, at the hour of freedom and safety, nearer to the source of my hopes than I had ever been. I held up my lamp, let the light play on the different objects as if it could tell me something. Still there came no movement from the other room. If Miss Tina was sleeping she was sleeping sound. Was she doing so – generous creature – on purpose to leave me the field? Did she know I was there and was she just keeping quiet to see what I would do – what I *could* do? Yet might I, when it came to that? She herself knew even better than I how little.

I stopped in front of the secretary, gaping at it vainly and no doubt grotesquely; for what had it to say to me after all? In the first place it was locked, and in the second it almost surely contained nothing in which I was interested. Ten to one the papers had been destroyed, and even if they hadn't the keen old woman wouldn't have put them in such a place as that after removing them from the green trunk – wouldn't have transferred them, with the idea of their safety on her brain, from the better hiding-place to the worse. The secretary was more conspicuous, more exposed in a room in which she could no longer mount guard. It opened with a key, but there was a small brass handle, like a button, as well: I saw this as I played my lamp over it. I did something more, for the climax of my crisis; I caught a glimpse of the possibility that Miss Tina wished me really to understand. If she didn't so wish me, if she wished me to keep away, why hadn't she locked the door of communication between the sitting-room and the sala? That would have been a definite sign that I was to leave them alone. If I didn't leave them alone she meant me to come for a purpose – a purpose now represented by the super-subtle inference that to oblige me she had unlocked the secretary. She hadn't left the key, but the lid would probably move if I touched the button. This possibility pressed me hard and I bent very close to judge. I didn't propose to do anything, not even – not in the least – to let down the lid; I only wanted to test my theory, to see if the cover *would* move. I touched the button with my hand – a mere touch would tell me; and as I did so – it is embarrassing for me to relate it – I looked over my shoulder. It was a chance, an instinct, for I had really heard nothing. I almost let my luminary drop and certainly I stepped back, straightening myself up at what I saw. Juliana stood there in her night-dress, by the doorway of her room, watching me; her hands were raised, she had lifted the everlasting curtain that covered half her face, and for the first, the last, the only time I beheld her extraordinary eyes. They glared at me; they were like the sudden drench, for a caught burglar, of a flood of gaslight; they made me horribly ashamed. I never shall forget her strange little bent white tottering figure, with its lifted head, her attitude, her expression; neither shall I forget the tone in which as I turned, looking at her, she hissed out passionately, furiously:

'Ah you publishing scoundrel!'

I can't now say what I stammered to excuse myself, to explain; but I went toward her to tell her I meant no harm. She waved me off with her old hands, retreating before me in horror; and the next thing I knew she had fallen back with a quick spasm, as if death had descended on her, into Miss Tina's arms.

## IX

I LEFT Venice the next morning, directly on learning that my hostess had not succumbed, as I feared at the moment, to the shock I had given her – the shock I may also say she had given me. How in the world could I have supposed her capable of getting out of bed by herself? I failed to see Miss Tina before going; I only saw the *donna*, whom I entrusted with a note for her younger mistress. In this note I mentioned that I should be absent but a few days. I went to Treviso, to Bassano, to Castelfranco; I took walks and drives and looked at musty old churches with ill-lighted pictures; I spent hours seated smoking at the doors of cafés, where there were flies and yellow curtains, on the shady side of sleepy little squares. In spite of these pastimes, which were mechanical and perfunctory, I scantly enjoyed my travels: I had had to gulp down a bitter draught and couldn't get rid of the taste. It had been devilish awkward, as the young men say, to be found by Juliana in the dead of night examining the attachment of her bureau; and it had not been less so to have to believe for a good many hours after that it was highly probable I had killed her. My humiliation galled me, but I had to make the best of it, had, in writing to Miss Tina, to minimise it, as well as account for the posture in which I had been discovered. As she gave me no word of answer I couldn't know what impression I made on her. It rankled for me that I had been called a publishing scoundrel, since certainly I did publish and no less certainly hadn't been very delicate. There was a moment when I stood convinced that the only way to purge my dishonour was to take myself straight away on the instant; to sacrifice my hopes and relieve the two poor women for ever of the oppression of my intercourse. Then I reflected that I had better try a short absence first, for I must already have had a sense (unexpressed and dim) that in disappearing completely it wouldn't be merely my own hopes I should condemn to extinction. It would perhaps answer if I kept dark long enough to give the elder lady time to believe herself rid of me. That she would wish to be rid of me after this – if I wasn't rid of her – was now not to be doubted: that midnight

monstrosity would have cured her of the disposition
with my company for the sake of my dollars. I said
that after all I couldn't abandon Miss Tina, and I c
to say this even while I noted that she quite ignored my
request – I had given her two or three addresses, at little t
*poste restante* – for some sign of her actual state. I would
have made my servant write me news but that he was unable to
manage a pen. Couldn't I measure the scorn of Miss Tina's
silence – little disdainful as she had ever been? Really the
soreness pressed; yet if I had scruples about going back I had
others about not doing so, and I wanted to put myself on a
better footing. The end of it was that I did return to Venice
on the twelfth day; and as my gondola gently bumped against
our palace steps a fine palpitation of suspense showed me the
violence my absence had done me.

I had faced about so abruptly that I hadn't even telegraphed
to my servant. He was therefore not at the station to meet me,
but he poked out his head from an upper window when I
reached the house. 'They have put her into earth, *quella vecchia*,' he said to me in the lower hall while he shouldered my
valise; and he grinned and almost winked as if he knew I
should be pleased with his news.

'She's dead!' I cried, giving him a very different look.

'So it appears, since they've buried her.'

'It's all over then? When was the funeral?'

'The other yesterday. But a funeral you could scarcely call it,
signore: *roba da niente – un piccolo passeggio brutto* of two
gondolas. Poveretta!' the man continued, referring apparently to
Miss Tina. His conception of funerals was that they were
mainly to amuse the living.

I wanted to know about Miss Tina, how she might be and
generally where; but I asked him no more questions till we had
got upstairs. Now that the fact had met me I took a bad view
of it, especially of the idea that poor Miss Tina had had to
manage by herself after the end. What did she know about
arrangements, about the steps to take in such a case? Poveretta
indeed! I could only hope the doctor had given her support and
that she hadn't been neglected by the old friends of whom she
had told me, the little band of the faithful whose fidelity consisted in coming to the house once a year. I elicited from my

servant that two old ladies and an old gentleman had in fact rallied round Miss Tina and had supported her – they had come for her in a gondola of their own – during the journey to the cemetery, the little red-walled island of tombs which lies to the north of the town and on the way to Murano. It appeared from these signs that the Misses Bordereau were Catholics, a discovery I had never made, as the old woman couldn't go to church and her niece, so far as I perceived, either didn't, or went only to early mass in the parish before I was stirring. Certainly even the priests respected their seclusion; I had never caught the whisk of the curato's skirt. That evening, an hour later, I sent my servant down with five words on a card to ask if Miss Tina would see me a few moments. She was not in the house, where he had sought her, he told me when he came back, but in the garden walking about to refresh herself and picking the flowers quite as if they belonged to her. He had found her there and she would be happy to see me.

I went down and passed half an hour with poor Miss Tina. She had always had a look of musty mourning, as if she were wearing out old robes of sorrow that wouldn't come to an end; and in this particular she made no different show. But she clearly had been crying, crying a great deal – simply, satisfyingly, refreshingly, with a primitive retarded sense of solitude and violence. But she had none of the airs or graces of grief, and I was almost surprised to see her stand there in the first dusk with her hands full of admirable roses and smile at me with reddened eyes. Her white face, in the frame of her mantilla, looked longer, leaner than usual. I hadn't doubted her being irreconcileably disgusted with me, her considering I ought to have been on the spot to advise her, to help her; and, though I believed there was no rancour in her composition and no great conviction of the importance of her affairs, I had prepared myself for a change in her manner, for some air of injury and estrangement, which should say to my conscience: 'Well, you're a nice person to have professed things!' But historic truth compels me to declare that this poor lady's dull face ceased to be dull, almost ceased to be plain, as she turned it gladly to her late aunt's lodger. That touched him extremely and he thought it simplified his situation until he found it didn't. I was as kind to her that evening as I knew how to be, and I walked about the garden with her as long as seemed good. There was no explanation of any sort between us; I didn't ask her why she hadn't answered my letter. Still less did I repeat what I had said to her in that communication; if she chose to let me suppose she had forgotten the position in which Miss Bordereau had surprised me and the effect of the discovery on the old woman, I was quite willing to take it that way: I was grateful to her for not treating me as if I had killed her aunt.

We strolled and strolled, though really not much passed between us save the recognition of her bereavement, conveyed in my manner and in the expression she had of depending on me now, since I let her see I still took an interest in her. Miss Tina's was no breast for the pride or the pretence of independence; she didn't in the least suggest that she knew at present what would become of her. I forbore to press on that question, however, for I certainly was not prepared to say that I would take charge of her. I was cautious; not ignobly, I think, for I felt her knowledge of life to be so small that in her unsophisticated vision there would be no reason why – since I seemed to pity her – I shouldn't somehow look after her. She told me how her aunt had died, very peacefully at the last, and how everything had been done afterwards by the care of her good friends – fortunately, thanks to me, she said, smiling, there was money in the house. She repeated that when once the 'nice' Italians like you they are your friends for life, and when we had gone into this she asked me about my *giro*, my impressions, my adventures, the places I had seen. I told her what I could, making it up partly, I'm afraid, as in my disconcerted state I had taken little in; and after she had heard me she exclaimed, quite as if she had forgotten her aunt and her sorrow, 'Dear, dear, how much I should like to do such things – to take an amusing little journey!' It came over me for the moment that I ought to propose some enterprise, say I would accompany her anywhere she liked; and I remarked at any rate that a pleasant excursion – to give her a change – might be managed: we would think of it, talk it over. I spoke never a word of the Aspern documents, asked no question as to what she had ascertained or what had otherwise happened with regard to them before Juliana's death. It wasn't that I wasn't on pins and needles to know, but that I thought it more decent not to show greed again so soon after the catastrophe. I hoped she herself would say something, but she never glanced that way, and I thought this natural at the time. Later on, however, that night, it occurred to me that her silence was matter for suspicion; since if she had talked of my movements, of anything so detached as the Giorgione at Castelfranco, she might have alluded to what she could easily remember was in my mind. It was not to be supposed the emotion produced by her aunt's death had blotted out the recollection that I was interested in that lady's relics, and I fidgeted afterwards as it came to me that her reticence might very possibly just mean that no relics survived. We separated in the garden – it was she who said she must go in; now that she was alone on the *piano nobile* I felt that (judged at any rate by Venetian ideas) I was on rather a different footing in regard to the invasion of it. As I shook hands with her for good-night I asked if she had some general plan, had thought over what she had best do. 'Oh yes, oh yes, but I haven't settled anything yet,' she replied quite cheerfully. Was her cheerfulness explained by the impression that I would settle for her?

I was glad the next morning that we had neglected practical questions, as this gave me a pretext for seeing her again immediately. There was a practical enough question now to be touched on. I owed it to her to let her know formally that of course I didn't expect her to keep me on as a lodger, as also to show some interest in her own tenure, what she might have on her hands in the way of a lease. But I was not destined, as befell, to converse with her for more than an instant on either of these points. I sent her no message; I simply went down to the sala and walked to and fro there. I knew she would come out; she would promptly see me accessible. Somehow I preferred not to be shut up with her; gardens and big halls seemed better places to talk. It was a splendid morning, with something in the air that told of the waning of the long Venetian summer; a freshness from the sea that stirred the flowers in the garden and made a pleasant draught in the house, less shuttered and darkened now than when the old woman was alive. It was the beginning of autumn, of the end of the golden months. With this it was the end of my experiment – or would be in the course of half an hour, when I should really have learned that my dream had been reduced to ashes. After that there would be nothing left for me but to go to the station; for seriously – and as it struck me in the morning light – I couldn't linger there to act as guardian to a piece of middle-aged female helplessness. If she hadn't saved the papers wherein should I be indebted to her? I think I winced a little as I asked myself how much, if she *had* saved them, I should have to recognise and, as it were, reward such a courtesy. Mightn't that service after all saddle me with a guardianship? If this idea didn't make me more uncomfortable as I walked up and down it was because I was convinced I had nothing to look to. If the old woman hadn't destroyed everything before she pounced on me in the parlour she had done so the next day.

It took Miss Tina rather longer than I had expected to act on my calculation; but when at last she came out she looked at me without surprise. I mentioned I had been waiting for her and she asked why I hadn't let her know. I was glad a few hours later on that I had checked myself before remarking that a friendly intuition might have told her: it turned to comfort for me that I hadn't played even to that mild extent on her sensibility. What I did say was virtually the truth – that I was too nervous, since I expected her now to settle my fate.

'Your fate?' said Miss Tina, giving me a queer look; and as she spoke I noticed a rare change in her. Yes, she was other than she had been the evening before – less natural and less easy. She had been crying the day before and was not crying now, yet she struck me as less confident. It was as if something had happened to her during the night, or at least as if she had thought of something that troubled her – something in particular that affected her relations with me, made them more embarrassing and more complicated. Had she simply begun to feel that her aunt's not being there now altered my position?

'I mean about our papers. *Are* there any? You must know now.'

'Yes, there are a great many; more than I supposed.' I was struck with the way her voice trembled as she told me this.

'Do you mean you've got them in there – and that I may see them?'

'I don't think you can see them,' said Miss Tina with an extraordinary expression of entreaty in her eyes, as if the dearest hope she had in the world now was that I wouldn't take them from her. But how could she expect me to make such a sacrifice as that after all that had passed between us? What had I come back to Venice for but to see them, to take them? My joy at learning they were still in existence was such that if the poor woman had gone down on her knees to beseech me never to mention them again I would have treated the proceeding as a bad joke. 'I've got them but I can't show them,' she lamentably added.

'Not even to me? Ah Miss Tina!' I broke into a tone of infiinite remonstrance and reproach.

She coloured and the tears came back to her eyes; I measured the anguish it cost her to take such a stand, which a dreadful sense of duty had imposed on her. It made me quite sick to find myself confronted with that particular obstacle; all the more that it seemed to me I had been distinctly encouraged to leave it out of account. I quite held Miss Tina to have assured me that if she had no greater hindrance than that—! 'You don't mean to say you made her a deathbed promise? It was precisely against your doing anything of that sort that I thought I was safe. Oh I would rather she had burnt the papers outright than have to reckon with such a treachery as that.'

'No, it isn't a promise,' said Miss Tina.

'Pray what is it then?'

She hung fire, but finally said: 'She tried to burn them, but I prevented it. She had hid them in her bed.'

'In her bed—?'

'Between the mattresses. That's where she put them when she took them out of the trunk. I can't understand how she did it, because Olimpia didn't help her. She tells me so and I believe her. My aunt only told her afterwards, so that she shouldn't undo the bed – anything but the sheets. So it was very badly made,' added Miss Tina simply.

'I should think so! And how did she try to burn them?'

'She didn't try much; she was too weak those last days. But she told me – she charged me. Oh it was terrible! She couldn't speak after that night. She could only make signs.'

'And what did you do?'

'I took them away. I locked them up.'

'In the secretary?'

'Yes, in the secretary,' said Miss Tina, reddening again.

'Did you tell her you'd burn them?'

'No, I didn't – on purpose.'

'On purpose to gratify me?'

'Yes, only for that.'

'And what good will you have done me if after all you won't show them?'

'Oh none. I know that – I know that,' she dismally sounded.

'And did she believe you had destroyed them?'

'I don't know what she believed at the last. I couldn't tell – she was too far gone.'

'Then if there was no promise and no assurance I can't see what ties you.'

'Oh she hated it so – she hated it so! She was so jealous. But here's the portrait – you may have that,' the poor woman announced, taking the little picture, wrapped up in the same manner in which her aunt had wrapped it, out of her pocket.

'I may have it – do you mean you give it to me?' I gasped as it passed into my hand.

'Oh yes.'

'But it's worth money – a large sum.'

'Well!' said Miss Tina, still with her strange look.

I didn't know what to make of it, for it could scarcely mean that she wanted to bargain like her aunt. She spoke as for making me a present. 'I can't take it from you as a gift,' I said, 'and yet I can't afford to pay you for it according to the idea Miss Bordereau had of its value. She rated it at a thousand pounds.'

'Couldn't we sell it?' my friend threw off.

'God forbid! I prefer the picture to the money.'

'Well then keep it.'

'You're very generous.'

'So are you.'

'I don't know why you should think so,' I returned; and this was true enough, for the good creature appeared to have in her mind some rich reference that I didn't in the least seize.

'Well, you've made a great difference for me,' she said.

I looked at Jeffrey Aspern's face in the little picture, partly in order not to look at that of my companion, which had begun to trouble me, even to frighten me a little – it had taken so very odd, so strained and unnatural a cast. I made no answer to this last declaration; I but privately consulted Jeffrey Aspern's delightful eyes with my own – they were so young and brilliant and yet so wise and so deep: I asked him what on earth was the matter with Miss Tina. He seemed to smile at me with mild mockery; he might have been amused at my case. I had got into a pickle for him – as if he needed it! He was unsatisfactory for the only moment since I had known him. Nevertheless, now that I held the little picture in my hand I felt it would be a precious possession. 'Is this a bribe to make me give up the papers?' I presently and all perversely asked. 'Much as I value this, you know, if I were to be obliged to choose the papers are what I should prefer. Ah but ever so much!'

'How can you choose – how can you choose?' Miss Tina returned slowly and woefully.

'I see! Of course there's nothing to be said if you regard the interdiction that rests on you as quite insurmountable. In this case it must seem to you that to part with them would be an impiety of the worst kind, a simple sacrilege!'

She shook her head, only lost in the queerness of her case. 'You'd understand if you had known her. I'm afraid,' she quavered suddenly – 'I'm afraid! She was terrible when she was angry.'

'Yes, I saw something of that, that night. She was terrible. Then I saw her eyes. Lord, they were fine!'

'I see them – they stare at me in the dark!' said Miss Tina.

'You've grown nervous with all you've been through.'

'Oh yes, very – very!'

'You mustn't mind; that will pass away,' I said kindly. Then I added resignedly, for it really seemed to me that I must accept the situation: 'Well, so it is, and it can't be helped. I must renounce.' My friend, at this, with her eyes on me, gave a low soft moan, and I went on: 'I only wish to goodness she had destroyed them: then there would be nothing more to say. And I can't understand why, with her ideas, she didn't.'

'Oh she lived on them!' said Miss Tina.

'You can imagine whether that makes me want less to see them,' I returned not quite so desperately. 'But don't let me stand here as if I had it in my soul to tempt you to anything base. Naturally, you understand, I give up my rooms. I leave

Venice immediately.' And I took up my hat, which I had placed on a chair. We were still rather awkwardly on our feet in the middle of the sala. She had left the door of the apartments open behind her, but had not led me that way.

A strange spasm came into her face as she saw me take my hat. 'Immediately – do you mean today?' The tone of the words was tragic – they were a cry of desolation.

'Oh no; not so long as I can be of the least service to you.'

'Well, just a day or two more – just two or three days,' she panted. Then controlling herself she added in another manner: 'She wanted to say something to me – the last day – something very particular. But she couldn't.'

'Something very particular?'

'Something more about the papers.'

'And did you guess – have you any idea?'

'No, I've tried to think – but I don't know. I've thought all kinds of things.'

'As for instance?'

'Well, that if you were a relation it would be different.'

I wondered. 'If I were a relation—?'

'If you weren't a stranger. Then it would be the same for you as for me. Anything that's mine would be yours, and you could do what you like. I shouldn't be able to prevent you – and you'd have no responsibility.'

She brought out this droll explanation with a nervous rush and as if speaking words got by heart. They gave me the impression of a subtlety which at first I failed to follow. But after a moment her face helped me to see further, and then the queerest of lights came to me. It was embarrassing, and I bent my head over Jeffrey Aspern's portrait. What an odd expression was in his face! 'Get out of it as you can, my dear fellow!' I put the picture into the pocket of my coat and said to Miss Tina: 'Yes, I'll sell it for you. I shan't get a thousand pounds by any means, but I shall get something good.'

She looked at me through pitiful tears, but seemed to try to smile as she returned: 'We can divide the money.'

'No, no, it shall be all yours.' Then I went on: 'I think I know what your poor aunt wanted to say. She wanted to give directions that her papers should be buried with her.'

Miss Tina appeared to weigh this suggestion; after which she answered with striking decision, 'Oh no, she wouldn't have thought that safe!'

'It seems to me nothing could be safer.'

'She had an idea that when people want to publish they're capable—!' And she paused, very red.

'Of violating a tomb? Mercy on us, what must she have thought of me!'

'She wasn't just, she wasn't generous!' my companion cried with sudden passion.

The light that had come into my mind a moment before spread further. 'Ah don't say that, for we *are* a dreadful race.' Then I pursued: 'If she left a will, that may give you some idea.'

'I've found nothing of the sort – she destroyed it. She was very fond of me,' Miss Tina added with an effect of extreme inconsequence. 'She wanted me to be happy. And if any person should be kind to me – she wanted to speak of that.'

I was almost awestricken by the astuteness with which the good lady found herself inspired, transparent astuteness as it was and stitching, as the phrase is, with white thread. 'Depend upon it she didn't want to make any provision that would be agreeable to *me*.'

'No, not to you, but quite to me. She knew I should like it if you could carry out your idea. Not because she cared for you, but because she did think of me,' Miss Tina went on with her unexpected persuasive volubility. 'You could see the things – you could use them.' She stopped, seeing I grasped the sense of her conditional – stopped long enough for me to give some sign that I didn't give. She must have been conscious, however, that though my face showed the greatest embarrassment ever painted on a human countenance it was not set as a stone, it was also full of compassion. It was a comfort to me a long time afterwards to consider that she couldn't have seen in me the smallest symptom of disrespect. 'I don't know what to do; I'm too tormented, I'm too ashamed!' she continued with vehemence. Then turning away from me and burying her face in her hands she burst into a flood of tears. If she didn't know what to do it may be imagined whether I knew better. I stood there dumb, watching her while her sobs resounded in the great empty hall. In a moment she was up at me again with her streaming eyes.

'I'd give you everything, and she'd understand, where she is – she'd forgive me!'

'Ah Miss Tina – ah Miss Tina,' I stammered for all reply. I didn't know what to do, as I say, but at a venture I made a wild vague movement in consequence of which I found myself at the door. I remember standing there and saying 'It wouldn't do, it wouldn't do!' – saying it pensively, awkwardly, grotesquely, while I looked away to the opposite end of the sala as at something very interesting. The next thing I remember is that I was downstairs and out of the house. My gondola was there and my gondolier, reclining on the cushions, sprang up as soon as he saw me. I jumped in and to his usual '*Dove commanda?*' replied, in a tone that made him stare: 'Anywhere, anywhere; out into the lagoon!'

He rowed me away and I sat there prostrate, groaning softly to myself, my hat pulled over my brow. What in the name of the preposterous did she mean if she didn't mean to offer me her hand? That was the price – that was the price! And did she think I wanted it, poor deluded infatuated extravagant lady? My gondolier, behind me, must have seen my ears red as I wondered, motionless there under the fluttering *tenda* with my hidden face, noticing nothing as we passed – wondered whether her delusion, her infatuation had been my own reckless work. Did she think I had made love to her even to get the papers? I hadn't, I hadn't; I repeated that over to myself for an hour, for two hours, till I was wearied if not convinced. I don't know where, on the lagoon, my gondolier took me; we floated aimlessly and with slow rare strokes. At last I became conscious that we were near the Lido, far up, on the right hand, as you turn your back to Venice, and I made him put me ashore. I wanted to walk, to move, to shed some of my bewilderment. I crossed the narrow strip and got to the sea-beach – I took my way toward Malamocco. But presently I flung myself down again on the warm sand, in the breeze, on the coarse dry grass. It took it out of me to think I had been so much at fault, that I had unwittingly but none the less deplorably trifled. But I hadn't given her cause – distinctly I hadn't. I had said to Mrs Prest that I would make love to her; but it had been a joke without consequences and I had never said it to my victim. I had been as kind as possible because I really liked her; but since when had that become a crime where a woman of such an age and such an appearance was concerned? I am far from remembering clearly the succession of events and feelings during this long day of confusion, which I spent entirely in wandering about, without going home, until late at night: it only comes back to me that there were moments when I pacified my conscience and others when I lashed it into pain. I didn't laugh all day – that I do recollect; the case, however it might have struck others, seemed to me so little amusing. I should have been better employed perhaps in taking in the comic side of it. At any rate, whether I had given cause or not, there was no doubt whatever that I couldn't pay the price. I couldn't accept the proposal. I couldn't, for a bundle of tattered papers, marry a ridiculous pathetic provincial old woman. It was a proof of how little she supposed the idea would come to me that she should have decided to suggest it herself in that practical argumentative heroic way – with the timidity, however, so much more striking than the boldness, that her reasons appeared to come first and her feelings afterward.

As the day went on I grew to wish I had never heard of Aspern's relics, and I cursed the extravagant curiosity that had put John Cumnor on the scent of them. We had more than enough material without them, and my predicament was the just punishment of that most fatal of human follies, our not having known when to stop. It was very well to say it was no predicament, that the way out was simple, that I had only to leave Venice by the first train in the morning, after addressing Miss Tina a note which should be placed in her hand as soon as I got clear of the house; for it was strong proof of my quandary that when I tried to make up the note to my taste in advance – I would put it on paper as soon as I got home, before going to bed – I couldn't think of anything but 'How can I thank you for the rare confidence you've placed in me?' That would never do; it sounded exactly as if an acceptance were to follow. Of course I might get off without writing at all, but that would be brutal, and my idea was still to exclude brutal solutions. As my confusion cooled I lost myself in wonder at the importance I had attached to Juliana's crumpled scraps; the thought of them became odious to me and I was as vexed with the old witch for the superstition that had prevented her from destroying them as I was with myself for having already spent more money than I could afford in attempting to control their fate. I forget what I did, where I went after leaving the Lido and at what hour or with what recovery of composure I made my way back to my boat. I only know that in the afternoon, when the air was aglow with the sunset, I was standing before the church of Saints John and Paul and looking up at the small square-jawed face of Bartolommeo Colleoni, the terrible *condottiere* who sits so sturdily astride of his huge bronze horse on the high pedestal on which Venetian gratitude maintains him. The statue is incomparable, the finest of all mounted figures, unless that of Marcus Aurelius, who rides benignant before the Roman Capitol, be finer: but I was not thinking of that; I only found myself staring at the triumphant captain as if he had had an oracle on his lips. The western light shines into all his grimness at that hour and makes it wonderfully personal. But he continued to look far over my head, at the red immersion of another day – he had seen so many go down into the lagoon through the centuries – and if he were thinking of battles and stratagems they were of a different quality from any I had to tell him of. He couldn't direct me what to do, gaze up at him as I might. Was it before this or after that I wandered about for an hour in the small canals, to the continued stupefaction of my gondolier, who had never seen me so restless and yet so void of a purpose and could extract from me no order but 'Go anywhere – everywhere – all over the place'? He reminded me that I had not lunched and expressed therefore respectfully the hope that I would dine earlier. He had had long periods of leisure during the day, when I had left the boat and rambled, so that I was not obliged to consider him, and I told him that till the morrow, for reasons, I should touch no meat. It was an effect of poor Miss Tina's proposal, not altogether auspicious, that I had quite lost my appetite. I don't know why it happened that on this occasion I was more than ever struck with that queer air of sociability, of cousinship and family life, which makes up half the expression of Venice. Without streets and vehicles, the uproar of wheels, the brutality of horses, and with its little winding ways where people crowd together, where voices sound as in the corridors of a house, where the human step circulates as if it skirted the angles of furniture and shoes never wear out, the place has the character of an immense collective apartment, in which Piazza San Marco is the most ornamented corner and palaces and churches, for the rest, play the part of great divans of repose, tables of entertainment, expanses of decoration. And somehow the splendid common domicile, familiar domestic and resonant, also resembles a theatre with its actors clicking over bridges and, in straggling processions, tripping along fondamentas. As you sit in your gondola the footways that in certain parts edge the canals assume to the eye the importance of a stage, meeting it at the same angle, and the Venetian figures, moving to and fro against the battered scenery of their little houses of comedy, strike you as members of an endless dramatic troupe.

I went to bed that night very tired and without being able to compose an address to Miss Tina. Was this failure the reason why I became conscious the next morning as soon as I awoke of a determination to see the poor lady again the first moment she would receive me? That had something to do with it, but what had still more was the fact that during my sleep the oddest revulsion had taken place in my spirit. I found myself aware of this almost as soon as I opened my eyes: it made me jump out of my bed with the movement of a man who remembers that he has left the house-door ajar or a candle burning under a shelf. Was I still in time to save my goods? That question was in my heart; for what had now come to pass was that in the unconscious cerebration of sleep I had swung back to a passionate appreciation of Juliana's treasure. The pieces composing it were now more precious than ever and a positive ferocity had come into my need to acquire them. The condition Miss Tina had attached to that act no longer appeared an obstacle worth thinking of, and for an hour this morning my repentant imagination brushed it aside. It was absurd I should be able to invent nothing; absurd to renounce so easily and turn away helpless from the idea that the only way to become possessed was to unite myself to her for life. I mightn't unite myself, yet I might still have what she had. I must add that by the time I sent down to ask if she would see me I had invented no alternative, though in fact I drew out my dressing in the interest of my wit. This failure was humiliating, yet what could the alternative be? Miss Tina sent back word I might come;

and as I descended the stairs and crossed the sala to her door – this time she received me in her aunt's forlorn parlour – I hoped she wouldn't think my announcement was to be 'favourable'. She certainly would have understood my recoil of the day before.

As soon as I came into the room I saw that she had done so, but I also saw something which had not been in my forecast. Poor Miss Tina's sense of her failure had produced a rare alteration in her, but I had been too full of stratagems and spoils to think of that. Now I took it in; I can scarcely tell how it startled me. She stood in the middle of the room with a face of mildness bent upon me, and her look of forgiveness, of absolution, made her angelic. It beautified her; she was younger; she was not a ridiculous old woman. This trick of her expression, this magic of her spirit, transfigured her, and while I still noted it I heard a whisper somewhere in the depths of my conscience: 'Why not, after all – why not?' It seemed to me I *could* pay the price. Still more distinctly however than the whisper I heard Miss Tina's own voice. I was so struck with the different effect she made on me that at first I wasn't clearly aware of what she was saying; then I recognised she had bade me good-bye – she said something about hoping I should be very happy.

'Good-bye – good-bye?' I repeated with an inflexion interrogative and probably foolish.

I saw she didn't feel the interrogation, she only heard the words: she had strung herself up to accepting our separation and they fell upon her ear as a proof. 'Are you going today?' she asked. 'But it doesn't matter, for whenever you go I shall not see you again. I don't want to.' And she smiled strangely, with an infinite gentleness. She had never doubted my having left her the day before in horror. How *could* she, since I hadn't come back before night to contradict, even as a simple form, even as an act of common humanity, such an idea? And now she had the force of soul – Miss Tina with force of soul was a new conception – to smile at me in her abjection.

'What shall you do – where shall you go?' I asked.

'Oh I don't know. I've done the great thing. I've destroyed the papers.'

'Destroyed them?' I wailed.

'Yes; what was I to keep them for? I burnt them last night, one by one, in the kitchen.'

'One by one?' I coldly echoed it.

'It took a long time – there were so many.' The room seemed to go round me as she said this and a real darkness for a moment descended on my eyes. When it passed Miss Tina was there still, but the transfiguration was over and she had changed back to a plain dingy elderly person. It was in this character she spoke as she said 'I can't stay with you longer, I can't'; and it was in this character she turned her back upon me, as I had turned mine upon her twenty-four hours before, and moved to the door of her room. Here she did what I hadn't done when I quitted her – she paused long enough to give me one look. I have never forgotten it and I sometimes still suffer from it, though it was not resentful. No, there was no resentment, nothing hard or vindictive in poor Miss Tina; for when, later, I sent her, as the price of the portrait of Jeffrey Aspern, a larger sum of money than I had hoped to be able to gather for her, writing to her that I had sold the picture, she kept it with thanks; she never sent it back. I wrote her that I had sold the picture, but I admitted to Mrs Prest at the time – I met this other friend in London that autumn – that it hangs above my writing-table. When I look at it I can scarcely bear my loss – I mean of the precious papers.

# THE PRIVATE LIFE

# THE PRIVATE LIFE

WE talked of London face to face with a great bristling primeval glacier. The hour and the scene were one of those impressions that make up a little in Switzerland for the modern indignity of travel – the promiscuities and vulgarities, the station and the hotel, the gregarious patience, the struggle for a scrappy attention, the reduction to a numbered state. The high valley was pink with the mountain rose, the cool air as fresh as if the world were young. There was a faint flush of afternoon on undiminished snows, and the fraternising tinkle of the unseen cattle came to us with a cropped and sun-warmed odour. The balconied inn stood on the very neck of the sweetest pass in the Oberland, and for a week we had had company and weather. This was felt to be great luck, for one would have made up for the other had either been bad.

The weather certainly would have made up for the company; but it wasn't subjected to this tax, for we had by a happy chance the *fleur des pois*: Lord and Lady Mellifont, Clare Vawdrey, the greatest (in the opinion of many) of our literary glories, and Blanche Adney, the greatest (in the opinion of all) of our theatrical. I mention these first because they were just the people whom in London, at that time, people tried to 'get'. People endeavoured to 'book' them six weeks ahead, yet on this occasion we had come in for them, we had all come in for each other, without the least wire-pulling. A turn of the game had pitched us together the last of August, and we recognised our luck by remaining so, under protection of the barometer. When the golden days were over – that would come soon enough – we should wind down opposite sides of the pass and disappear over the crest of surrounding heights. We were of the same general communion, chalk-marked for recognition by signs from the same alphabet. We met, in London, with irregular frequency; we were more or less governed by the laws and the language, the traditions and the shibboleths of the same dense social state. I think all of us, even the ladies, 'did' something, though we pretended we didn't when it was mentioned. Such things aren't mentioned indeed in London, but it was our innocent pleasure to be different here. There had to be some way to show the difference, inasmuch as we were under the impression that this was our annual holiday. We felt at any rate that the conditions were more human than in London, or at least that we ourselves were. We were frank about this, we talked about it: it was what we were talking about as we looked at the flushing glacier, just as some one called attention to the prolonged absence of Lord Mellifont and Mrs Adney. We were seated on the terrace of the inn, where there were benches and little tables, and those of us most bent on showing with what a rush we had returned to nature were, in the queer Germanic fashion, having coffee before meat.

The remark about the absence of our two companions was not taken up, not even by Lady Mellifont, not even by little Adney, the fond composer; for it had been dropped only in the briefest intermission of Clare Vawdrey's talk. (This celebrity was 'Clarence' only on the title-page.) It was just that revelation of our being after all human that was his theme. He asked the company whether, candidly, everyone hadn't been tempted to say to everyone else: 'I had no idea you were really so nice.' I had had, for my part, an idea that *he* was, and even a good deal nicer, but that was too complicated to go into then, besides it's exactly my story. There was a general understanding among us that when Vawdrey talked we should be silent, and not, oddly enough, because he at all expected it. He didn't, for of all copious talkers he was the most understanding, the least greedy and professional. It was rather the religion of the host, of the hostess, that prevailed among us; it was their own idea, but they always looked for a listening circle when the great novelist dined with them. On the occasion I allude to there was probably no one present with whom in London he hadn't dined, and we felt the force of this habit. He had dined even with me; and on the evening of that dinner, as on this Alpine afternoon, I had been at no pains to hold my tongue, absorbed as I inveterately was in a study of the question that always rose before me to such a height in his fair square strong stature.

This question was all the more tormenting that I'm sure he never suspected himself of imposing it, any more than he had

ever observed that every day of his life everyone listened to him
at dinner. He used to be called 'subjective and introspective' in
the weekly papers, but if that meant he was avid of tribute no
distinguished man could in society have been less so. He never
talked about himself; and this was an article on which, though
it would have been tremendously worthy of him, he apparently
never even reflected. He had his hours and his habits, his tailor
and his hatter, his hygiene and his particular wine, but all
these things together never made up an attitude. Yet they
constituted the only one he ever adopted, and it was easy for
him to refer to our being 'nicer' abroad than at home. *He* was
exempt from variations, and not a shade either less or more nice
in one place than in another. He differed from other people,
but never from himself – save in the extraordinary sense I shall
throw my light upon – and he struck me as having neither
moods nor sensibilities nor preferences. He might have been
always in the same company, so far as he recognised any
influence from age or condition or sex: he addressed himself to
women exactly as he addressed himself to men, and gossiped
with all men alike, talking no better to clever folk than to dull.
I used to wail to myself over his way of liking one subject –
so far as I could tell – precisely as much as another: there were
some I hated so myself. I never found him anything but loud
and liberal and cheerful, and I never heard him utter a paradox
or express a shade or play with an idea. That fancy about our
being 'human' was, in his conversation, quite an exceptional
flight. His opinions were sound and second-rate, and of his
perceptions it was too mystifying to think. I envied him his
magnificent health.

Vawdrey had marched with his even pace and his perfectly
good conscience into the flat country of anecdote, where stories
are visible from afar like windmills and sign-posts; but I observed
after a little that Lady Mellifont's attention wandered. I happened to be sitting next her. I noticed that her eyes rambled a
little anxiously over the lower slopes of the mountains. At last,
after looking at her watch, she said to me: 'Do you know where
they went?'

'Do you mean Mrs Adney and Lord Mellifont?'

'Lord Mellifont and Mrs Adney.' Her ladyship's speech seemed
– unconsciously indeed – to correct me, but it didn't occur to

me that this might be an effect of jealousy. I imputed to her no
such vulgar sentiment: in the first place because I liked her,
and in the second because it would always occur to one rather
quickly to put Lord Mellifont, whatever the connexion, first.
He *was* first – extraordinarily first. I don't say greatest or wisest
or most renowned, but essentially at the top of the list and the
head of the table. That's a position by itself, and his wife was
naturally accustomed to see him in it. My phrase had sounded
as if Mrs Adney had taken him; but it was not possible for him
to be taken – he only took. No one, in the nature of things,
could know this better than Lady Mellifont. I had originally
been rather afraid of her, thinking her, with her stiff silence and
the extreme blackness of almost everything that made up her
person, somewhat hard, even a little saturnine. Her paleness
seemed slightly grey and her glossy black hair metallic, even
as the brooches and bands and combs with which it was inveterately adorned. She was in perpetual mourning and wore
numberless ornaments of jet and onyx, a thousand clicking
chains and bugles and beads. I had heard Mrs Adney call her
the Queen of Night, and the term was descriptive if you took
the night for cloudy. She had a secret, and if you didn't find it
out as you knew her better you at least felt sure she was gentle
unaffected and limited, as well as rather submissively sad. She
was like a woman with a painless malady. I told her that I had
merely seen her husband and his companion stroll down the
glen together about an hour before, and suggested that Mr
Adney would perhaps know something of their intentions.

Vincent Adney, who, though fifty years old, looked like a
good little boy on whom it had been impressed that children
shouldn't talk in company, acquitted himself with remarkable
simplicity and taste of the position of husband of a great expo-
nent of comedy. When all was said about her making it easy
for him one couldn't help admiring the charmed affection with
which he took everything for granted. It's difficult for a husband
not on the stage, or at least in the theatre, to be graceful about
a wife so conspicuous there; but Adney did more than carry it
off, the awkwardness – he taught it ever so oddly to make *him*
interesting. He set his beloved to music; and you remember how
genuine his music could be – the only English compositions I
ever saw a foreigner care for. His wife was in them somewhere

always; they were a free rich translation of the impression she produced. She seemed, as one listened, to pass laughing, with loosened hair and the gait of a wood-nymph, across the scene. He had been only a little fiddler at her theatre, always in his place during the acts; but she had made him something rare and brave and misunderstood. Their superiority had become a kind of partnership, and their happiness was a part of the happiness of their friends. Adney's one discomfort was that he couldn't write a play for his wife, and the only way he meddled with her affairs was by asking impossible people if *they* couldn't.

Lady Mellifont, after looking across at him a moment, re-marked to me that she would rather not put any question to him. She added the next minute: 'I had rather people shouldn't see I'm nervous.'

'*Are* you nervous?'

'I always become so if my husband's away from me for any time.'

'Do you imagine something has happened to him?

'Yes, always. Of course I'm used to it.'

'Do you mean his tumbling over precipices – that sort of thing?'

'I don't know exactly *what* I fear: it's the general sense that he'll never come back.'

She said so much and withheld so much that the only way to treat her idiosyncrasy seemed the jocular. 'Surely he'll never forsake you!' I laughed.

She looked at the ground a moment. 'Oh at bottom I'm easy.'

'Nothing can ever happen to a man so accomplished, so infallible, so armed at all points,' I went on in the same spirit.

'Oh you don't know how he's armed!' she returned with such an odd quaver that I could account for it only by her being nervous. The idea was confirmed by her moving just afterwards, changing her seat rather pointlessly, not as if to cut our conver-sation short, but because she was worried. I could scarcely enter into her feeling, though I was presently relieved to see Mrs Adney come toward us. She had in her hand a big bunch of wild flowers, but was not closely attended by Lord Mellifont. I quickly saw, however, that she had no disaster to announce; yet as I knew there was a question Lady Mellifont would like to hear answered, without wishing to ask it, I expressed to her at once the hope that his lordship hadn't remained in a crevasse.

'Oh no; he left me but three minutes ago. He has gone into the house.' Blanche Adney rested her eyes on mine an instant – a mode of intercourse to which no man, for himself, could ever object. The interest on this occasion was quickened by the particular thing the eyes happened to say. What they usually said was only: 'Oh yes, I'm charming, I know, but don't make a fuss about it. I only want a new part – I do, I do, I do!' At present they added dimly, surreptitiously and of course sweetly – since that was the way they did everything: 'It's all right, but something did happen. Perhaps I'll tell you later.' She turned to Lady Mellifont, and the transition to simple gaiety suggested her mastery of her profession. 'I've brought him safe. We had a charming walk.'

'I'm so very glad,' said Lady Mellifont with her faint smile; continuing vaguely, as she got up: 'He must have gone to dress for dinner. Isn't it rather near?' She moved away to the hotel in her leavetaking simplifying fashion, and the rest of us, at the mention of dinner, looked at each other's watches as if to shift the responsibility for such grossness. The head-waiter, essentially, like all head-waiters, a man of the world, allowed us hours and places of our own, so that in the evening, apart under the lamp, we formed a compact, an indulged little circle. But it was only the Mellifonts who 'dressed' and as to whom it was recognised that they naturally *would* dress: she exactly in the same manner as on any other evening of her ceremonious existence – she wasn't a woman whose habits could take account of anything so mutable as fitness – and he, on the other hand, with remarkable adjustment and suitability. He was almost as much a man of the world as the head-waiter, and spoke almost as many languages; but he abstained from courting a comparison of dresscoats and white waistcoats, analysing the occasion in a much finer way – into black velvet and blue velvet and brown velvet, for instance, into delicate harmonies of necktie and subtle laxities of shirt. He had a costume for every function and a moral for every costume; and his functions and costumes and morals were ever a part of the amusement of life – a part at any rate of its beauty and romance – for an immense circle of spectators. For his particular friends indeed these things were more than an amusement; they were a topic, a social support and of course in addition a constant theme for speculative suspense. If his wife hadn't been present before dinner they were what the rest of us probably would have been putting our heads together about.

Clare Vawdrey had a fund of anecdote on the whole question: he had known Lord Mellifont almost from the beginning. It was a peculiarity of this nobleman that there could be no conversation about him that didn't instantly take the form of anecdote, and a still further distinction that there could apparently be no anecdote that wasn't on the whole to his honour. At whatever moment he came into a room people might say frankly: 'Of course we were telling stories about you!' As consciences go, in London, the general conscience would have been good. Moreover it would have been impossible to imagine his taking such a tribute otherwise than amiably, for he was always as unperturbed as an actor with the right cue. He had never in his life needed the prompter – his very embarrassments had been rehearsed. For myself, when he was talked about I had always had a sense of our speaking of the dead: it had the mark of that peculiar accumulation of relish. His reputation was a kind of gilded obelisk, as if he had been buried beneath it; the body of legend and reminiscence of which he was to be the subject had crystallised in advance.

This ambiguity sprang, I suppose, from the fact that the mere sound of his name and air of his person, the general expectation he created, had somehow a pitch so romantic and abnormal. The experience of his urbanity always came later; the prefigurement, the legend paled then before the reality. I remember that on the evening I refer to the reality struck me as supreme. The handsomest man of his period could never have looked better, and he sat among us like a bland conductor controlling by an harmonious play of arm an orchestra still a little rough. He directed the conversation by gestures as irresistible as they were vague; one felt as if without him it wouldn't have had anything to call a tone. This was essentially what he contributed to any occasion – what he contributed above all to English public life. He pervaded it, he coloured it, he embellished it, and without him it would have lacked, comparatively speaking, a vocabulary. Certainly it wouldn't have had a style, for a style was what it had in having Lord Mellifont.

He was a style. I was freshly struck with it as, in the *salle-à-manger* of the little Swiss inn, we resigned ourselves to inevitable veal. Confronted with *his* high form – I must parenthesise that it wasn't confronted much – Clare Vawdrey's talk suggested the reporter contrasted with the bard. It was interesting to watch the shock of characters from which of an evening so much would be expected. There was however no concussion – it was all muffled and minimised in Lord Mellifont's tact. It was rudimentary with him to find the solution of such a problem in playing the host, assuming responsibilities that carried with them their sacrifice. He had indeed never been a guest in his life; he was the host, the patron, the moderator at every board. If there was a defect in his manner – and I suggest this under my breath – it was that he had a little more art than any conjunction, even the most complicated, could possibly require. At any rate one made one's reflexions in noticing how the accomplished peer handled the case and how the sturdy man of letters hadn't a suspicion that the case – and least of all he himself as part of it – was handled. Lord Mellifont expended treasures of tact, and Clare Vawdrey never dreamed he was doing it.

Vawdrey had no suspicion of any such precaution even when Blanche Adney asked him if he really didn't see by this time his third act – an enquiry into which she introduced a subtlety of her own. She had settled it for him that he was to write her a play and that the heroine, should he but do his duty, would be the part for which she had immemorially longed. She was forty years old – this could be no secret to those who had admired her from the first – and might now reach out her hand and touch her uttermost goal. It gave a shade of tragic passion – perfect actress of comedy as she was – to her desire not to miss the great thing. The years had passed, and still she had missed it; none of the things she had done was the thing she had dreamed of, so that at present she had no more time to lose. This was the canker in the rose, the ache beneath the smile. It made her touching – made her melancholy more arch than her mirth. She had done the old English and the new French, and had charmed for a while her generation; but she was haunted by the vision of a bigger chance, of something truer to the conditions that lay near her. She was tired of

Sheridan and she hated Bowdler; she called for a canvas of a finer grain. The worst of it, to my sense, was that she would never extract her modern comedy from the great mature novelist, who was as incapable of producing it as he was of threading a needle. She coddled him, she talked to him, she made love to him, as she frankly proclaimed; but she dwelt in illusions – she would have to live and die with Bowdler.

It is difficult to be cursory over this charming woman, who was beautiful without beauty and complete with a dozen deficiencies. The perspective of the stage made her over, and in society she was like the model off the pedestal. She was the picture walking about, which to the artless social mind was a perpetual surprise – a miracle. People thought she told them the secrets of the pictorial nature, in return for which they gave her relaxation and tea. She told them nothing and she drank the tea; but they had all the same the best of the bargain. Vawdrey was really at work on a play; but if he had begun it because he liked her I think he let it drag for the same reason. He secretly felt the atrocious difficulty and hung off, for illusion's sake, from the point of tests and tribulations. In spite of which nothing could be so agreeable as to have such a question open with Blanche Adney, and from time to time he doubtless put something very good into the play. If he deceived Mrs Adney it was only because in her despair she was determined to be deceived. To her appeal about their third act he replied that before dinner he had written a splendid passage.

'Before dinner?' I said. 'Why, *cher grand maître*, before dinner you were holding us all spellbound on the terrace.'

My words were a joke, because I thought his had been; but for the first time that I could remember I noted in his face a shade of confusion. He looked at me hard, throwing back his head quickly, the least bit like a horse who has been pulled up short. 'Oh it was before that,' he returned naturally enough.

'Before that you were playing billiards with *me*,' Lord Mellifont threw off.

'Then it must have been yesterday,' said Vawdrey.

But he was in a tight place. 'You told me this morning you did nothing yesterday,' Blanche objected.

'I don't think I really know when I do things.' He looked vaguely, without helping himself, at a dish just offered him.

'It's enough if *we* know,' smiled Lord Mellifont.

'I don't believe you've written a line,' said Blanche Adney.

'I think I could repeat you the scene.' And Vawdrey took refuge in *haricots verts*.

'Oh do – oh do!' two or three of us cried.

'After dinner, in the salon, it will be a high *régal*,' Lord Mellifont declared.

'I'm not sure, but I'll try,' Vawdrey went on.

'Oh you lovely sweet man!' exclaimed the actress, who was practising what she believed to be Americanisms and was resigned even to an American comedy.

'But there must be this condition,' said Vawdrey: 'you must make your husband play.'

'Play while you're reading? Never!'

'I've too much vanity,' said Adney.

The direction of Lord Mellifont's fine eyes distinguished him. 'You must give us the overture before the curtain rises. That's a peculiarly delightful moment.'

'I shan't read – I shall just speak,' said Vawdrey.

'Better still, let me go and get your manuscript,' Blanche suggested.

Vawdrey replied that the manuscript didn't matter; but an hour later, in the salon, we wished he might have had it. We sat expectant, still under the spell of Adney's violin. His wife, in the foreground, on an ottoman, was all impatience and profile, and Lord Mellifont, in the chair – it was always *the* chair, Lord Mellifont's – made our grateful little group feel like a social science congress or a distribution of prizes. Suddenly, instead of beginning, our tame lion began to roar out of tune – he had clean forgotten every word. He was very sorry, but the lines absolutely wouldn't come to him; he was utterly ashamed, but his memory was a blank. He didn't look in the least ashamed – Vawdrey had never looked ashamed in his life; he was only imperturbably and merrily natural. He protested that he had never expected to make such a fool of himself, but we felt that this wouldn't prevent the incident's taking its place among his jolliest reminiscences. It was only *we* who were humiliated, as if he had played us a premeditated trick. This was an occasion, if ever, for Lord Mellifont's tact, which descended on us all like balm: he told us, in his charming

artistic way, his way of bridging over arid intervals (he had a
*débit* – there was nothing to approach it in England – like the
actors of the Comédie Française) of his own collapse on a
momentous occasion, the delivery of an address to a mighty
multitude, when, finding he had forgotten his memoranda, he
fumbled, on the terrible platform, the cynosure of every eye,
fumbled vainly in irreproachable pockets for indispensable notes.
But the point of his story was finer than that of our other
entertainer's easy fiasco; for he sketched with a few light
gestures the brilliancy of a performance which had risen superior
to embarrassment, had resolved itself, we were left to divine,
into an effort recognised at the moment as not absolutely a
blot on what the public was so good as to call his reputation.

'Play up – play up!' cried Blanche Adney, tapping her
husband and remembering how on the stage a *contretemps* is
always drowned in music. Adney threw himself upon his fiddle,
and I said to Clare Vawdrey that his mistake could easily be
corrected by his sending for the manuscript. If he'd tell me
where it was I'd immediately fetch it from his room. To this he
replied: 'My dear fellow, I'm afraid there *is* no manuscript.'

'Then you've not written anything?'

'I'll write it tomorrow.'

'Ah you trifle with us!' I said in much mystification.

He seemed at this to think better of it. 'If there *is* anything
you'll find it on my table.'

One of the others, at the moment, spoke to him, and Lady
Mellifont remarked audibly, as to correct gently our want of
consideration, that Mr Adney was playing something very
beautiful. I had noticed before how fond she appeared of music;
she always listened to it in a hushed transport. Vawdrey's attention was drawn away, but it didn't seem to me the words
he had just dropped constituted a definite permission to go to
his room. Moreover I wanted to speak to Blanche Adney; I had
something to ask her. I had to await my chance, however, as we
remained silent a while for her husband, after which the conversation became general. It was our habit to go early to bed,
but a little of the evening was still left. Before it quite waned
I found on opportunity to tell Blanche that Vawdrey had given
me leave to put my hand on his manuscript. She adjured me,
by all I held sacred, to bring it at once, to give it to her; and

her insistence was proof against my suggestion that it would now be too late for him to begin to read: besides which the charm was broken – the others wouldn't care. It wasn't, she assured me, too late for *her* to begin; therefore I was to possess myself without more delay of the precious pages. I told her she should be obeyed in a moment, but I wanted her first to satisfy my just curiosity. What had happened before dinner, while she was on the hills with Lord Mellifont?

'How do you know anything happened?'

'I saw it in your face when you came back.'

'And they call me an actress!' my friend cried.

'What do they call *me*?' I asked.

'You're a searcher of hearts – that frivolous thing an observer.'

'I wish you'd let an observer write you a play!' I broke out.

'People don't care for what you write: you'd break any run of luck.'

'Well, I see plays all round me,' I declared; 'the air is full of them tonight.'

'The air? Thank you for nothing! I only wish my table-drawers were.'

'Did he make love to you on the glacier?' I went on.

She stared – then broke into the graduated ecstasy of her laugh. 'Lord Mellifont, poor dear? What a funny place! It would indeed be the place for *our* love!'

'Did he fall into a crevasse?' I continued.

Blanche Adney looked at me again as she had done – so unmistakeably though briefly – when she came up before dinner with her hands full of flowers. 'I don't know into what he fell. I'll tell you tomorrow.'

'He did come down then?'

'Perhaps he went up,' she laughed. 'It's really strange.'

'All the more reason you should tell me tonight.'

'I must think it over; I must puzzle it out.'

'Oh if you want conundrums I'll throw in another,' I said. 'What's the matter with the Master?'

'The master of what?'

'Of every form of dissimulation. Vawdrey hasn't written a line.'

'Go and get his papers and we'll see.'

'I don't like to expose him,' I said.

'Why not, if I expose Lord Mellifont?'

'Oh I'd do anything for that,' I allowed. 'But why should Vawdrey have made a false statement? It's very curious.'

'It's very curious,' Blanche Adney repeated with a musing air and her eyes on Lord Mellifont. Then rousing herself she added: 'Go and look in his room.'

'In Lord Mellifont's?'

She turned to me quickly. '*That* would be a way!'

'A way to what?'

'To find out – to find out!' She spoke gaily and excitedly, but suddenly checked herself. 'We're talking awful nonsense.'

'We're mixing things up, but I'm struck with your idea. Get Lady Mellifont to let you.'

'Oh *she* has looked!' Blanche brought out with the oddest dramatic expression. Then after a movement of her beautiful uplifted hand, as if to brush away a fantastic vision, she added imperiously: 'Bring me the scene – bring me the scene!'

'I go for it,' I answered; 'but don't tell me I can't write a play.'

She left me, but my errand was arrested by the approach of a lady who had produced a birthday-book – we had been threatened with it for several evenings – and who did me the honour to solicit my autograph. She had been asking the others and couldn't decently leave me out. I could usually remember my name, but it always took me long to recall my date, and even when I had done so I was never very sure. I hesitated between two days, remarking to my petitioner that I would sign on both if it would give her any satisfaction. She opined that I had surely been born but once, and I replied of course that on the day I made her acquaintance I had been born again. I mention the feeble joke only to show that, with the obligatory inspection of the other autographs, we gave some minutes to this transaction. The lady departed with her book, and I then found the company had scattered. I was alone in the little salon that had been appropriated to our use. My first impression was one of disappointment: if Vawdrey had gone to bed I didn't wish to disturb him. While I hesitated however I judged that my friend must still be afoot. A window was open and the sound of voices outside came in to me: Blanche was on the terrace with her dramatist and they were talking about the stars. I went to the window for a glimpse – the Alpine night was splendid. My friends had stepped out together; Mrs Adney had picked up a cloak; she looked as I had seen her look in the wing of the theatre. They were silent a while, and I heard the roar of a neighbouring torrent. I turned back into the room, and its quiet lamplight gave me an idea. Our companions had dispersed – it was late for a pastoral country – and we three should have the place to ourselves. Clare Vawdrey had written his scene, which couldn't but be splendid; and his reading it to us there at such an hour would be a thing always to remember. I'd bring down his manuscript and meet the two with it as they came in.

I quitted the salon for this purpose; I had been in his room and knew it was on the second floor, the last in a long corridor. A minute later my hand was on the knob of the door, which I naturally pushed open without knocking. It was equally natural that in the absence of its occupant the room should be dark; the more so as, the end of the corridor being at that hour unlighted, the obscurity was not immediately diminished by the opening of the door. I was only aware at first that I had made no mistake and that, the window-curtains not being drawn, I had before me a couple of vague star-lighted apertures. Their aid, however, was not sufficient to enable me to find what I had come for, and my hand, in my pocket, was already on the little box of matches that I always carried for cigarettes. Suddenly I withdrew it with a start, uttering an ejaculation, an apology. I had entered the wrong room; a glance prolonged for three seconds showed me a figure seated at a table near one of the windows – a figure I had at first taken for a travelling-rug thrown over a chair. I retreated with a sense of intrusion; but as I did so I took in more rapidly than it takes me to express it, first that this was Vawdrey's room and second that, surprisingly, its occupant himself sat before me. Checking myself on the threshold I was briefly bewildered, but before I knew it I had called out: 'Hullo, is that you, Vawdrey?'

He neither turned nor answered me, but my question received an immediate and practical reply in the opening of a door on the other side of the passage. A servant with a candle had come out of the opposite room, and in this flitting illumination I definitely recognised the man whom an instant before I had to the best of my belief left below in conversation with Mrs Adney. His back was half-turned to me and he bent over the table in the attitude of writing, but I took in at every pore his identity. 'I beg your pardon – I thought you were downstairs,' I said; and as the person before me gave no sign of hearing I added: 'If you're busy I won't disturb you.' I backed out, closing the door – I had been in the place, I suppose, less than a minute. I had a sense of mystification which however deepened infinitely the next instant. I stood there with my hand still on the knob of the door, overtaken by the oddest impression of my life. Vawdrey was seated at his table, and it was a very natural place for him; but why was he writing in the dark and why hadn't he answered me? I waited a few seconds for the sound of some movement, to see if he wouldn't rouse himself from his abstraction – a fit conceivable in a great writer – and call out 'Oh my dear fellow, is it you?' But I heard only the still-ness, I felt only the star-lighted dusk of the room, with the unexpected presence it enclosed. I turned away, slowly retracing my steps, and came confusedly downstairs. The lamp still burned in the salon, but the room was empty. I passed round to the door of the hotel and stepped out. Empty too was the terrace. Blanche Adney and the gentleman with her had apparently come in. I hung about five minutes – then I went to bed.

# II

I SLEPT badly, for I was agitated. On looking back at these queer occurrences (you'll see presently *how* queer!) I perhaps suppose myself more affected than in fact; for great anomalies are never so great at first as after we've reflected on them. It takes us time to use up explanations. I was vaguely nervous – I had been sharply startled; but there was nothing I couldn't clear up by asking Blanche Adney, the first thing in the morning, who had been with her on the terrace. Oddly enough, however, when the morning dawned – it dawned admirably – I felt less desire to satisfy myself on this point than to escape, to brush away the shadow of my stupefaction. I saw the day would be splendid, so that the fancy took me to spend it, as I had spent happy days of youth, in a lonely mountain ramble. I dressed early, partook of conventional coffee, put a big roll into one pocket and a small flask into the other, and, with a stout stick in my hand, went forth into the high places. My story isn't closely concerned with the charming hours I passed there – hours of the kind that make intense memories. If I roamed away half of them on the shoulders of the hills, I lay on the sloping grass for the other half and, with my cap pulled over my eyes – save a peep for immensities of view – listened, in the bright stillness, to the mountain bee and felt most things sink and dwindle. Clare Vawdrey grew small, Blanche Adney grew dim, Lord Mellifont grew old, and before the day was over I forgot I had ever been puzzled. When in the late afternoon I made my way down to the inn there was nothing I wanted so much to learn as that dinner was at hand. Tonight I dressed, in a manner, and by the time I was presentable they were all at table.

In their company again my little problem came back to me, so that I was curious to see if Vawdrey wouldn't look at me with a certain queerness. But he didn't look at me at all; which gave me a chance both to be patient and to wonder why I should hesitate to ask him my question across the table. I did hesitate, and with the consciousness of doing so came back a little of the agitation I had left behind me, or below me, during the day. I wasn't ashamed of my scruple, however: it was only a fine discretion. What I vaguely felt was that a public enquiry wouldn't have been fair. Lord Mellifont was there, of course, to mitigate with his perfect manner all consequences; but I think it was present to me that with these particular elements his lordship wouldn't be at home. The moment we got up therefore I approached Mrs Adney, asking her whether, as the evening was lovely, she wouldn't take a turn with me outside.

'You've walked a hundred miles; hadn't you better be quiet?' she replied.

'I'd walk a hundred miles more to get you to tell me something.'

She looked at me an instant with a little of the odd consciousness I had sought, but hadn't found, in Clare Vawdrey's eyes. 'Do you mean what became of Lord Mellifont?'

'Of Lord Mellifont?' With my new speculation I had lost that thread.

'Where's your memory, foolish man? We talked of it last evening.'

'Ah yes!' I cried, recalling; 'we shall have lots to discuss.' I drew her out to the terrace and, before we had gone three steps, said to her: 'Who was with you here last night?'

'Last night?' – she was as wide of the mark as I had been.

'At ten o'clock – just after our company broke up. You came out here with a gentleman. You talked about the stars.'

She stared a moment, then gave her laugh. 'Are you jealous of dear Vawdrey?'

'Then it was he?'

'Certainly it was he.'

'And how long did he stay?'

She laughed again. 'You have it badly! He stayed about a quarter of an hour – perhaps rather more. We walked some distance. He talked about his play. There you have it all. That is the only witchcraft I have used.'

Well, it wasn't enough for me; so 'What did Vawdrey do afterwards?' I continued.

'I haven't the least idea. I left him and went to bed.'

'At what time did you go to bed?'

'At what time did *you*? I happen to remember that I parted from Mr Vawdrey at ten twenty-five,' said Mrs Adney. 'I came back into the salon to pick up a book, and I noticed the clock.'

'In other words you and Vawdrey distinctly lingered here from about five minutes past ten till the hour you mention?'

'I don't know how distinct we were, but we were very jolly. Où voulez-vous en venir?' Blanche Adney asked.

'Simply to this, dear lady: that at the time your companion was occupied in the manner you describe he was also engaged in literary composition in his own room.'

She stopped short for it, and her eyes had a sheen in the darkness. She wanted to know if I challenged her veracity; and I replied that on the contrary I backed it up – it made the case so interesting. She returned that this would only be if she should back up mine; which however I had no difficulty in persuading her to do after I had related to her circumstantially the incident of my quest of the manuscript – the manuscript which at the time, for a reason I could now understand, appeared to have passed so completely out of her own head.

'His talk made me forget it – I forgot I sent you for it. He made up for his fiasco in the salon: he declaimed me the scene,' said Blanche. She had dropped on a bench to listen to me and, as we sat there, had briefly cross-examined me. Then she broke out into fresh laughter. 'Oh the eccentricities of genius!'

'Yes indeed! They seem greater even than I supposed.'

'Oh the mysteries of greatness!'

'You ought to know all about them, but they take me by surprise,' I declared.

'Are you absolutely certain it was Vawdrey?' my companion asked.

'If it wasn't he who in the world was it? That a strange gentleman, looking exactly like him and of like literary pursuits, should be sitting in his room at that hour of the night and writing at his table *in the dark*,' I insisted, 'would be practically as wonderful as my own contention.'

'Yes, why in the dark?' my friend mused.

'Cats can see in the dark,' I said.

She smiled at me dimly. 'Did it look like a cat?'

'No, dear lady, but I'll tell you what it did look like – it looked like the author of Vawdrey's admirable works. It looked infinitely more like him than our friend does himself,' I pronounced.

'Do you mean it was somebody he gets to do them?'

'Yes, while he dines out and disappoints you.'

'Disappoints me?' she murmured artlessly.

'Disappoints *me* – disappoints everyone who looks in him for the genius that created the pages they adore. Where is it in his talk?'

'Ah last night he was splendid,' said the actress.

'He's always splendid, as your morning bath is splendid, or a sirloin of beef, or the railway-service to Brighton. But he's never rare.'

'I see what you mean.'

I could have hugged her – and perhaps I did. 'That's what makes you such a comfort to talk to. I've often wondered – now I know. There are two of them.'

'What a delightful idea!'

'One goes out, the other stays at home. One's the genius, the other's the bourgeois, and it's only the bourgeois whom we personally know. He talks, he circulates, he's awfully popular, he flirts with you—'

'Whereas it's the genius *you* are privileged to flirt with!' Mrs Adney broke in. 'I'm much obliged to you for the distinction.'

I laid my hand on her arm. 'See him yourself. Try it, test it, go to his room.'

'Go to his room? It wouldn't be proper!' she cried in the manner of her best comedy.

'Anything's proper in such an enquiry. If you see him it settles it.'

'How charming – to settle it!' She thought a moment, then sprang up. 'Do you mean *now*?'

'Whenever you like.'

'But suppose I should find the wrong one?' she said with an exquisite effect.

'The wrong one? Which one do you call the right?'

'The wrong one for a lady to go and see. Suppose I shouldn't find – the genius?'

'Oh I'll look after the other,' I returned. Then as I had happened to glance about me I added: 'Take care – here comes Lord Mellifont.'

'I wish you'd look after *him*,' she said with a drop of her voice.

'What's the matter with him?'

'That's just what I was going to tell you.'

'Tell me now. He's not coming.'

Blanche looked a moment. Lord Mellifont, who appeared to have emerged from the hotel to smoke a meditative cigar, had paused at a distance from us and stood admiring the wonders of the prospect, discernible even in the dusk. We strolled slowly in another direction, and she presently resumed: 'My idea's almost as droll as yours.'

'I don't call mine droll: it's beautiful.'

'There's nothing so beautiful as the droll,' Mrs Adney returned.

'You take a professional view. But I'm all ears.' My curiosity was indeed alive again.

'Well then, my dear friend, if Clare Vawdrey's double – and I'm bound to say I think that the more of him the better – his lordship there has the opposite complaint: he isn't even whole.'

We stopped once more, simultaneously. 'I don't understand.'

'No more do I. But I've a fancy that if there are two of Mr Vawdrey, there isn't so much as one, all told, of Lord Mellifont.'

I considered a moment, then I laughed out. 'I think I see what you mean!'

'That's what makes *you* a comfort.' She didn't, alas, hug me, but she promptly went on. 'Did you ever see him alone?'

I tried to remember. 'Oh yes – he has been to see me.'

'Ah then he wasn't alone.'

'And I've been to see *him* – in his study.'

'Did he know you were there?'

'Naturally – I was announced.'

She glared at me like a lovely conspirator. 'You mustn't *be* announced!' With this she walked on.

I rejoined her, breathless. 'Do you mean one must come upon him when he doesn't know it?'

'You must take him unawares. You must go to his room – that's what you must do.'

If I was elated by the way our mystery opened out I was also, pardonably, a little confused. 'When I know he's not there?'

'When you know he *is*.'

'And what shall I see?'

'You won't see anything!' she cried as we turned round.

We had reached the end of the terrace and our movement brought us face to face with Lord Mellifont, who, addressing himself again to his walk, had now, without indiscretion, overtaken us. The sight of him at that moment was illuminating, and it kindled a great backward train, connecting itself with one's general impression of the personage. As he stood there smiling at us and waving a practised hand into the transparent night – he introduced the view as if it had been a candidate and 'supported' the very Alps – as he rose before us in the delicate fragrance of his cigar and all his other delicacies and fragrances, with more perfections somehow heaped on his handsome head than one had ever seen accumulated before or elsewhere, he struck me as so essentially, so conspicuously and uniformly the public character that I read in a flash the answer to Blanche's riddle. He was all public and had no corresponding private life, just as Clare Vawdrey was all private and had no corresponding public. I had heard only half my companion's tale, yet as we joined Lord Mellifont – he had followed us, liking Mrs Adney, but it was always to be conceived of him that he accepted society rather than sought it – as we participated for half an hour in the distributed wealth of his discourse I felt with unabashed duplicity that we had, as it were, found him out. I was even more deeply diverted by that whisk of the curtain to which the actress had just treated me than I had been by my own discovery; and if I wasn't ashamed of my share of her secret any more than of having divided my own with her – though my own was, of the two mysteries, the more glorious for the personage involved – this was because there was no cruelty in my advantage, but on the contrary an extreme tenderness and a positive compassion. Oh he was safe with me, and I felt moreover rich and enlightened, as if I had suddenly got the universe into my pouch. I had learned what an affair of the spot and the moment a great appearance may be. It would doubtless be too much to say that I had always suspected the possibility, in the background of his lordship's being, of some such beautiful instance; but it's at least a fact that, patronising as such words may sound, I had been conscious of a certain reserve of indulgence for him. I had secretly pitied him for the perfection of his performance, had wondered what blank face such a mask had to cover, what was left to him for the immitigable hours in which a man sits down with himself, or, more serious still, with that intenser self his lawful wife. How was he at home and what did he do when he was alone? There was something in Lady Mellifont that gave a point to these researches – something that suggested how even to her he must have been still the public character and she beset with similar questionings. She had never cleared them up: that was her eternal trouble. We therefore knew more than she did, Blanche Adney and I; but we wouldn't tell her for the world, nor would she probably thank us for doing so. She preferred the relative grandeur of uncertainty. She wasn't at home with him, so she couldn't say; and with her he wasn't alone, so he couldn't show her. He represented to his wife and was a hero to his servants, and what one wanted to arrive at was what really became of him when no eye could see – and *a fortiori* no soul admire. He relaxed and rested presumably; but how utter a blank mustn't it take to repair such a plenitude of presence! – how intense an *entr'acte* to make possible more such performances! Lady Mellifont was too proud to pry, and as she had never looked through a keyhole she remained dignified and unrelieved.

It may have been a fancy of mine that Mrs Adney drew out our companion, or it may be that the practical irony of our relation to him at such a moment made me see him more vividly: at any rate he never had struck me as so dissimilar from what he would have been if we hadn't offered him a reflexion of his image. We were only a concourse of two, but he had never been more public. His perfect manner had never been more perfect, his remarkable tact never more remarkable, his one conceivable *raison d'être*, the absolute singleness of his identity, never more attested. I had a tacit sense that it would all be in the morning papers, with a leader, and also a secretly exhilarating one that I knew something that wouldn't be, that never could be, though any enterprising journal would give me a fortune for it. I must add, however, that in spite of my enjoyment – it was almost sensual, like that of a consummate dish or an unprecedented pleasure – I was eager to be alone

again with Mrs Adney, who owed me an anecdote. This proved
impossible that evening, for some of the others came out to
see what he found so absorbing; and then Lord Mellifont bespoke
a little music from the fiddler, who produced his violin and
played to us divinely, on our platform of echoes, face to face
with the ghosts of the mountains. Before the concert was over
I missed our actress and, glancing into the window of the salon,
saw her established there with Vawdrey, who was reading out
from a manuscript. The great scene had apparently been
achieved and was doubtless the more interesting to Blanche
from the new lights she had gathered about its author. I
judged discreet not to disturb them, and went to bed without
seeing her again. I looked out for her betimes the next morning
and, as the promise of the day was fair, proposed to her that
we should take to the hills, reminding her of the high obligation
she had incurred. She recognised the obligation and gratified
me with her company, but before we had strolled ten yards up
the pass she broke out with intensity: 'My dear friend, you've
no idea how it works in me! I can think of nothing else.'

'Than your theory about Lord Mellifont?'

'Oh bother Lord Mellifont! I allude to yours about Mr
Vawdrey, who's much the more interesting person of the two.
I'm fascinated by that vision of his – what-do-you-call-it?'

'His alternate identity?'

'His other self: that's easier to say.'

'You accept it then, you adopt it?'

'Adopt it? I rejoice in it! It became tremendously vivid to
me last evening.'

'While he read to you there?'

'Yes, as I listened to him, watched him. It simplified everything, explained everything.'

I rose to my triumph. 'That's indeed the blessing of it. Is the
scene very fine?'

'Magnificent, and he reads beautifully.'

'Almost as well as the other one writes!' I laughed.

This made her stop a moment, laying her hand on my arm.
'You utter my very impression! I felt he was reading me the
work of another.'

'In a manner that was such a service to the other,' I concurred.

'Such a totally different person,' said Blanche. We talked

of this difference as we went on, and of what a wealth it constituted, what a resource for life, such a duplication of character.

'It ought to make him live twice as long as other people,' I made out.

'Ought to make which of them?'

'Well, both; for after all they're members of a firm, and one of them would never be able to carry on the business without the other. Moreover mere survival would be dreadful for either.'

She was silent a little; after which she exclaimed: 'I don't know – I wish he *would* survive!'

'May I on my side enquire which?'

'If you can't guess I won't tell you.'

'I know the heart of woman. You always prefer the other.'

She halted again, looking round her. 'Off here, away from my husband, I *can* tell you. I'm in love with him!'

'Unhappy woman, he has no passions,' I answered.

'That's exactly why I adore him. Doesn't a woman with my history know the passions of others for insupportable? An actress, poor thing, can't care for any love that's not all on *her* side; she can't afford to be repaid. My marriage proves that: a pretty one, a lucky one like ours, is ruinous. Do you know what was in my mind last night and all the while Mr Vawdrey read me those beautiful speeches? An insane desire to see the author.' And dramatically, as if to hide her shame, Blanche Adney passed on.

'We'll manage that,' I returned. 'I want another glimpse of him myself. But meanwhile please remember that I've been waiting more than forty-eight hours for the evidence that supports your sketch, intensely suggestive and plausible, of Lord Mellifont's private life.'

'Oh Lord Mellifont doesn't interest me.'

'He did yesterday,' I said.

'Yes, but that was before I fell in love. You blotted him out with *your* story.'

'You'll make me sorry I told it. Come,' I pleaded, 'if you don't let me know how your idea came into your head I shall imagine you simply made it up.'

'Let me recollect then, while we wander in this velvet gorge.'

We stood at the entrance of a charming crooked valley, a portion of the level floor of which formed the bed of a stream that was smooth with swiftness. We turned into it, and the soft walk beside the clear torrent drew us on and on; till suddenly, as we continued and I waited for my companion to remember, a bend of the ravine showed us Lady Mellifont coming toward us. She was alone, under the canopy of her parasol, drawing her sable train over the turf; and in this form, on the devious ways, she was a sufficiently rare apparition. She mostly took out a footman, who marched behind her on the highroads and whose livery was strange to the rude rustics. She blushed on seeing us, as if she ought somehow to justify her being there; she laughed vaguely and described herself as abroad but for a small early stroll. We stood together thus, exchanging plati- tudes, and then she told us how she had counted a little on finding her husband.

'Is he in this quarter?' I asked.

'I supposed he would be. He came out an hour ago to sketch.'

'Have you been looking for him?' Mrs Adney put to her.

'A little; not very much,' said Lady Mellifont.

Each of the women rested her eyes with some intensity, as it seemed to me, on the eyes of the other. 'We'll look for him for you, if you like,' said Blanche.

'Oh it doesn't matter. I thought I'd join him.'

'He won't make his sketch if you don't,' my companion hinted.

'Perhaps he will if *you* do,' said Lady Mellifont.

'Oh I dare say he'll turn up,' I interposed.

'He certainly will if he knows we're here!' Blanche retorted.

'Will you wait while we search?' I asked of Lady Mellifont.

She repeated that it was of no consequence; upon which Mrs Adney went on: 'We'll go into the matter for our own pleasure.'

'I wish you a pleasant excursion,' said her ladyship, and was turning away when I sought to know if we should inform her husband she was near. 'That I've followed him?' She demurred a moment and then jerked out oddly: 'I think you had better not.' With this she took leave of us, floating a little stiffly down the gorge.

My companion and I watched her retreat; after which we exchanged a stare and a light ghost of a laugh rippled from the actress's lips. 'She might be walking in the shrubberies at Mellifont!'

I had my view. 'She suspects it, you know.'

'And she doesn't want him to guess it. There won't be any sketch.'

'Unless we overtake him,' I suggested. 'In that case we shall find him producing one, in the very most graceful and established attitude, and the queer thing is that it will be brilliant.'

'Let us leave him alone – he'll have to come home without it,' my friend contributed.

'He'd rather never come home. Oh he'll find a public!'

'Perhaps he'll do it for the cows,' Blanche risked; and as I was on the point of rebuking her profanity she went on: 'That's simply what I happened to discover.'

'What are you speaking of?'

'The incident of day before yesterday.'

I jumped at it. 'Ah let's have it at last!'

'That's all it was – that I was like Lady Mellifont: I couldn't find him.'

'Did you lose him?'

'He lost *me* – that appears to be the way of it. He supposed me gone. And then—!' But she paused, looking – that is smiling – volumes.

'You did find him, however,' I said as I wondered, 'since you came home with him.'

'It was he who found *me*. That again is what must happen. He's there from the moment he knows somebody else is.'

'I understand his intermissions,' I returned on short reflexion, 'but I don't quite seize the law that governs them.'

Ah Blanche had quite mastered it! 'It's a fine shade, but I caught it at that moment. I had started to come home, I was tired and had insisted on his not coming back with me. We had found some rare flowers – those I brought home – and it was he who had discovered almost all of them. It amused him very much, and I knew he wanted to get more; but I was weary and I quitted him. He let me go – where else would have been his tact? – and I was too stupid then to have guessed that from the moment I wasn't there no flower would be – *could* be – gathered. I started homeward, but at the end of three minutes I found I had brought away his penknife – he had lent it to me trim a branch – and I knew he'd need it. I turned back a few steps to call him, but before I spoke I looked about for him. You can't understand what happened then without having the scene before you.'

'You must take me there,' I said.

'We may see the wonder here. The place was simply one that offered no chance for concealment – a great gradual hillside without obstructions or cavities or bushes or trees. There were some rocks below me, behind which I myself had disappeared, but from which on coming back I immediately emerged again.'

'Then he must have seen you.'

'He was too absent, too utterly gone, as gone as a candle blown out; for some reason best known to himself. It was probably some moment of fatigue – he's getting on, you know, so that with the sense of returning solitude the reaction had been proportionately great, the extinction proportionately complete. At any rate the stage was as bare as your hand.'

'Couldn't he have been somewhere else?'

'He couldn't have been, in the time, anywhere but just where I had left him. Yet the place was utterly empty – as empty as this stretch of valley in front of us. He had vanished – he had ceased to be. But as soon as my voice rang out – I uttered his name – he rose before me like the rising sun.'

'And where did the sun rise?'

'Just where it ought to – just where he would have been and where I should have seen him had he been like other people.'

I had listened with the deepest interest, but it was my duty to think of objections. 'How long a time elapsed between the moment you were sure of his absence and the moment you called?'

'Oh but a few seconds. I don't pretend it was long.'

'Long enough for you to be really certain?' I said.

'Certain he wasn't there?'

'Yes, and that you weren't mistaken, weren't the victim of some hocus-pocus of your eyesight.'

'I may have been mistaken – but I feel too strongly I wasn't. At any rate that's just why I want you to look in his room.'

I thought a moment. 'How *can* I – when even his wife doesn't dare to?'

'She *wants* to; propose it to her. It wouldn't take much to make her. She does suspect.'

I thought another moment. 'Did he seem to know?'

'That I had missed him and might have immensely wondered? So it struck me – but with it too that he probably thought he had been quick enough. He has, you see, to think that – to take it mostly for granted.'

Ah – I lost myself – who could say? 'But did you speak at least of his disappearance?'

'Heaven forbid – *y pensez-vous*? It seemed to me too strange.'

'Quite right. And how did he look?'

Trying to think it out again and reconstitute her miracle, Blanche Adney gazed abstractedly up the valley. Suddenly she brought out: 'Just as he looks now!' and I saw Lord Mellifont stand before us with his sketch-block. I took in as we met him that he appeared neither suspicious nor blank: he simply stood there, as he stood always everywhere, for the principal feature of the scene. Naturally he had no sketch to show us, but nothing could better have rounded off our actual conception of him than the way he fell into position as we approached. He had been selecting his point of view – he took possession of it with a flourish of the pencil. He leaned against a rock; his beautiful little box of water-colours reposed on a natural table beside him, a ledge of the bank which showed how inveterately nature ministered to his convenience. He painted while he talked and he talked while he painted; and if the painting was as miscellaneous as the talk, the talk would equally have graced an album. We stayed while the exhibition went on, and the conscious profiles of the peaks might to our apprehension have been interested in his success. They grew as black as silhouettes in paper, sharp against a livid sky from which, how-ever, there would be nothing to fear till Lord Mellifont's sketch should be finished. All nature deferred to him and the very elements waited. Blanche Adney communed with me dumbly, and I could read the language of her eyes: 'Oh if *we* could only do it as well as that! He fills the stage in a way that beats us.' We could no more have left him than we could have quitted the theatre till the play was over; but in due time we turned round with him and strolled back to the inn, before the door of which his lordship, glancing again at his picture, tore the fresh leaf from the block and presented it with a few happy words to our friend. Then he went into the house; and a moment later, looking up from where we stood, we saw him, above, at the window of his sitting-room – he had the best apartments – watching the signs of the weather.

'He'll have to rest after this,' Blanche said, dropping her eyes on her water-colour.

'Indeed he will!' I raised mine to the window: Lord Mellifont had vanished. 'He's already reabsorbed.'

'Reabsorbed?' I could see the actress was now thinking of something else.

'Into the immensity of things. He has lapsed again. The entr'acte has begun.'

'It ought to be long.' She surveyed the terrace and as at that moment the head-waiter appeared in the doorway she suddenly turned to address him. 'Have you seen Mr Vawdrey lately?'

The man immediately approached. 'He left the house five minutes ago – for a walk, I think. He went down the pass; he had a book.'

I was watching the ominous clouds. 'He had better have had an umbrella.'

The waiter smiled. 'I recommended him to take one.'

'Thank you,' Blanche said; and the Oberkellner withdrew. Then she went on abruptly: 'Will you do me a favour?'

'Yes, if you'll do me one. Let me see if your picture's signed.'

She glanced at the sketch before giving it to me. 'For a wonder it isn't.'

'It ought to be, for full value. May I keep it a while?'

'Yes, if you'll do what I ask. Take an umbrella and go after Mr Vawdrey.'

'To bring him to Mrs Adney?'

'To keep him out – as long as you can.'

'I'll keep him as long as the rain holds off.'

'Oh never mind the rain!' my companion cried.

'Would you have us drenched?'

'Without remorse.' Then with a strange light in her eyes: 'I'm going to try.'

'To try?'

'To see the real one. Oh if I can get at him!' she broke out with passion.

'Try, try!' I returned. 'I'll keep our friend all day.'

'If I can get at the one who does it' – and she paused with shining eyes – 'if I can have it out with him I shall get another act, I shall have my part!'

'I'll keep Vawdrey for ever!' I called after her as she passed quickly into the house.

Her audacity was communicable and I stood there in a glow of excitement. I looked at Lord Mellifont's water-colour and I looked at the gathering storm; I turned my eyes again to his lordship's windows and then I bent them on my watch. Vawdrey had so little the start of me that I should have time to overtake him, time even if I should take five minutes to go up to Lord Mellifont's sitting-room – where we had all been hospitably received – and say to him, as a messenger, that Mrs Adney begged he would bestow on his sketch the high consecration of his signature. As I again considered this work of art I noted there was something it certainly did lack: what else then but so noble an autograph? It was my duty without loss of time to make the deficiency good, and in accordance with this view I instantly re-entered the hotel. I went up to Lord Mellifont's apartments; I reached the door of his salon. Here, however, I was met by a difficulty with which my extravagance hadn't counted. If I were to knock I should spoil everything; yet was I prepared to dispense with this ceremony? I put myself the question and it embarrassed me; I turned my little picture round and round, but it gave me no answer I wanted. I wanted it to say 'Open the door gently, gently, without a sound, yet very quickly: then you'll see what you'll see.' I had gone so far as to lay my hand on the knob when I became aware (having my wits so about me) that exactly in the manner I was thinking of – gently, gently, without a sound – another door had moved, and on the opposite side of the hall. At the same instant I found myself smiling rather constrainedly at Lady Mellifont, who seeing me, had checked herself by the threshold of her room. For a moment, as she stood there, we exchanged two or three ideas that were the more singular for being so unspoken. We had caught each other hovering and to that extent understood each other; but as I stepped over to her –

so that we were separated from the sitting-room by the width of the hall – her lips formed the almost soundless entreaty: 'Don't!' I could see in her conscious eyes everything the word expressed – the confession of her own curiosity and the dread of the consequences of mine. '*Don't!*' she repeated as I stood before her. From the moment my experiment could strike her as an act of violence I was ready to renounce it; yet I thought I caught from her frightened face a still deeper betrayal – a possibility of disappointment if I should give way. It was as if she had said: 'I'll let you do it if you'll take the responsibility. Yes, with someone else I'd surprise him. But it would never do for him to think it was I.'

'We soon found Lord Mellifont,' I observed in allusion to our encounter with her an hour before, 'and he was so good as to give this lovely sketch to Mrs Adney, who has asked me to come up and beg him to put in the omitted signature.'

Lady Mellifont took the drawing from me, and I could guess the struggle that went on in her while she looked at it. She waited to speak; then I felt all her delicacies and dignities, all her old timidities and pieties obstruct her great chance. She turned away from me and, with the drawing, went back to her room. She was absent for a couple of minutes, and when she reappeared I could see she had vanquished her temptation, that even with a kind of resurgent horror she had shrunk from it. She had deposited the sketch in the room. 'If you'll kindly leave the picture with me I'll see that Mrs Adney's request is attended to,' she said with great courtesy and sweetness, but in a manner that put an end to our colloquy.

I assented, with a somewhat artificial enthusiasm perhaps, and then, to ease off our separation, remarked that we should have a change of weather.

'In that case we shall go – we shall go immediately,' the poor lady returned. I was amused at the eagerness with which she made this declaration: it appeared to represent a coveted flight into safety, an escape with her threatened secret. I was the more surprised therefore when, as I was turning away, she put out her hand to take mine. She had the pretext of bidding me farewell, but as I shook hands with her on this supposition I felt that what the movement really conveyed was: 'I thank you for the help you'd have given me, but it's better as it is.

If I should know, who would help me then?' As I went to my room to get my umbrella I said to myself: 'She's sure, but she won't put it to the proof.'

A quarter of an hour later I had overtaken Clare Vawdrey in the pass, and shortly after this we found ourselves looking for refuge. The storm hadn't only completely gathered, but had broken at the last with extraordinary force. We scrambled up a hillside to an empty cabin, a rough structure that was hardly more than a shed for the protection of cattle. It was a tolerable shelter however, and it had fissures through which we could see the show, watch the grand rage of nature. Our entertainment lasted an hour – an hour that has remained with me as full of odd disparities. While the lightning played with the thunder and the rain gushed in on our umbrellas, I said to myself that Clare Vawdrey was disappointing. I don't know exactly what I should have predicated of a great author exposed to the fury of the elements, I can't say what particular Manfred attitude I should have expected my companion to assume, but it struck me somehow that I shouldn't have looked to him to regale me in such a situation with stories – which I had already heard – about the celebrated Lady Ringrose. Her ladyship formed the subject of Vawdrey's conversation during this prodigious scene, though before it was quite over he had launched out on Mr Chafer, the scarcely less notorious reviewer. It broke my heart to hear a man like Vawdrey talk of reviewers. The lightning projected a hard clearness upon the truth, familiar to me for years, to which the last day or two had added transcendent support – the irritating certitude that for personal relations this admirable genius thought his second-best good enough. It *was*, no doubt, as society was made, but there was a contempt in the distinction which couldn't fail to be galling to an admirer. The world was vulgar and stupid, and the real man would have been a fool to come out for it when he could gossip and dine by deputy. None the less my heart sank as I felt him practise this economy. I don't know exactly what I wanted; I suppose I wanted him to make an exception for *me* – for me all alone, and all handsomely and tenderly, in the vast horde of the dull. I almost believed he would have done so had he known how I worshipped his talent. But I had never been able to translate this to him, and his application of his principle was relentless.

At any rate I was more than ever sure that at such an hour his chair at home at least wasn't empty: *there* was the Manfred attitude, *there* were the responsive flashes. I could only envy Mrs Adney her presumable enjoyment of them.

The weather drew off at last and the rain abated sufficiently to allow us to emerge from our asylum and make our way back to the inn, where we found on our arrival that our prolonged absence had produced some agitation. It was judged apparently that the storm had placed us in a predicament. Several of our friends were at the door, who seemed just disconcerted to note we were only drenched. Clare Vawdrey, for some reason, had had the greater soaking, and he took a straight course to his room. Blanche Adney was among the persons collected to look out for us, but as the subject of our speculation came toward her she shrank from him without a greeting; with a movement that I measured as almost one of coldness she turned her back on him and went quickly into the salon. Wet as I was I went in after her; on which she immediately flung round and faced me. The first thing I saw was that she had never been so beautiful. There was a light of inspiration in her, and she broke out to me in the quickest whisper, which was at the same time the loudest cry I have ever heard: 'I've got my *part!*'

'You went to his room – I was right?'

'Right?' Blanche Adney repeated. 'Ah my dear fellow!' she murmured.

'He was there – you saw him?'

'He saw *me*. It was the hour of my life!'

'It must have been the hour of his, if you were half as lovely as you are at this moment.'

'He's splendid,' she pursued as if she didn't hear me. 'He *is* the one who does it!' I listened, immensely impressed, and she added: 'We understood each other.'

'By flashes of lightning?'

'Oh I didn't see the lightning then!'

'How long were you there?' I asked with admiration.

'Long enough to tell him I adore him.'

'Ah that's what I've never been able to tell him!' I quite wailed.

'I shall have my part – I shall have my part!' she continued with triumphant indifference; and she flung round the room with the joy of a girl, only checking herself to say: 'Go and change your clothes.'

'You shall have Lord Mellifont's signature,' I said.

'Oh hang Lord Mellifont's signature! He's far nicer than Mr Vawdrey,' she went on irrelevantly.

'Lord Mellifont?' I pretended to enquire.

'Confound Lord Mellifont!' And Blanche Adney, in her elation, brushed by me, whisking again through the open door. Just outside of it she came upon her husband; whereupon with a charming cry of 'We're talking of *you*, my love!' she threw herself upon him and kissed him.

I went to my room and changed my clothes, but I remained there till the evening. The violence of the storm had passed over us, but the rain had settled down to a drizzle. On descending to dinner I saw the change in the weather had already broken up our party. The Mellifonts had departed in a carriage and four, they had been followed by others, and several vehicles had been bespoken for the morning. Blanche Adney's was one of them, and on the pretext that she had preparations to make she quitted us directly after dinner. Clare Vawdrey asked me what was the matter with her – she suddenly appeared to dislike him. I forget what answer I gave, but I did my best to comfort him by driving away with him the next day. Blanche had vanished when we came down; but they made up their quarrel in London, for he finished his play, which she produced. I must add that she is still nevertheless in want of the great part. I've a beautiful one in my head, but she doesn't come to see me to stir me up about it. Lady Mellifont always drops me a kind word when we meet, but that doesn't console me.

# THE MIDDLE YEARS

# THE MIDDLE YEARS

## I

THE April day was soft and bright, and poor Dencombe, happy in the conceit of reasserted strength, stood in the garden of the hotel, comparing, with a deliberation in which however there was still something of languor, the attractions of easy strolls. He liked the feeling of the south so far as you could have it in the north, he liked the sandy cliffs and the clustered pines, he liked even the colourless sea. 'Bournemouth as a health-resort' had sounded like a mere advertisement, but he was thankful now for the commonest conveniences. The sociable country post-man, passing through the garden, had just given him a small parcel which he took out with him, leaving the hotel to the right and creeping to a bench he had already haunted, a safe recess in the cliff. It looked to the south, to the tinted walls of the Island, and was protected behind by the sloping shoulder of the down. He was tired enough when he reached it, and for a moment was disappointed; he was better of course, but better, after all, than what? He should never again, as at one or two great moments of the past, be better than himself. The infinite of life was gone, and what remained of the dose a small glass scored like a thermometer by the apothecary. He sat and stared at the sea, which appeared all surface and twinkle, far shallower than the spirit of man. It was the abyss of human illusion that was the real, the tideless deep. He held his packet, which had come by book-post, unopened on his knee, liking, in the lapse of so many joys – his illness had made him feel his age – to know it was there, but taking for granted there could be no complete renewal of the pleasure, dear to young experience, of seeing one's self 'just out'. Dencombe, who had a reputation, had come out too often and knew too well in advance how he should look.

His postponement associated itself vaguely, after a little, with a group of three persons, two ladies and a young man, whom, beneath him, straggling and seemingly silent, he could see move slowly together along the sands. The gentleman had his head bent over a book and was occasionally brought to a stop by the charm of this volume, which, as Dencombe could perceive even at a distance, had a cover alluringly red. Then his companions, going a little further, waited for him to come up, poking their parasols into the beach, looking around them at the sea and sky and clearly sensible of the beauty of the day. To these things the young man with the book was still more clearly indifferent; lingering, credulous, absorbed, he was an object of envy to an observer from whose connexion with literature all such artlessness had faded. One of the ladies was large and mature; the other had the spareness of comparative youth and of a social situation possibly inferior. The large lady carried back Dencombe's imagination to the age of crinoline; she wore a hat of the shape of a mushroom, decorated with a blue veil, and had the air, in her aggressive amplitude, of clinging to a vanished fashion or even a lost cause. Presently her companion produced from under the folds of a mantle a limp portable chair which she stiffened out and of which the large lady took possession. This act, and something in the movement of either party, at once characterised the performers – they performed for Dencombe's recreation – as opulent matron and humble dependent. Where moreover was the virtue of an approved novelist if one couldn't establish a relation between such figures? the clever theory for instance that the young man was the son of the opulent matron and that the humble dependent, the daughter of a clergyman or an officer, nourished a secret passion for him. Was that not visible from the way she stole behind her protectress to look back at him? – back to where he had let himself come to a full stop when his mother sat down to rest. His book was a novel, it had the catchpenny binding; so that while the romance of life stood neglected at his side he lost himself in that of the circulating library. He moved mechanically to where the sand was softer and ended by plumping down in it to finish his chapter at his ease. The humble dependent, discouraged by his remoteness, wandered with a martyred droop of the head in another direction, and the exorbitant lady, watching the waves, offered a confused resemblance to a flying-machine that had broken down.

When his drama began to fail Dencombe remembered that he had after all another pastime. Though such promptitude on the part of the publisher was rare he was already able to draw from its wrapper his 'latest', perhaps his last. The cover of 'The Middle Years' was duly meretricious, the smell of the fresh pages the very odour of sanctity; but for the moment he went no further – he had become conscious of a strange alienation. He had forgotten what his book was about. Had the assault of his old ailment, which he had so fallaciously come to Bourne-mouth to ward off, interposed utter blankness as to what had preceded it? He had finished the revision of proof before quitting London, but his subsequent fortnight in bed had passed the sponge over colour. He couldn't have chanted to himself a single sentence, couldn't have turned with curiosity or confidence to any particular page. His subject had already gone from him, leaving scarce a superstition behind. He uttered a low moan as he breathed the chill of this dark void, so desperately it seemed to represent the completion of a sinister process. The tears filled his mild eyes; something precious had passed away. This was the pang that had been sharpest during the last few years – the sense of ebbing time, of shrinking opportunity; and now he felt not so much that his last chance was going as that it was gone indeed. He had done all he should ever do, and yet hadn't done what he wanted. This was the laceration – that practically his career was over: it was as violent as a grip at his throat. He rose from his seat nervously – a creature hunted by a dread; then he fell back in his weakness and nervously opened his book. It was a single volume; he preferred single volumes and aimed at a rare compression. He began to read and, little by little, in this occupation, was pacified and reassured. Everything came back to him, but came back with a wonder, came back above all with a high and magnificent beauty. He read his own prose, he turned his own leaves, and had as he sat there with the spring sunshine on the page an emotion peculiar and intense. His career was over, no doubt, but it was over, when all was said, with *that*.

He had forgotten during his illness the work of the previous year; but what he had chiefly forgotten was that it was extra-ordinarily good. He dived once more into his story and was drawn down, as by a siren's hand, to where, in the dim underworld of fiction, the great glazed tank of art, strange silent subjects float. He recognised his motive and surrendered to his talent. Never probably had that talent, such as it was, been so fine. His difficulties were still there, but what was also there, to his perception, though probably, alas! to nobody's else, was the art that in most cases had surmounted them. In his surprised enjoyment of this ability he had a glimpse of a possible reprieve. Surely its force wasn't spent – there was life and service in it yet. It hadn't come to him easily, it had been backward and roundabout. It was the child of time, the nursling of delay; he had struggled and suffered for it, making sacrifices not to be counted, and now that it was really mature was it to cease to yield, to confess itself brutally beaten? There was an infinite charm for Dencombe in feeling as he had never felt before that diligence *vincit omnia*. The result produced in his little book was somehow a result beyond his conscious intention: it was as if he had planted his genius, had trusted his method, and they had grown up and flowered with this sweetness. If the achieve-ment had been real, however, the process had been painful enough. What he saw so intensely today, what he felt as a nail driven in, was that only now, at the very last, had he come into possession. His development had been abnormally slow, almost grotesquely gradual. He had been hindered and retarded by experience, he had for long periods only groped his way. It had taken too much of his life to produce too little of his art. The art had come, but it had come after everything else. At such a rate a first existence was too short – long enough only to collect material; so that to fructify, to use the material, one should have a second age, an extension. This extension was what poor Dencombe sighed for. As he turned the last leaves of his volume he murmured 'Ah for another go, ah for a better chance!'

The three persons drawing his attention to the sands had vanished and then reappeared; they had now wandered up a path, an artificial and easy ascent, which led to the top of the cliff. Dencombe's bench was halfway down, on a sheltered ledge, and the large lady, a massive heterogeneous person with bold black eyes and kind red cheeks, now took a few moments to rest. She wore dirty gauntlets and immense diamond ear-rings; at first she looked vulgar, but she contradicted this announce-

ment in an agreeable off-hand tone. While her companions stood
waiting for her she spread her skirts on the end of Dencombe's
seat. The young man had gold spectacles, through which, with
his finger still in his red-covered book, he glanced at the volume,
bound in the same shade of the same colour, lying on the lap
of the original occupant of the bench. After an instant Dencombe felt him struck with a resemblance; he had recognised
the gilt stamp on the crimson cloth, was reading 'The Middle
Years' and now noted that somebody else had kept pace with
him. The stranger was startled, possibly even a little ruffled,
to find himself not the only person favoured with an early
copy. The eyes of the two proprietors met a moment, and
Dencombe borrowed amusement from the expression of those of
his competitor, those, it might even be inferred, of his admirer.
They confessed to some resentment – they seemed to say: 'Hang
it, has he got it *already*? Of course he's a brute of a reviewer!'
Dencombe shuffled his copy out of sight while the opulent
matron, rising from her repose, broke out: 'I feel already the
good of this air!'

'I can't say I do,' said the angular lady. 'I find myself quite
let down.'

'I find myself horribly hungry. At what time did you order
luncheon?' her protectress pursued.

The young person put the question by. 'Doctor Hugh always
orders it.'

'I ordered nothing to-day – I'm going to make you diet,' said
their comrade.

'Then I shall go home and sleep. *Qui dort dine!*'

'Can I trust you to Miss Vernham?' asked Doctor Hugh of
his elder companion.

'Don't I trust *you*?' she archly enquired.

'Not too much!' Miss Vernham, with her eyes on the ground,
permitted herself to declare. 'You must come with us at least
to the house,' she went on while the personage on whom they
appeared to be in attendance began to mount higher. She had
got a little out of ear-shot; nevertheless Miss Vernham became,
so far as Dencombe was concerned, less distinctly audible to
murmur to the young man: 'I don't think you realise all you
owe the Countess!'

Absently, a moment, Doctor Hugh caused his gold-rimmed

spectacles to shine at her. 'Is that the way I strike you? I see – I see!'

'She's awfully good to us,' continued Miss Vernham, compelled by the lapse of the other's motion to stand there in spite of his discussion of private matters. Of what use would it have been that Dencombe should be sensitive to shades hadn't he detected in that arrest a strange influence from the quiet old convalescent in the great tweed cape? Miss Vernham appeared suddenly to become aware of some such connexion, for she added in a moment: 'If you want to sun yourself here you can come back after you've seen us home.'

Doctor Hugh, at this, hesitated, and Dencombe, in spite of a desire to pass for unconscious, risked a covert glance at him. What his eyes met this time, as happened, was, on the part of the young lady, a queer stare, naturally vitreous, which made her remind him of some figure – he couldn't name it – in a play or a novel, some sinister governess or tragic old maid. She seemed to scan him, to challenge him, to say out of general spite: 'What have you got to do with us?' At the same instant the rich humour of the Countess reached them from above: 'Come, come, my little lambs; you should follow your old *bergère!*' Miss Vernham turned away for it, pursuing the ascent, and Doctor Hugh, after another mute appeal to Dencombe and a minute's evident demur, deposited his book on the bench as if to keep his place, or even as a gage of earnest return, and bounded without difficulty up the rougher part of the cliff.

Equally innocent and infinite are the pleasures of observation and the resources engendered by the trick of analysing life. It amused poor Dencombe, as he dawdled in his tepid air-bath, to believe himself awaiting a revelation of something at the back of a fine young mind. He looked hard at the book on the end of the bench, but wouldn't have touched it for the world. It served his purpose to have a theory that shouldn't be exposed to refutation. He already felt better of his melancholy; he had, according to his old formula, put his head at the window. A passing Countess could draw off the fancy when, like the elder of the ladies who had just retreated, she was as obvious as the giantess of a caravan. It was indeed general views that were terrible; short ones, contrary to an opinion sometimes expressed, were the refuge, were the remedy. Doctor Hugh couldn't possibly be anything but a reviewer who had understandings for early copies with publishers or with newspapers. He reappeared in a quarter of an hour with visible relief at finding Dencombe on the spot and the gleam of white teeth in an embarrassed but generous smile. He was perceptibly disappointed at the eclipse of the other copy of the book; it made a pretext the less for speaking to the quiet gentleman. But he spoke notwithstanding; he held up his own copy and broke out pleadingly: 'Do say, if you have occasion to speak of it, that it's the best thing he has done yet!'

Dencombe responded with a laugh: 'Done yet' was so amusing to him, made such a grand avenue of the future. Better still, the young man took *him* for a reviewer. He pulled out 'The Middle Years' from under his cape, but instinctively concealed any telltale look of fatherhood. This was partly because a person was always a fool for insisting to others on his work. 'Is that what you're going to say yourself?' he put to his visitor.

'I'm not quite sure I shall write anything. I don't, as a regular thing – I enjoy in peace. But it's awfully fine.'

Dencombe just debated. If the young man had begun to abuse him he would have confessed on the spot to his identity, but there was no harm in drawing out any impulse to praise. He drew it out with such success that in a few moments his new acquaintance, seated by his side, was confessing candidly that the works of the author of the volume before them were the only ones he could read a second time. He had come the day before from London, where a friend of his, a journalist, had lent him his copy of the last, the copy sent to the office of the journal and already the subject of a 'notice' which, as was pretended there – but one had to allow for 'swagger' – it had taken a full quarter of an hour to prepare. He intimated that he was ashamed for his friend, and in the case of a work demanding and repaying study, of such inferior manners; and, with his fresh appreciation and his so irregular wish to express it, he speedily became for poor Dencombe a remarkable, a delightful apparition. Chance had brought the weary man of letters face to face with the greatest admirer in the new generation of whom it was supposable he might boast. The admirer in truth was mystifying, so rare a case was it to find a bristling young

doctor – he looked like a German physiologist – enamoured of
literary form. It was an accident, but happier than most accidents, so that Dencombe, exhilarated as well as confounded,
spent half an hour in making his visitor talk while he kept
himself quiet. He explained his premature possession of 'The
Middle Years' by an allusion to the friendship of the publisher,
who, knowing he was at Bournemouth for his health, had
paid him this graceful attention. He allowed he had been ill,
for Doctor Hugh would infallibly have guessed it; he even went
so far as to wonder if he mightn't look for some hygienic 'tip'
from a personage combining so bright an enthusiasm with a
presumable knowledge of the remedies now in vogue. It would
shake his faith a little perhaps to have to take a doctor seriously
who could take *him* so seriously, but he enjoyed this gushing
modern youth and felt with an acute pang that there would still
be work to do in a world in which such odd combinations were
presented. It wasn't true, what he had tried for renunciation's
sake to believe, that all the combinations were exhausted. They
weren't by any means – they were infinite: the exhaustion was
in the miserable artist.

Doctor Hugh, an ardent physiologist, was saturated with the
spirit of the age – in other words he had just taken his degree;
but he was independent and various, he talked like a man who
would have preferred to love literature best. He would fain
have made fine phrases, but nature had denied him the trick.
Some of the finest in 'The Middle Years' had struck him in-
ordinately, and he took the liberty of reading them to Dencombe in support of his plea. He grew vivid, in the balmy air,
to his companion, for whose deep refreshment he seemed to
have been sent; and was particularly ingenuous in describing
how recently he had become acquainted, and how instantly
infatuated, with the only man who had put flesh between the
ribs of an art that was starving on superstitions. He hadn't yet
written to him – he was deterred by a strain of respect. Dencombe at this moment rejoiced more inwardly than ever that
he had never answered the photographers. His visitor's attitude
promised him a luxury of intercourse, though he was sure a
due freedom for Doctor Hugh would depend not a little on the
Countess. He learned without delay what type of Countess was
involved, mastering as well the nature of the tie that united

the curious trio. The large lady, an Englishwoman by birth and the daughter of a celebrated baritone, whose taste *minus* his talent she had inherited, was the widow of a French nobleman and mistress of all that remained of the handsome fortune, the fruit of her father's earnings, that had constituted her dower. Miss Vernham, an odd creature but an accomplished pianist, was attached to her person at a salary. The Countess was generous, independent, eccentric; she travelled with her minstrel and her medical man. Ignorant and passionate she had nevertheless moments in which she was almost irresistible. Dencombe saw her sit for her portrait in Doctor Hugh's free sketch, and felt the picture of his young friend's relation to her frame itself in his mind. This young friend, for a representative of the new psychology, was himself easily hypnotised, and if he became abnormally communicative it was only a sign of his real subjection. Dencombe did accordingly what he wanted with him, even without being known as Dencombe.

Taken ill on a journey in Switzerland the Countess had picked him up at an hotel, and the accident of his happening to please her had made her offer him, with her imperious liberality, terms that couldn't fail to dazzle a practitioner without patients and whose resources had been drained dry by his studies. It wasn't the way he would have proposed to spend his time, but it was time that would pass quickly, and meanwhile she was wonderfully kind. She exacted perpetual attention, but it was impossible not to like her. He gave details about his queer patient, a 'type' if there ever was one, who had in connexion with her flushed obesity, and in addition to the morbid strain of a violent and aimless will, a grave organic disorder; but he came back to his loved novelist, whom he was so good as to pronounce more essentially a poet than many of those who went in for verse, with a zeal excited, as all his indiscretion had been excited, by the happy chance of Dencombe's sympathy and the coincidence of their occupation. Dencombe had confessed to a slight personal acquaintance with the author of 'The Middle Years,' but had not felt himself as ready as he could have wished when his companion, who had never yet encountered a being so privileged, began to be eager for particulars. He even divined in Doctor Hugh's eye at that moment a glimmer of suspicion. But the young man was too

inflamed to be shrewd and repeatedly caught up the book to
exclaim: 'Did you notice this?' or 'Weren't you immensely
struck with that?' 'There's a beautiful passage toward the end,'
he broke out; and again he laid his hand on the volume. As
he turned the pages he came upon something else, while Dencombe saw him suddenly change colour. He had taken up as it
lay on the bench Dencombe's copy instead of his own, and his
neighbour at once guessed the reason of his start. Doctor Hugh
looked grave an instant; then he said: 'I see you've been
altering the text!' Dencombe was a passionate corrector, a
fingerer of style; the last thing he ever arrived at was a form
final for himself. His ideal would have been to publish secretly,
and then, on the published text, treat himself to the terrified
revise, sacrificing always a first edition and beginning for
posterity and even for the collectors, poor dears, with a second.
This morning, in 'The Middle Years', his pencil had pricked a
dozen lights. He was amused at the effect of the young man's
reproach; for an instant it made him change colour. He stammered at any rate ambiguously, then through a blur of ebbing
consciousness saw Doctor Hugh's mystified eyes. He only had
time to feel he was about to be ill again – that emotion, excitement, fatigue, the heat of the sun, the solicitation of the air,
had combined to play him a trick, before, stretching out a hand
to his visitor with a plaintive cry, he lost his senses altogether.

Later he knew he had fainted and that Doctor Hugh had got
him home in a Bath-chair, the conductor of which, prowling
within hail for custom, had happened to remember seeing him
in the garden of the hotel. He had recovered his perception on
the way, and had, in bed that afternoon, a vague recollection
of Doctor Hugh's young face, as they went together, bent over
him in a comforting laugh and expressive of something more
than a suspicion of his identity. That identity was ineffaceable
now, and all the more that he was rueful and sore. He had been
rash, been stupid, had gone out too soon, stayed out too long.
He oughtn't to have exposed himself to strangers, he ought to
have taken his servant. He felt as if he had fallen into a hole
too deep to descry any little patch of heaven. He was confused
about the time that had passed – he pieced the fragments
together. He had seen his doctor, the real one, the one who
had treated him from the first and who had again been very

kind. His servant was in and out on tiptoe, looking very wise after the fact. He said more than once something about the sharp young gentleman. The rest was vagueness in so far as it wasn't despair. The vagueness, however, justified itself by dreams, dozing anxieties from which he finally emerged to the consciousness of a dark room and a shaded candle.

'You'll be all right again – I know all about you now,' said a voice near him that he felt to be young. Then his meeting with Doctor Hugh came back. He was too discouraged to joke about it yet, but made out after a little that the interest was intense for his visitor. 'Of course I can't attend you professionally – you've got your own man, with whom I've talked and who's excellent,' Doctor Hugh went on. 'But you must let me come to see you as a good friend. I've just looked in before going to bed. You're doing beautifully, but it's a good job I was with you on the cliff. I shall come in early to-morrow. I want to do something for you. I want to do everything. You've done a tremendous lot for me.' The young man held his hand, hanging over him, and poor Dencombe, weakly aware of this living pressure, simply lay there and accepted his devotion. He couldn't do anything less – he needed help too much.

The idea of the help he needed was very present to him that night, which he spent in a lucid stillness, an intensity of thought that constituted a reaction from his hours of stupor. He was lost, he was lost – he was lost if he couldn't be saved. He wasn't afraid of suffering, of death, wasn't even in love with life; but he had had a deep demonstration of desire. It came over him in the long quiet hours that only with 'The Middle Years' had he taken his flight; only on that day, visited by soundless processions, had he recognised his kingdom. He had had a revelation of his range. What he dreaded was the idea that his reputation should stand on the unfinished. It wasn't with his past but with his future that it should properly be concerned. Illness and age rose before him like spectres with pitiless eyes: how was he to bribe such fates to give him the second chance? He had had the one chance that all men have – he had had the chance of life. He went to sleep again very late, and when he awoke Doctor Hugh was sitting at hand. There was already by this time something beautifully familiar in him.

'Don't think I've turned out your physician,' he said; 'I'm

acting with his consent. He has been here and seen you. Somehow he seems to trust me. I told him how we happened to come together yesterday, and he recognises that I've a peculiar right.'

Dencombe felt his own face pressing. 'How have you squared the Countess?'

The young man blushed a little, but turned it off. 'Oh never mind the Countess!'

'You told me she was very exacting.'

Doctor Hugh had a wait. 'So she is.'

'And Miss Vernham's an *intrigante*.'

'How do you know that?'

'I know everything. One *has* to, to write decently!'

'I think she's mad,' said limpid Doctor Hugh.

'Well, don't quarrel with the Countess – she's a present help to you.'

'I don't quarrel,' Doctor Hugh returned. 'But I don't get on with silly women.' Presently he added: 'You seem very much alone.'

'That often happens at my age. I've outlived, I've lost by the way.'

Doctor Hugh faltered; then surmounting a soft scruple: 'Whom have you lost?'

'Everyone.'

'Ah no,' the young man breathed, laying a hand on his arm.

'I once had a wife – I once had a son. My wife died when my child was born, and my boy, at school, was carried off by typhoid.'

'I wish I'd been there!' cried Doctor Hugh.

'Well – if you're here!' Dencombe answered with a smile that, in spite of dimness, showed how he valued being sure of his companion's whereabouts.

'You talk strangely of your age. You're not old.'

'Hypocrite – so early!'

'I speak physiologically.'

'That's the way I've been speaking for the last five years, and it's exactly what I've been saying to myself. It isn't till we *are* old that we begin to tell ourselves we're not.'

'Yet I know I myself am young,' Doctor Hugh returned.

'Not so well as I!' laughed his patient, whose visitor indeed would have established the truth in question by the honesty with which he changed the point of view, remarking that it must be one of the charms of age – at any rate in the case of high distinction – to feel that one has laboured and achieved. Doctor Hugh employed the common phrase about earning one's rest, and it made poor Dencombe for an instant almost angry. He recovered himself, however, to explain, lucidly enough, that if, ungraciously, he knew nothing of such a balm, it was doubtless because he had wasted inestimable years. He had followed literature from the first, but he had taken a lifetime to get abreast of her. Only to-day at last had he begun to *see*, so that all he had hitherto shown was a movement without a direction. He had ripened too late and was so clumsily consti-tuted that he had had to teach himself by mistakes.

'I prefer your flowers then to other people's fruit, and your mistakes to other people's successes,' said gallant Doctor Hugh. 'It's for your mistakes I admire you.'

'You're happy – you don't know,' Dencombe answered.

Looking at his watch the young man had got up; he named the hour of the afternoon at which he would return. Dencombe warned him against committing himself too deeply, and ex-pressed again all his dread of making him neglect the Countess – perhaps incur her displeasure.

'I want to be like you – I want to learn by mistakes!' Doctor Hugh laughed.

'Take care you don't make too grave a one! But do come back,' Dencombe added with the glimmer of a new idea.

'You should have had more vanity!' His friend spoke as if he knew the exact amount required to make a man of letters normal.

'No, no – I only should have had more time. I want another go.'

'Another go?'

'I want an extension.'

'An extension?' Again Doctor Hugh repeated Dencombe's words, with which he seemed to have been struck.

'Don't you know? – I want to what they call "live".'

The young man, for good-bye, had taken his hand, which closed with a certain force. They looked at each other hard. 'You *will* live,' said Doctor Hugh.

'Don't be superficial. It's too serious!'

'You *shall* live!' Dencombe's visitor declared, turning pale.

'Ah that's better!' And as he retired the invalid, with a troubled laugh, sank gratefully back.

All that day and all the following night he wondered if it mightn't be arranged. His doctor came again, his servant was attentive, but it was to his confident young friend that he felt himself mentally appeal. His collapse on the cliff was plausibly explained and his liberation, on a better basis, promised for the morrow; meanwhile, however, the intensity of his meditations kept him tranquil and made him indifferent. The idea that occupied him was none the less absorbing because it was a morbid fancy. Here was a clever son of the age, ingenious and ardent, who happened to have set him up for connoisseurs to worship. This servant of his altar had all the new learning in science and all the old reverence in faith; wouldn't he therefore put his knowledge at the disposal of his sympathy, his craft at the disposal of his love? Couldn't he be trusted to invent a remedy for a poor artist to whose art he had paid a tribute? If he couldn't the alternative was hard: Dencombe would have to surrender to silence unvindicated and undivined. The rest of the day and all the next he toyed in secret with this sweet futility. Who would work the miracle for him but the young man who could combine such lucidity with such passion? He thought of the fairy-tales of science and charmed himself into forgetting that he looked for a magic that was not of this world. Doctor Hugh was an apparition, and that placed him above the law. He came and went while his patient, who now sat up, followed him with supplicating eyes. The interest of knowing the great author had made the young man begin 'The Middle Years' afresh and would help him to find a richer sense between its covers. Dencombe had told him what he 'tried for'; with all his intelligence, on a first perusal, Doctor Hugh had failed to guess it. The baffled celebrity wondered then who in the world *would* guess it: he was amused once more at the diffused massive weight that could be thrown into the missing of an intention. Yet he wouldn't rail at the general mind to-day – consoling as that ever had been: the revelation of his own slowness had seemed to make all stupidity sacred.

Doctor Hugh, after a little, was visibly worried, confessing, on enquiry, to a source of embarrassment at home. 'Stick to the Countess – don't mind me,' Dencombe said repeatedly; for his companion was frank enough about the large lady's attitude. She was so jealous that she had fallen ill – she resented such a breach of allegiance. She paid so much for his fidelity that she must have it all: she refused him the right to other sympathies, charged him with scheming to make her die alone, for it was needless to point out how little Miss Vernham was a resource in trouble. When Doctor Hugh mentioned that the Countess would already have left Bournemouth if he hadn't kept her in bed, poor Dencombe held his arm tighter and said with decision: 'Take her straight away.' They had gone out together, walking back to the sheltered nook in which, the other day, they had met. The young man, who had given his companion a personal support, declared with emphasis that his conscience was clear – he could ride two horses at once. Didn't he dream for his future of a time when he should have to ride five hundred? Longing equally for virtue, Dencombe replied that in that golden age no patient would pretend to have contracted with him for his whole attention. On the part of the Countess wasn't such an avidity lawful? Doctor Hugh denied it, said there was no contract, but only a free under-standing, and that a sordid servitude was impossible to a generous spirit; he liked moreover to talk about art, and that was the subject on which, this time, as they sat together on the sunny bench, he tried most to engage the author of 'The Middle Years'. Dencombe, soaring again a little on the weak wings of convalescence and still haunted by that happy notion of an organised rescue, found another strain of eloquence to plead the cause of a certain splendid 'last manner', the very citadel, as it would prove, of his reputation, the stronghold into which his real treasure would be gathered. While his listener gave up the morning and the great still sea ostensibly waited he had a wondrous explanatory hour. Even for himself he was inspired as he told what his treasure would consist of; the precious metals he would dig from the mine, the jewels rare, strings of pearls, he would hang between the columns of his temple. He was wondrous for himself, so thick his convictions crowded, but still more wondrous for Doctor Hugh, who assured him none the less that the very pages he had just published were already encrusted with gems. This admirer, however, panted for the combinations to come and, before the face of the beautiful day, renewed to Dencombe his guarantee that his profession would hold itself responsible for such a life. Then he suddenly clapped his hand upon his watch-pocket and asked leave to absent himself for half an hour. Dencombe waited there for his return, but was at last recalled to the actual by the fall of a shadow across the ground. The shadow darkened into that of Miss Vernham, the young lady in attendance on the Countess; whom Dencombe, recognising her, perceived so clearly to have come to speak to him that he rose from his bench to acknowledge the civility. Miss Vernham indeed proved not particularly civil; she looked strangely agitated, and her type was now unmistakeable.

'Excuse me if I do ask,' she said, 'whether it's too much to hope that you may be induced to leave Doctor Hugh alone.' Then before our poor friend, greatly disconcerted, could protest: 'You ought to be informed that you stand in his light – that you may do him a terrible injury.'

'Do you mean by causing the Countess to dispense with his services?'

'By causing her to disinherit him.' Dencombe stared at this, and Miss Vernham pursued, in the gratification of seeing she could produce an impression: 'It has depended on himself to come into something very handsome. He has had a grand prospect, but I think you've succeeded in spoiling it.'

'Not intentionally, I assure you. Is there no hope the accident may be repaired?' Dencombe asked.

'She was ready to do anything for him. She takes great fancies, she lets herself go – it's her way. She has no relations, she's free to dispose of her money, and she's very ill,' said Miss Vernham for a climax.

'I'm very sorry to hear it,' Dencombe stammered.

'Wouldn't it be possible for you to leave Bournemouth? That's what I've come to see about.'

He sank to his bench. 'I'm very ill myself, but I'll try!'

Miss Vernham still stood there with her colourless eyes and the brutality of her good conscience. 'Before it's too late, please!' she said; and with this she turned her back, in order, quickly, as if it had been a business to which she could spare but a precious moment, to pass out of his sight.

Oh yes, after this Dencombe was certainly very ill. Miss Vernham had upset him with her rough fierce news; it was the sharpest shock to him to discover what was at stake for a penniless young man of fine parts. He sat trembling on his bench, staring at the waste of waters, feeling sick with the directness of the blow. He was indeed too weak, too unsteady, too alarmed; but he would make the effort to get away, for he couldn't accept the guilt of interference and his honour was really involved. He would hobble home, at any rate, and then think what was to be done. He made his way back to the hotel and, as he went, had a characteristic vision of Miss Vernham's great motive. The Countess hated women of course – Dencombe was lucid about that; so the hungry pianist had no personal hopes and could only console herself with the bold conception of helping Doctor Hugh in order to marry him after he should get his money or else induce him to recognise her claim for compensation and buy her off. If she had befriended him at a fruitful crisis he would really, as a man of delicacy – and she knew what to think of that point – have to reckon with her.

At the hotel Dencombe's servant insisted on his going back to bed. The invalid had talked about catching a train and had begun with orders to pack; after which his racked nerves had yielded to a sense of sickness. He consented to see his physician, who immediately was sent for, but he wished it to be understood that his door was irrevocably closed to Doctor Hugh. He had his plan, which was so fine that he rejoiced in it after getting back to bed. Doctor Hugh, suddenly finding himself snubbed without mercy, would, in natural disgust and to the joy of Miss Vernham, renew his allegiance to the Countess. When his physician arrived Dencombe learned that he was feverish and that this was very wrong: he was to cultivate calmness and try, if possible, not to think. For the rest of the day he wooed stupidity; but there was an ache that kept him sentient, the probable sacrifice of his 'extension,' the limit of his course. His medical adviser was anything but pleased; his successive relapses were ominous. He charged this personage to put out a strong hand and take Doctor Hugh off his mind – it would contribute so much to his being quiet. The agitating name, in his room, was not mentioned again, but his security was a smothered fear, and it was not confirmed by the receipt, at ten o'clock that evening, of a telegram which his servant opened and read him and to which, with an address in London, the signature of Miss Vernham was attached. 'Beseech you to use all influence to make our friend join us here in the morning. Countess much the worse for dreadful journey, but everything may still be saved.' The two ladies had gathered themselves up and had been capable in the afternoon of a spiteful revolution. They had started for the capital, and if the elder one, as Miss Vernham had announced, was very ill, she had wished to make it clear that she was proportionately reckless. Poor Dencombe, who was not reckless and who only desired that everything should indeed be 'saved', sent this missive straight off to the young man's lodging and had on the morrow the pleasure of knowing that he had quitted Bournemouth by an early train.

Two days later he pressed in with a copy of a literary journal in his hand. He had returned because he was anxious and for the pleasure of flourishing the great review of 'The Middle Years'. Here at least was something adequate – it rose to the occasion; it was an acclamation, a reparation, a critical attempt to place the author in the niche he had fairly won. Dencombe accepted and submitted; he made neither objection nor enquiry, for old complications had returned and he had had two dismal days. He was convinced not only that he should never again leave his bed, so that his young friend might pardonably remain, but that the demand he should make on the patience of beholders would be of the most moderate. Doctor Hugh had been to town, and he tried to find in his eyes some confession that the Countess was pacified and his legacy clinched; but all he could see there was the light of his juvenile joy in two or three of the phrases of the newspaper. Dencombe couldn't read them, but when his visitor had insisted on repeating them more than once he was able to shake an unintoxicated head. 'Ah no – but they would have been true of what I *could* have done!'

'What people "could have done" is mainly what they've in fact done,' Doctor Hugh contended.

'Mainly, yes; but I've been an idiot!' Dencombe said.

Doctor Hugh did remain; the end was coming fast. Two days later his patient observed to him, by way of the feeblest of jokes, that there would now be no question whatever of a second chance. At this the young man stared; then he exclaimed: 'Why it has come to pass – it has come to pass! The second chance has been the public's – the chance to find the point of view, to pick up the pearl!'

'Oh the pearl!' poor Dencombe uneasily sighed. A smile as cold as a winter sunset flickered on his drawn lips as he added: 'The pearl is the unwritten – the pearl is the unalloyed, the *rest*, the lost!'

From that hour he was less and less present, heedless to all appearance of what went on round him. His disease was definitely mortal, of an action as relentless, after the short arrest that had enabled him to fall in with Doctor Hugh, as a leak in a great ship. Sinking steadily, though this visitor, a man of rare resources, now cordially approved by his physician, showed endless art in guarding him from pain, poor Dencombe kept no reckoning of favour or neglect, betrayed no symptom of regret or speculation. Yet toward the last he gave a sign of having noticed how for two days Doctor Hugh hadn't been in his room, a sign that consisted of his suddenly opening his eyes to put a question. Had he spent those days with the Countess?

'The Countess is dead,' said Doctor Hugh. 'I knew that in a particular contingency she wouldn't resist. I went to her grave.'

Dencombe's eyes opened wider. 'She left you "something handsome"?'

The young man gave a laugh almost too light for a chamber of woe. 'Never a penny. She roundly cursed me.'

'Cursed you?' Dencombe wailed.

'For giving her up. I gave her up for *you*. I had to choose,' his companion explained.

'You chose to let a fortune go?'

'I chose to accept, whatever they might be, the consequences of my infatuation,' smiled Doctor Hugh. Then as a larger pleasantry: 'The fortune be hanged! It's your own fault if I can't get your things out of my head.'

The immediate tribute to his humour was a long bewildered moan; after which, for many hours, many days, Dencombe lay motionless and absent. A response so absolute, such a glimpse of a definite result and such a sense of credit, worked together in his mind and, producing a strange commotion, slowly altered and transfigured his despair. The sense of cold submersion left him – he seemed to float without an effort. The incident was extraordinary as evidence, and it shed an intenser light. At the last he signed to Doctor Hugh to listen and, when he was down on his knees by the pillow, brought him very near. 'You've made me think it all a delusion.'

'Not your glory, my dear friend,' stammered the young man.

'Not my glory – what there is of it! It *is* glory – to have been tested, to have had our little quality and cast our little spell. The thing is to have made somebody care. You happen to be crazy of course, but that doesn't affect the law.'

'You're a great success!' said Doctor Hugh, putting into his young voice the ring of a marriage-bell.

Dencombe lay taking this in; then he gathered strength to speak once more. 'A second chance – *that's* the delusion. There never was to be but one. We work in the dark – we do what we can – we give what we have. Our doubt is our passion and our passion is our task. The rest is the madness of art.'

'If you've doubted, if you've despaired, you've always "done" it,' his visitor subtly argued.

'We've done something or other,' Dencombe conceded.

'Something or other is everything. It's the feasible. It's *you!*'

'Comforter!' poor Dencombe ironically sighed.

'But it's true,' insisted his friend.

'It's true. It's frustration that doesn't count.'

'Frustration's only life,' said Doctor Hugh.

'Yes, it's what passes.' Poor Dencombe was barely audible, but he had marked with the words the virtual end of his first and only chance.

# THE DEATH OF THE LION

# THE DEATH OF THE LION

## I

I HAD simply, I suppose, a change of heart, and it must have begun when I received my manuscript back from Mr Pinhorn. Mr Pinhorn was my 'chief', as he was called in the office: he had accepted the high mission of bringing the paper up. This was a weekly periodical, which had been supposed to be almost past redemption when he took hold of it. It was Mr Deedy who had let the thing down so dreadfully: he was never mentioned in the office now save in connexion with that misdemeanour. Young as I was I had been in a manner taken over from Mr Deedy, who had been owner as well as editor; forming part of a promiscuous lot, mainly plant and office-furniture, which poor Mrs Deedy, in her bereavement and depression, parted with at a rough valuation. I could account for my continuity but on the supposition that I had been cheap. I rather resented the practice of fathering all flatness on my late protector, who was in his unhonoured grave; but as I had my way to make I found matter enough for complacency in being on a 'staff'. At the same time I was aware of my exposure to suspicion as a product of the old lowering system. This made me feel I was doubly bound to have ideas, and had doubtless been at the bottom of my proposing to Mr Pinhorn that I should lay my lean hands on Neil Paraday. I remember how he looked at me – quite, to begin with, as if he had never heard of this celebrity, who indeed at that moment was by no means in the centre of the heavens; and even when I had knowingly explained he expressed but little confidence in the demand for any such stuff. When I had reminded him that the great principle on which we were supposed to work was just to create the demand we required, he considered a moment and then returned: 'I see – you want to write him up.'

'Call it that if you like.'

'And what's your inducement?'

'Bless my soul – my admiration!'

Mr Pinhorn pursed up his mouth. 'Is there much to be done with him?'

'Whatever there is we should have it all to ourselves, for he hasn't been touched.'

This argument was effective and Mr Pinhorn responded. 'Very well, touch him.' Then he added: 'But where can you do it?'

'Under the fifth rib!'

Mr Pinhorn stared. 'Where's that?'

'You want me to go down and see him?' I asked when I had enjoyed his visible search for the obscure suburb I seemed to have named.

'I don't "want" anything – the proposal's your own. But you must remember that that's the way we do things now,' said Mr Pinhorn with another dig at Mr Deedy.

Unregenerate as I was I could read the queer implications of this speech. The present owner's superior virtue as well as his deeper craft spoke in his reference to the late editor as one of that baser sort who deal in false representations. Mr Deedy would as soon have sent me to call on Neil Paraday as he would have published a 'holiday-number'; but such scruples presented themselves as mere ignoble thrift to his successor, whose own sincerity took the form of ringing door-bells and whose definition of genius was the art of finding people at home. It was as if Mr Deedy had published reports without his young men's having, as Pinhorn would have said, really been there. I was unregenerate, as I have hinted, and couldn't be concerned to straighten out the journalistic morals of my chief, feeling them indeed to be an abyss over the edge of which it was better not to peer. Really to be there this time moreover was a vision that made the idea of writing something subtle about Neil Paraday only the more inspiring. I would be as considerate as even Mr Deedy could have wished, and yet I should be as present as only Mr Pinhorn could conceive. My allusion to the sequestered manner in which Mr Paraday lived – it had formed part of my explanation, though I knew of it only by hearsay – was, I could divine, very much what had made Mr Pinhorn nibble. It struck him as inconsistent with the success of his paper that anyone should be so sequestered as that. And then wasn't an immediate exposure of everything just what the public wanted? Mr Pinhorn effectually called me to order by reminding me of the promptness with which I had met Miss Braby at Liverpool on her return from her fiasco in the States. Hadn't we published, while its freshness and flavour were unimpaired, Miss Braby's own version of that great international episode? I felt somewhat uneasy at this lumping of the actress and the author, and I confess that after having enlisted Mr Pinhorn's sympathies I procrastinated a little. I had succeeded better than I wished, and I had, as it happened, work nearer at hand. A few days later I called on Lord Crouchley and carried off in triumph the most unintelligible statement that had yet appeared of his lordship's reasons for his change of front. I thus set in motion in the daily papers columns of virtuous verbiage. The following week I ran down to Brighton for a chat, as Mr Pinhorn called it, with Mrs Bounder, who gave me, on the subject of her divorce, many curious particulars that had not been articulated in court. If ever an article flowed from the primal fount it was that article on Mrs Bounder. By this time, however, I became aware that Neil Paraday's new book was on the point of appearing and that its approach had been the ground of my original appeal to Mr Pinhorn, who was now annoyed with me for having lost so many days. He bundled me off – we would at least not lose another. I've always thought his sudden alertness a remarkable example of the journalistic instinct. Nothing had occurred, since I first spoke to him, to create a visible urgency, and no enlightenment could possibly have reached him. It was a pure case of professional *flair* – he had smelt the coming glory as an animal smells its distant prey.

I MAY as well say at once that this little record pretends in no degree to be a picture either of my introduction to Mr Paraday or of certain proximate steps and stages. The scheme of my narrative allows no space for these things, and in any case a prohibitory sentiment would hang about my recollection of so rare an hour. These meagres notes are essentially private, so that if they see the light the insidious forces that, as my story itself shows, make at present for publicity will simply have overmastered my precautions. The curtain fell lately enough on the lamentable drama. My memory of the day I alighted at Mr Paraday's door is a fresh memory of kindness, hospitality, compassion, and of the wonderful illuminating talk in which the welcome was conveyed. Some voice of the air had taught me the right moment, the moment of his life at which an act of unexpected young allegiance might most come home to him. He had recently recovered from a long, grave illness. I had gone to the neighbouring inn for the night, but I spent the evening in his company, and he insisted the next day on my sleeping under his roof. I hadn't an indefinite leave: Mr Pinhorn supposed us to put our victims through on the gallop. It was later, in the office, that the rude motions of the jig were set to music. I fortified myself, however, as my training had taught me to do, by the conviction that nothing could be more advantageous for my article than to be written in the very atmosphere. I said nothing to Mr Paraday about it, but in the morning, after my removal from the inn, while he was occupied in his study, as he had notified me he should need to be, I committed to paper the main heads of my impression. Then thinking to commend myself to Mr Pinhorn by my celerity, I walked out and posted my little packet before luncheon. Once my paper was written I was free to stay on, and if it was calculated to divert attention from my levity in so doing I could reflect with satisfaction that I had never been so clever. I don't mean to deny of course that I was aware it was much too good for Mr Pinhorn; but I was equally conscious that Mr Pinhorn had the supreme shrewdness of recognising from time to time the cases in which an article was not too bad only because it was too good. There was

nothing he loved so much as to print on the right occasion a
thing he hated. I had begun my visit to the great man on a
Monday, and on the Wednesday his book came out. A copy of it
arrived by the first post, and he let me go out into the garden
with it immediately after breakfast. I read it from beginning to
end that day, and in the evening he asked me to remain with
him the rest of the week and over the Sunday.

That night my manuscript came back from Mr Pinhorn,
accompanied with a letter the gist of which was the desire to
know what I meant by trying to fob off on him such stuff.
That was the meaning of the question, if not exactly its form,
and it made my mistake immense to me. Such as this mistake
was I could now only look it in the face and accept it. I knew
where I had failed, but it was exactly where I couldn't have
succeeded. I had been sent down to be personal and then in
point of fact hadn't been personal at all: what I had dispatched
to London was just a little finicking feverish study of my
author's talent. Anything less relevant to Mr Pinhorn's purpose
couldn't well be imagined, and he was visibly angry at my
having (at his expense, with a second-class ticket) approached
the subject of our enterprise only to stand off so helplessly. For
myself, I knew but too well what had happened, and how a
miracle – as pretty as some old miracle of legend – had been
wrought on the spot to save me. There had been a big brush
of wings, the flash of an opaline robe, and then, with a great
cool stir of the air, the sense of an angel's having swooped
down and caught me to his bosom. He held me only till the
danger was over, and it all took place in a minute. With my
manuscript back on my hands I understood the phenomenon
better, and the reflexions I made on it are what I meant, at the
beginning of this anecdote, by my change of heart. Mr Pinhorn's
note was not only a rebuke decidedly stern, but an invitation
immediately to send him – it was the case to say so – the
genuine article, the revealing and reverberating sketch to the
promise of which, and of which alone, I owed my squandered
privilege. A week or two later I recast my peccant paper and,
giving it a particular application to Mr Paraday's new book,
obtained for it the hospitality of another journal, where, I must
admit, Mr Pinhorn was so far vindicated as that it attracted
not the least attention.

# III

I WAS frankly, at the end of three days, a very prejudiced critic, so that one morning when, in the garden, my great man had offered to read me something I quite held my breath as I listened. It was the written scheme of another book – something put aside long ago, before his illness, but that he had lately taken out again to reconsider. He had been turning it round when I came down on him, and it had grown magnificently under this second hand. Loose liberal confident, it might have passed for a great gossiping eloquent letter – the overflow into talk of an artist's amorous plan. The theme I thought singularly rich, quite the strongest he had yet treated; and this familiar statement of it, full too of fine maturities, was really, in summarised splendour, a mine of gold, a precious independent work. I remember rather profanely wondering whether the ultimate production could possibly keep at the pitch. His reading of the fond epistle, at any rate, made me feel as if I were, for the advantage of posterity, in close correspondence with him – were the distinguished person to whom it had been affectionately addressed. It was a high distinction simply to be told such things. The idea he now communicated had all the freshness, the flushed fairness, of the conception untouched and untried: it was Venus rising from the sea and before the airs had blown upon her. I had never been so throbbingly present at such an unveiling. But when he had tossed the last bright word after the others, as I had seen cashiers in banks, weighing mounds of coin, drop a final sovereign into the tray, I knew a sudden prudent alarm.

'My dear master, how, after all, are you going to do it? It's infinitely noble, but what time it will take, what patience and independence, what assured, what perfect conditions! Oh for a lone isle in a tepid sea!'

'Isn't this practically a lone isle, and aren't you, as an encircling medium, tepid enough?' he asked, alluding with a laugh to the wonder of my young admiration and the narrow limits of his little provincial home. 'Time isn't what I've lacked hitherto: the question hasn't been to find it, but to use it. Of course my illness made, while it lasted, a great hole – but I dare say there would have been a hole at any rate. The earth we tread has more pockets than a billiard-table. The great thing is now to keep on my feet.'

'That's exactly what I mean.'

Neil Paraday looked at me with eyes – such pleasant eyes as he had – in which, as I now recall their expression, I seem to have seen a dim imagination of his fate. He was fifty years old, and his illness had been cruel, his convalescence slow. 'It isn't as if I weren't all right.'

'Oh if you weren't all right I wouldn't look at you!' I tenderly said.

We had both got up, quickened as by this clearer air, and he had lighted a cigarette. I had taken a fresh one, which with an intenser smile, by way of answer to my exclamation, he applied to the flame of his match. 'If I weren't better I shouldn't have thought of *that!*' He flourished his script in his hand.

'I don't want to be discouraging, but that's not true,' I returned. 'I'm sure that during the months you lay here in pain you had visitations sublime. You thought of a thousand things. You think of more and more all the while. That's what makes you, if you'll pardon my familiarity, so respectable. At a time when so many people are spent you come into your second wind. But, thank God, all the same, you're better! Thank God too you're not, as you were telling me yesterday, "successful". If *you* weren't a failure what would be the use of trying? That's my one reserve on the subject of your recovery – that it makes you "score", as the newspapers say. It looks well in the newspapers, and almost anything that does that's horrible. "We are happy to announce that Mr Paraday, the celebrated author, is again in the enjoyment of excellent health." Somehow I shouldn't like to see it.'

'You won't see it; I'm not in the least celebrated – my obscurity protects me. But couldn't you bear even to see I was dying or dead?' my host enquired.

'Dead – *passe encore*; there's nothing so safe. One never knows what a living artist may do – one has mourned so many. However, one must make the worst of it. You must be as dead as you can.'

'Don't I meet that condition in having just published a book?'

'Adequately, let us hope; for the book's verily a masterpiece.'

At this moment the parlour-maid appeared in the door that opened from the garden: Paraday lived at no great cost, and the frisk of petticoats, with a timorous 'Sherry, sir?' was about his modest mahogany. He allowed half his income to his wife, from whom he had succeeded in separating without redundancy of legend. I had a general faith in his having behaved well, and I had once, in London, taken Mrs Paraday down to dinner. He now turned to speak to the maid, who offered him, on a tray, some card or note, while, agitated, excited, I wandered to the end of the precinct. The idea of his security became supremely dear to me, and I asked myself if I were the same young man who had come down a few days before to scatter him to the four winds. When I retraced my steps he had gone into the house, and the woman – the second London post had come in – had placed my letters and a newspaper on a bench. I sat down there to the letters, which were a brief business, and then, without heeding the address, took the paper from its envelope. It was the journal of highest renown, *The Empire* of that morning. It regularly came to Paraday, but I remembered that neither of us had yet looked at the copy already delivered. This one had a great mark on the 'editorial' page, and, uncrumpling the wrapper, I saw it to be directed to my host and stamped with the name of his publishers. I instantly divined that *The Empire* had spoken of him, and I've not forgotten the odd little shock of the circumstance. It checked all eagerness and made me drop the paper a moment. As I sat there conscious of a palpitation I think I had a vision of what was to be. I had also a vision of the letter I would presently address to Mr Pinhorn, breaking, as it were, with Mr Pinhorn. Of course, however, the next minute the voice of *The Empire* was in my ears.

The article wasn't, I thanked heaven, a review; it was a 'leader', the last of three, presenting Neil Paraday to the human race. His new book, the fifth from his hand, had been but a day or two out, and *The Empire*, already aware of it, fired, as if on the birth of a prince, a salute of a whole column. The guns had been booming these three hours in the house without our suspecting them. The big blundering newspaper had discovered him, and now he was proclaimed and anointed and crowned. His place was assigned him as publicly as if a fat usher with a wand had pointed to the topmost chair; he was to pass up and still up, higher and higher, between the watching faces and the envious sounds – away up to the dais and the throne. The article was 'epoch-making', a landmark in his life; he had taken rank at a bound, waked up a national glory. A national glory was needed, and it was an immense convenience he was there. What all this meant rolled over me, and I fear I grew a little faint – it meant so much more than I could say 'yea' to on the spot. In a flash, somehow, all was different; the tremendous wave I speak of had swept something away. It had knocked down, I suppose, my little customary altar, my twinkling tapers and my flowers, and had reared itself into the likeness of a temple vast and bare. When Neil Paraday should come out of the house he would come out a contemporary. That was what had happened: the poor man was to be squeezed into his horrible age. I felt as if he had been overtaken on the crest of the hill and brought back to the city. A little more and he would have dipped down the short cut to posterity and escaped.

# IV

WHEN he came out it was exactly as if he had been in custody, for beside him walked a stout man with a big black beard, who, save that he wore spectacles, might have been a policeman, and in whom at a second glance I recognised the highest contemporary enterprise.

'This is Mr Morrow,' said Paraday, looking, I thought, rather white: 'he wants to publish heaven knows what about me.'

I winced as I remembered that this was exactly what I myself had wanted. 'Already?' I cried with a sort of sense that my friend had fled to me for protection.

Mr Morrow glared, agreeably, through his glasses: they suggested the electric headlights of some monstrous modern ship, and I felt as if Paraday and I were tossing terrified under his bows. I saw his momentum was irresistible. 'I was confident that I should be the first in the field. A great interest is naturally felt in Mr Paraday's surroundings,' he heavily observed.

'I hadn't the least idea of it,' said Paraday, as if he had been told he had been snoring.

'I find he hasn't read the article in *The Empire*', Mr Morrow remarked to me. 'That's so very interesting – it's something to start with,' he smiled. He had begun to pull off his gloves, which were violently new, and to look encouragingly round the little garden. As a 'surrounding' I felt how I myself had already been taken in; I was a little fish in the stomach of a bigger one. 'I represent,' our visitor continued, 'a syndicate of influential journals, no less than thirty-seven, whose public – whose publics, I may say – are in peculiar sympathy with Mr Paraday's line of thought. They would greatly appreciate any expression of his views on the subject of the art he so nobly exemplifies. In addition to my connexion with the syndicate just mentioned I hold a particular commission from *The Tatler*, whose most prominent department, "Smatter and Chatter" – I dare say you've often enjoyed it – attracts such attention. I was honoured only last week, as a representative of *The Tatler*, with the confidence of Guy Walsingham, the brilliant author of "Obsessions". She pronounced herself thoroughly pleased with my sketch of her method; she went so far as to say that I had made her genius more comprehensible even to herself.'

Neil Paraday had dropped on the garden-bench and sat there at once detached and confounded; he looked hard at a bare spot in the lawn, as if with an anxiety that had suddenly made him grave. His movement had been interpreted by his visitor as an invitation to sink sympathetically into a wicker chair that stood hard by, and while Mr Morrow so settled himself I felt he had taken official possession and that there was no undoing it. One had heard of unfortunate people's having 'a man in the house', and this was just what *we* had. There was a silence of a moment, during which we seemed to acknowledge in the only way that was possible the presence of universal fate; the sunny stillness took no pity, and my thought, as I was sure Paraday's was doing, performed within the minute a great distant revolution. I saw just how emphatic I should make my rejoinder to Mr Pinhorn, and that having come, like Mr Morrow, to betray, I must remain as long as possible to save. Not because I had brought my mind back, but because our visitor's last words were in my ear, I presently enquired with gloomy irrelevance if Guy Walsingham were a woman.

'Oh yes, a mere pseudonym – rather pretty, isn't it? – and convenient, you know, for a lady who goes in for the larger latitude. "Obsessions, by Miss So-and-so", would look a little odd, but men are more naturally indelicate. Have you peeped into "Obsessions"?' Mr Morrow continued sociably to our companion.

Paraday, still absent, remote, made no answer, as if he hadn't heard the question: a form of intercourse that appeared to suit the cheerful Mr Morrow as well as any other. Imperturbably bland, he was a man of resources – he only needed to be on the spot. He had pocketed the whole poor place while Paraday and I were wool-gathering, and I could imagine that he had already got his 'heads'. His system, at any rate, was justified by the inevitability with which I replied, to save my friend the trouble: 'Dear no – he hasn't read it. He doesn't read such things!' I unwarily added.

'Things that are *too* far over the fence, eh?' I was indeed a godsend to Mr Morrow. It was the psychological moment; it determined the appearance of his note-book, which, however, he at first kept slightly behind him, even as the dentist approaching his victim keeps the horrible forceps. 'Mr Paraday holds with the good old proprieties – I see!' And thinking of the thirty-seven influential journals, I found myself, as I found poor Paraday, helplessly assisting at the promulgation of this ineptitude. 'There's no point on which distinguished views are so acceptable as on this question – raised perhaps more strikingly than ever by Guy Walsingham – of the permissibility of the larger latitude. I've an appointment, precisely in connexion with it, next week, with Dora Forbes, author of "The Other Way Round", which everybody's talking about. Has Mr Paraday glanced at "The Other Way Round"?' Mr Morrow now frankly appealed to me. I took on myself to repudiate the supposition, while our companion, still silent, got up nervously and walked away. His visitor paid no heed to his withdrawal, but opened out the note-book with a more fatherly pat. 'Dora Forbes, I gather, takes the ground, the same as Guy Walsingham's, that the larger latitude has simply got to come. He holds that it has got to be squarely faced. Of course his sex makes him a less prejudiced witness. But an authoritative word from Mr Paraday – from the point of view of *his* sex, you know – would go right round the globe. He takes the line that we *haven't* got to face it?'

I was bewildered: it sounded somehow as if there were three sexes. My interlocutor's pencil was poised, my private responsibility great. I simply sat staring, none the less, and only found presence of mind to say: 'Is this Miss Forbes a gentleman?'

Mr Morrow had a subtle smile. 'It wouldn't be "Miss" – there's a wife!'

'I mean is she a man?'

'The wife?' – Mr Morrow was for a moment as confused as myself. But when I explained that I alluded to Dora Forbes in person he informed me, with visible amusement at my being so out of it, that this was the 'pen-name' of an indubitable male – he had a big red moustache. 'He goes in for the slight mystification because the ladies are such popular favourites. A great deal of interest is felt in his acting on that idea – which *is* clever, isn't it? – and there's every prospect of its being widely imitated.' Our host at this moment joined us again, and Mr Morrow remarked invitingly that he should be happy to make a note of any observation the movement in question, the bid for success under a lady's name, might suggest to Mr Paraday. But the poor man, without catching the allusion, excused himself, pleading that, though greatly honoured by his visitor's interest, he suddenly felt unwell and should have to take leave of him – have to go and lie down and keep quiet. His young friend might be trusted to answer for him, but he hoped Mr Morrow didn't expect great things even of his young friend. His young friend, at this moment, looked at Neil Paraday with an anxious eye, greatly wondering if he were doomed to be ill again; but Paraday's own kind face met his question reassuringly, seemed to say in a glance intelligible enough: 'Oh I'm not ill, but I'm scared; get him out of the house as quietly as possible.' Getting newspaper-men out of the house was odd business for an emissary of Mr Pinhorn, and I was so exhilarated by the idea of it that I called after him as he left us: 'Read the article in *The Empire* and you'll soon be all right!'

# V

'DELICIOUS my having come down to tell him of it!' Mr Morrow ejaculated. 'My cab was at the door twenty minutes after *The Empire* had been laid on my breakfast-table. Now what have you got for me?' he continued, dropping again into his chair, from which, however, he the next moment eagerly rose. 'I was shown into the drawing-room, but there must be more to see – his study, his literary sanctum, the little things he has about, or other domestic objects and features. He wouldn't be lying down on his study-table? There's great interest always felt in the scene of an author's labours. Sometimes we're favoured with very delightful peeps. Dora Forbes showed me all his table-drawers, and almost jammed my hand into one into which I made a dash! I don't ask that of you, but if we could talk things over right there where he sits I feel as if I should get the keynote.'

I had no wish whatever to be rude to Mr Morrow, I was much too initiated not to tend to more diplomacy; but I had a quick inspiration, and I entertained an insurmountable, an almost superstitious objection to his crossing the threshold of my friend's little lonely shabby consecrated workshop. 'No, no – we shan't get at his life that way,' I said. 'The way to get at his life is to – But wait a moment!' I broke off and went quickly into the house, whence I in three minutes reappeared before Mr Morrow with the two volumes of Paraday's new book. 'His life's here,' I went on, 'and I'm so full of this admirable thing that I can't talk of anything else. The artist's life's his work, and this is the place to observe him. What he has to tell us he tells us with *this* perfection. My dear sir, the best interviewer's the best reader.'

Mr Morrow good-humouredly protested. 'Do you mean to say that no other source of information should be open to us?'

'None other till this particular one – by far the most copious – has been quite exhausted. Have you exhausted it, my dear sir? Had you exhausted it when you came down here? It seems to me in our time almost wholly neglected, and something should surely be done to restore its ruined credit. It's the course to which the artist himself at every step, and with such pathetic confidence, refers us. This last book of Mr Paraday's is full of revelations.'

'Revelations?' panted Mr Morrow, whom I had forced again into his chair.

'The only kind that count. It tells you with a perfection that seems to me quite final all the author thinks, for instance, about the advent of the "larger latitude".'

'Where does it do that?' asked Mr Morrow, who had picked up the second volume and was insincerely thumbing it.

'Everywhere – in the whole treatment of his case. Extract the opinion, disengage the answer – those are the real acts of homage.'

Mr Morrow, after a minute, tossed the book away. 'Ah but you mustn't take me for a reviewer.'

'Heaven forbid I should take you for anything so dreadful! You came down to perform a little act of sympathy, and so, I may confide to you, did I. Let us perform our little act together. These pages overflow with the testimony we want: let us read them and taste them and interpret them. You'll of course have perceived for yourself that one scarcely does read Neil Paraday till one reads him aloud; he gives out to the ear an extraordinary full tone, and it's only when you expose it confidently to that test that you really get near his style. Take up your book again and let me listen, while you pay it out, to that wonderful fifteenth chapter. If you feel you can't do it justice, compose yourself to attention while I produce for you – I think I can! – this scarcely less admirable ninth.'

Mr Morrow gave me a straight look which was as hard as a blow between the eyes; he had turned rather red, and a question had formed itself in his mind which reached my sense as distinctly as if he had uttered it: 'What sort of a damned fool are you?' Then he got up, gathering together his hat and gloves, buttoning his coat, projecting hungrily all over the place the big transparency of his mask. It seemed to flare over Fleet Street and somehow made the actual spot distressingly humble: there was so little for it to feed on unless he counted the blisters of our stucco or saw his way to do something with the roses. Even the poor roses were common kinds. Presently his eyes fell on the manuscript from which Paraday had been reading to me and which still lay on the bench. As my own followed them I saw it looked promising, looked pregnant, as if it gently throbbed with the life the reader had given it. Mr Morrow indulged in a nod at it and a vague thrust of his umbrella. 'What's that?'

'Oh it's a plan – a secret.'

'A secret!' There was an instant's silence, and then Mr Morrow made another movement. I may have been mistaken, but it affected me as the translated impulse of the desire to lay hands on the manuscript, and this led me to indulge in a quick anticipatory grab which may very well have seemed ungraceful, or even impertinent, and which at any rate left Mr Paraday's two admirers very erect, glaring at each other while one of them held a bundle of papers well behind him. An instant later Mr Morrow quitted me abruptly, as if he had really carried something off with him. To reassure myself, watching his broad back recede, I only grasped my manuscript the tighter. He went to the back door of the house, the one he had come out from, but on trying the handle he appeared to find it fastened. So he passed round into the front garden, and by listening intently enough I could presently hear the outer gate close behind him with a bang. I thought again of the thirty-seven influential journals and wondered what would be his revenge. I hasten to add that he was magnanimous: which was just the most dreadful thing he could have been. The Tatler published a charming chatty familiar account of Mr Paraday's 'Home-life', and on the wings of the thirty-seven influential journals it went, to use Mr Morrow's own expression, right round the globe.

## VI

A WEEK later, early in May, my glorified friend came up to town, where, it may be veraciously recorded, he was the king of the beasts of the year. No advancement was ever more rapid, no exaltation more complete, no bewilderment more teachable. His book sold but moderately, though the article in *The Empire* had done unwonted wonders for it; but he circulated in person to a measure that the libraries might well have envied. His formula had been found – he was a 'revelation'. His momentary terror had been real, just as mine had been – the overclouding of his passionate desire to be left to finish his work. He was far from unsociable, but he had the finest conception of being let alone that I've ever met. For the time, none the less, he took his profit where it seemed most to crowd on him, having in his pocket the portable sophistries about the nature of the artist's task. Observation too was a kind of work and experience a kind of success; London dinners were all material and London ladies were fruitful toil. 'No one has the faintest conception of what I'm trying for,' he said to me, 'and not many have read three pages that I've written; but I must dine with them first – they'll find out why when they've time.' It was rather rude justice perhaps; but the fatigue had the merit of being a new sort, while the phantasmagoric town was probably after all less of a battlefield than the haunted study. He once told me that he had had no personal life to speak of since his fortieth year, but had had more than was good for him before. London closed the parenthesis and exhibited him in relations; one of the most inevitable of these being that in which he found himself to Mrs Weeks Wimbush, wife of the boundless brewer and proprietress of the universal menagerie. In this establishment, as everybody knows, on occasions when the crush is great, the animals rub shoulders freely with the spectators and the lions sit down for whole evenings with the lambs.

It had been ominously clear to me from the first that in Neil Paraday this lady, who, as all the world agreed, was tremendous fun, considered that she had secured a prime attraction, a creature of almost heraldic oddity. Nothing could exceed her enthusiasm over her capture, and nothing could exceed the confused apprehensions it excited in me. I had an instinctive fear of her which I tried without effect to conceal from her victim, but which I let her notice with perfect impunity. Paraday heeded it, but she never did, for her conscience was that of a romping child. She was a blind violent force to which I could attach no more idea of responsibility than to the creaking of a sign in the wind. It was difficult to say what she conduced to but circulation. She was constructed of steel and leather, and all I asked of her for our tractable friend was not to do him to death. He had consented for a time to be of india-rubber, but my thoughts were fixed on the day he should resume his shape or at least get back into his box. It was evidently all right, but I should be glad when it was well over. I had a special fear – the impression was ineffaceable of the hour, when, after Mr Morrow's departure, I had found him on the sofa in his study. That pretext of indisposition had not in the least been meant as a snub to the envoy of *The Tatler* – he had gone to lie down in very truth. He had felt a pang of his old pain, the result of the agitation wrought in him by this forcing open of a new period. His old programme, his old ideal even had to be changed. Say what one would, success was a complication and recognition had to be reciprocal. .The monastic life, the pious illumination of the missal in the convent-cell were things of the gathered past. It didn't engender despair, but at least it required adjustment. Before I left him on that occasion we had passed a bargain, my part of which was that I should make it my business to take care of him. Let whoever would represent the interest in his presence (I must have had a mystical prevision of Mrs Weeks Wimbush) I should represent the interest in his work – or otherwise expressed in his absence. These two interests were in their essence opposed; and I doubt, as youth is fleeting, if I shall ever again know the intensity of joy with which I felt that in so good a cause I was willing to make myself odious.

One day in Sloane Street I found myself questioning Paraday's landlord, who had come to the door in answer to my knock. Two vehicles, a barouche and a smart hansom, were drawn up before the house.

'In the drawing-room, sir? Mrs Weeks Wimbush.'

'And in the dining-room?'

'A young lady, sir – waiting: I think a foreigner.'

It was three o'clock, and on days when Paraday didn't lunch out he attached a value to these appropriated hours. On which days, however, didn't the dear man lunch out? Mrs Wimbush, at such a crisis, would have rushed round immediately after her own repast. I went into the dining-room first, postponing the pleasure of seeing how, upstairs, the lady of the barouche would, on my arrival, point the moral of my sweet solicitude. No one took such an interest as herself in his doing only what was good for him, and she was always on the spot to see that he did it. She made appointments with him to discuss the best means of economising his time and protecting his privacy. She further made his health her special business, and had so much sympathy with my own zeal for it that she was the author of pleasing fictions on the subject of what my devotion had led me to give up. I gave up nothing (I don't count Mr Pinhorn) because I had nothing, and all I had as yet achieved was to find myself also in the menagerie. I had dashed in to save my friend, but I had got domesticated and wedged; so that I could do little more for him than exchange with him over people's heads looks of intense but futile intelligence.

# VII

THE young lady in the dining-room had a brave face, black hair, blue eyes, and in her lap a big volume. 'I've come for his autograph,' she said when I had explained to her that I was under bonds to see people for him when he was occupied. 'I've been waiting half an hour, but I'm prepared to wait all day.' I don't know whether it was this that told me she was American, for the propensity to wait all day is not in general characteristic of her race. I was enlightened probably not so much by the spirit of the utterance as by some quality of its sound. At any rate I saw she had an individual patience and a lovely frock, together with an expression that played among her pretty features like a breeze among flowers. Putting her book on the table she showed me a massive album, showily bound and full of autographs of price. The collection of faded notes, of still more faded 'thoughts', of quotations, platitudes, signatures, represented a formidable purpose.

I could only disclose my dread of it. 'Most people apply to Mr Paraday by letter, you know.'

'Yes, but he doesn't answer. I've written three times.'

'Very true,' I reflected; 'the sort of letter you mean goes straight into the fire.'

'How do you know the sort I mean?' My interlocutress had blushed and smiled, and in a moment she added: 'I don't believe he gets many like them!'

'I'm sure they're beautiful, but he burns without reading.' I didn't add that I had convinced him he ought to.

'Isn't he then in danger of burning things of importance?'

'He would perhaps be so if distinguished men hadn't an infallible nose for nonsense.'

She looked at me a moment – her face was sweet and gay. 'Do *you* burn without reading too?' – in answer to which I assured her that if she'd trust me with her repository I'd see that Mr Paraday should write his name in it.

She considered a little. 'That's very well, but it wouldn't make me see him.'

'Do you want very much to see him?' It seemed ungracious

to catechise so charming a creature, but somehow I had never yet taken my duty to the great author so seriously.

'Enough to have come from America for the purpose.'

I stared. 'All alone?'

'I don't see that that's exactly your business, but if it will make me more seductive I'll confess that I'm quite by myself. I had to come alone or not come at all.'

She was interesting; I could imagine she had lost parents, natural protectors – could conceive even she had inherited money. I was at a pass of my own fortunes when keeping hansoms at doors seemed to me pure swagger. As a trick of this bold and sensitive girl, however, it became romantic – a part of the general romance of her freedom, her errand, her inno-cence. The confidence of young Americans was notorious, and I speedily arrived at a conviction that no impulse could have been more generous than the impulse that had operated here. I foresaw at that moment that it would make her my peculiar charge, just as circumstances had made Neil Paraday. She would be another person to look after, so that one's honour would be concerned in guiding her straight. These things became clearer to me later on; at the instant I had scepticism enough to observe to her, as I turned the pages of her volume, that her net had all the same caught many a big fish. She appeared to have had fruitful access to the great ones of the earth; there were people moreover whose signatures she had presumably secured without a personal interview. She couldn't have worried George Wash-ington and Friedrich Schiller and Hannah More. She met this argument, to my surprise, by throwing up the album without a pang. It wasn't even her own; she was responsible for none of its treasures. It belonged to a girl-friend in America, a young lady in a western city. This young lady had insisted on her bringing it, to pick up more autographs: she thought they might like to see, in Europe, in what company they would be. The 'girl-friend', the western city, the immortal names, the curious errand, the idyllic faith, all made a story as strange to me, and as beguiling, as some tale in the Arabian Nights. Thus it was that my informant had encumbered herself with the ponderous tome; but she hastened to assure me that this was the first time she had brought it out. For her visit to Mr Paraday it had simply been a pretext. She didn't really care a straw that he should write his name; what she did want was to look straight into his face.

I demurred a little. 'And why do you require to do that?'

'Because I just love him!' Before I could recover from the agitating effect of this crystal ring my companion had continued: 'Hasn't there ever been any face that *you've* wanted to look into?'

How could I tell her so soon how much I appreciated the opportunity of looking into hers? I could only assent in general to the proposition that there were certainly for everyone such yearnings, and even such faces; and I felt the crisis demand all my lucidity, all my wisdom. 'Oh yes, I'm a student of physiognomy. Do you mean,' I pursued, 'that you've a passion for Mr Paraday's books?'

'They've been everything to me and a little more beside – I know them by heart. They've completely taken hold of me. There's no author about whom I'm in such a state as I'm in about Neil Paraday.'

'Permit me to remark then,' I presently returned, 'that you're one of the right sort.'

'One of the enthusiasts? Of course I am!'

'Oh there are enthusiasts who are quite of the wrong. I mean you're one of those to whom an appeal can be made.'

'An appeal?' Her face lighted as if with the chance of some great sacrifice.

If she was ready for one it was only waiting for her, and in a moment I mentioned it. 'Give up this crude purpose of seeing him. Go away without it. That will be far better.'

She looked mystified, then turned visibly pale. 'Why, hasn't he any personal charm?' The girl was terrible and laughable in her bright directness.

'Ah that dreadful word "personal"!' I wailed; 'we're dying of it, for you women bring it out with murderous effect. When you meet with a genius as fine as this idol of ours let him off the dreary duty of being a personality as well. Know him only by what's best in him and spare him for the same sweet sake.'

My young lady continued to look at me in confusion and mistrust, and the result of her reflexion on what I had just said was to make her suddenly break out: 'Look here, sir – what's the matter with him?'

'The matter with him is that if he doesn't look out people will eat a great hole in his life.'

She turned it over. 'He hasn't any disfigurement?'

'Nothing to speak of!'

'Do you mean that social engagements interfere with his occupations?'

'That but feebly expresses it.'

'So that he can't give himself up to his beautiful imagination?'

'He's beset, badgered, bothered – he's pulled to pieces on the pretext of being applauded. People expect him to give them his time, his golden time, who wouldn't themselves give five shillings for one of his books.'

'Five? I'd give five thousand!'

'Give your sympathy – give your forbearance. Two thirds of those who approach him only do it to advertise themselves.'

'Why it's too bad!' the girl exclaimed with the face of an angel. 'It's the first time I was ever called crude!' she laughed.

I followed up my advantage. 'There's a lady with him now who's a terrible complication, and who yet hasn't read, I'm sure, ten pages he ever wrote.'

My visitor's wide eyes grew tenderer. 'Then how does she talk—?'

'Without ceasing. I only mention her as a single case. Do you want to know how to show a superlative consideration? Simply avoid him.'

'Avoid him?' she despairingly breathed.

'Don't force him to have to take account of you; admire him in silence, cultivate him at a distance and secretly appropriate his message. Do you want to know,' I continued, warming to my idea, 'how to perform an act of homage really sublime?' Then as she hung on my words: 'Succeed in never seeing him at all!'

'Never at all?' – she suppressed a shriek for it.

'The more you get into his writings the less you'll want to, and you'll be immensely sustained by the thought of the good you're doing him.'

She looked at me without resentment or spite, and at the truth I had put before her with candour, credulity, pity. I was afterwards happy to remember that she must have gathered from my face the liveliness of my interest in herself. 'I think I see what you mean.'

'Oh I express it badly, but I should be delighted if you'd let me come to see you – to explain it better.'

She made no response to this, and her thoughtful eyes fell on the big album, on which she presently laid her hands as if to take it away. 'I did use to say out West that they might write a little less for autographs – to all the great poets, you know – and study the thoughts and style a little more.'

'What do they care for the thoughts and style? They didn't even understand you. I'm not sure,' I added, 'that I do myself, and I dare say that you by no means make me out.'

She had got up to go, and though I wanted her to succeed in not seeing Neil Paraday I wanted her also, inconsequently, to remain in the house. I was at any rate far from desiring to hustle her off. As Mrs Weeks Wimbush, upstairs, was still saving our friend in her own way, I asked my young lady to let me briefly relate, in illustration of my point, the little incident of my having gone down into the country for a profane purpose and been converted on the spot to holiness. Sinking again into her chair to listen she showed a deep interest in the anecdote. Then thinking it over gravely she returned with her odd intonation: 'Yes, but you do see him!' I had to admit that this was the case; and I wasn't so prepared with an effective attenuation as I could have wished. She eased the situation off, however, by the charming quaintness with which she finally said: 'Well, I wouldn't want him to be lonely!' This time she rose in earnest, but I persuaded her to let me keep the album to show Mr Paraday. I assured her I'd bring it back to her myself. 'Well, you'll find my address somewhere in it on a paper!' she sighed all resignedly at the door.

# VIII

I BLUSH to confess it, but I invited Mr Paraday that very day to transcribe into the album one of his most characteristic passages. I told him how I had got rid of the strange girl who had brought it – her ominous name was Miss Hurter and she lived at an hotel; quite agreeing with him moreover as to the wisdom of getting rid with equal promptitude of the book itself. This was why I carried it to Albemarle Street no later than on the morrow. I failed to find her at home, but she wrote to me and I went again: she wanted so much to hear more about Neil Paraday. I returned repeatedly, I may briefly declare, to supply her with this information. She had been immensely taken, the more she thought of it, with that idea of mine about the act of homage: it had ended by filling her with a generous rapture. She positively desired to do something sublime for him, though indeed I could see that, as this particular flight was difficult, she appreciated the fact that my visits kept her up. I had it on my conscience to keep her up; I neglected nothing that would contribute to it, and her conception of our cherished author's independence became at last as fine as his very own. 'Read him, read him – *that* will be an education in decency,' I constantly repeated; while, seeking him in his works even as God in nature, she represented herself as convinced that, according to my assurance, this was the system that had, as she expressed it, weaned her. We read him together when I could find time, and the generous creature's sacrifice was fed by our communion. There were twenty selfish women about whom I told her and who stirred her to a beautiful rage. Immediately after my first visit her sister, Mrs Milsom, came over from Paris, and the two ladies began to present, as they called it, their letters. I thanked our stars that none had been presented to Mr Paraday. They received invitations and dined out, and some of these occasions enabled Fanny Hurter to perform, for consistency's sake, touching feats of submission. Nothing indeed would now have induced her even to look at the object of her admiration. Once, hearing his name announced at a party, she instantly left the room by another door and then straightway quitted the house. At another time when I was at the opera with them – Mrs Milsom had invited me to their box – I attempted to point Mr Paraday out to her in the stalls. On this she asked her sister to change places with her and, while that lady devoured the great man through a powerful glass, presented, all the rest of the evening, her inspired back to the house. To torment her tenderly I pressed the glass upon her, telling her how wonderfully near it brought our friend's handsome head. By way of answer she simply looked at me in charged silence, letting me see that tears had gathered in her eyes. These tears, I may remark, produced an effect on me of which the end is not yet. There was a moment when I felt it my duty to mention them to Neil Paraday, but I was deterred by the reflexion that there were questions more relevant to his happiness.

These questions indeed, by the end of the season, were reduced to a single one – the question of reconstituting so far as might be possible the conditions under which he had produced his best work. Such conditions could never all come back, for there was a new one that took up too much place; but some perhaps were not beyond recall. I wanted above all things to see him sit down to the subject he had, on my making his acquaintance, read me that admirable sketch of. Something told me there was no security but in his doing so before the new factor, as we used to say at Mr Pinhorn's, should render the problem incalculable. It only half-reassured me that the sketch itself was so copious and so eloquent that even at the worst there would be the making of a small but complete book, a tiny volume which, for the faithful, might well become an object of adoration. There would even not be wanting critics to declare, I foresaw, that the plan was a thing to be more thankful for than the structure to have been reared on it. My impatience for the structure, none the less, grew and grew with the interruptions. He had on coming up to town begun to sit for his portrait to a young painter, Mr Rumble, whose little game, as we also used to say at Mr Pinhorn's, was to be the first to perch on the shoulders of renown. Mr Rumble's studio was a circus in which the man of the hour, and still more the woman, leaped through the hoops of his showy frames almost as electrically as they burst into telegrams and 'specials'. He pranced into the exhibitions on their back; he was the reporter on canvas,

the Vandyke up to date, and there was one roaring year in
which Mrs Bounder and Miss Braby, Guy Walsingham and
Dora Forbes proclaimed in chorus from the same pictured walls
that no one had yet got ahead of him.

Paraday had been promptly caught and saddled, accepting
with characteristic good humour his confidential hint that to
figure in his show was not so much a consequence as a cause
of immortality. From Mrs Wimbush to the last 'representative'
who called to ascertain his twelve favourite dishes, it was the
same ingenuous assumption that he would rejoice in the reper-
cussion. There were moments when I fancied I might have had
more patience with them if they hadn't been so fatally ben-
evolent. I hated at all events Mr Rumble's picture, and had
my bottled resentment ready when, later on, I found my dis-
tracted friend had been stuffed by Mrs Wimbush into the
mouth of another cannon. A young artist in whom she was
intensely interested, and who had no connexion with Mr
Rumble, was to show how far *he* could make him go. Poor
Paraday, in return, was naturally to write something somewhere about the young artist. She played her victims against
each other with admirable ingenuity, and her establishment was
a huge machine in which the tiniest and the biggest wheels
went round to the same treadle. I had a scene with her in which
I tried to express that the function of such a man was to
exercise his genius – not to serve as a hoarding for pictorial
posters. The people I was perhaps angriest with were the
editors of magazines who had introduced what they called new
features, so aware were they that the newest feature of all
would be to make him grind their axes by contributing his
views on vital topics and taking part in the periodical prattle
about the future of fiction. I made sure that before I should
have done with him there would scarcely be a current form
of words left me to be sick of; but meanwhile I could make
surer still of my animosity to bustling ladies for whom he
drew the water that irrigated their social flower-beds.

I had a battle with Mrs Wimbush over the artist she protected, and another over the question of a certain week, at the
end of July, that Mr Paraday appeared to have contracted to
spend with her in the country. I protested against this visit;
I intimated that he was too unwell for hospitality without a

*nuance*, for caresses without imagination; I begged he might rather take the time in some restorative way. A sultry air of promises, of ponderous parties, hung over his August, and he would greatly profit by the interval of rest. He hadn't told me he was ill again – that he had had a warning; but I hadn't needed this, for I found his reticence his worst symptom. The only thing he said to me was that he believed a comfortable attack of something or other would set him up: it would put out of the question everything but the exemptions he prized. I'm afraid I shall have presented him as a martyr in a very small cause if I fail to explain that he surrendered himself much more liberally than I surrendered him. He filled his lungs, for the most part, with the comedy of his queer fate: the tragedy was in the spectacles through which I chose to look. He was conscious of inconvenience, and above all of a great renouncement; but how could he have heard a mere dirge in the bells of his accession? The sagacity and the jealousy were mine, and his the impressions and the harvest. Of course, as regards Mrs Wimbush, I was worsted in my encounters, for wasn't the state of his health the very reason for his coming to her at Prestidge? Wasn't it precisely at Prestidge that he was to be coddled, and wasn't the dear Princess coming to help her to coddle him? The dear Princess, now on a visit to England, was of a famous foreign house, and, in her gilded cage, with her retinue of keepers and feeders, was the most expensive specimen in the good lady's collection. I don't think her august presence had had to do with Paraday's consenting to go, but it's not impossible he had operated as a bait to the illustrious stranger. The party had been made up for him, Mrs Wimbush averred, and everyone was counting on it, the dear Princess most of all. If he was well enough he was to read them something absolutely fresh, and it was on that particular prospect the Princess had set her heart. She was so fond of genius in *any* walk of life, and was so used to it and understood it so well: she was the greatest of Mr Paraday's admirers, she devoured everything he wrote. And then he read like an angel. Mrs Wimbush reminded me that he had again and again given her, Mrs Wimbush, the privilege of listening to him.

I looked at her a moment. 'What has he read to you?' I crudely enquired.

For a moment too she met my eyes, and for the fraction of a moment she hesitated and coloured. 'Oh all sorts of things!'

I wondered if this were an imperfect recollection or only a perfect fib, and she quite understood my unuttered comment on her measure of such things. But if she could forget Neil Paraday's beauties she could of course forget my rudeness, and three days later she invited me, by telegraph, to join the party at Prestidge. This time she might indeed have had a story about what I had given up to be near the master. I addressed from that fine residence several communications to a young lady in London, a young lady whom, I confess, I quitted with reluctance and whom the reminder of what she herself could give up was required to make me quit at all. It adds to the gratitude I owe her on other grounds that she kindly allows me to transcribe from my letters a few of the passages in which that hateful sojourn is candidly commemorated.

# IX

'I SUPPOSE I ought to enjoy the joke of what's going on here,' I wrote, 'but somehow it doesn't amuse me. Pessimism on the contrary possesses me and cynicism deeply engages. I positively feel my own flesh sore from the brass nails in Neil Paraday's social harness. The house is full of people who like him, as they mention, awfully, and with whom his talent for talking nonsense has prodigious success. I delight in his nonsense myself; why is it therefore that I grudge these happy folk their artless satisfaction? Mystery of the human heart – abyss of the critical spirit! Mrs Wimbush thinks she can answer that question, and as my want of gaiety has at last worn out her patience she has given me a glimpse of her shrewd guess. I'm made restless by the selfishness of the insincere friend – I want to monopolise Paraday in order that he may push me on. To be intimate with him's a feather in my cap; it gives me an importance that I couldn't naturally pretend to, and I seek to deprive him of social refreshment because I fear that meeting more disinterested people may enlighten him as to my real motive. All the disinterested people here are his particular admirers and have been carefully selected as such. There's supposed to be a copy of his last book in the house, and in the hall I come upon ladies, in attitudes, bending gracefully over the first volume. I discreetly avert my eyes, and when I next look round the precarious joy has been superseded by the book of life. There's a sociable circle or a confidential couple, and the relinquished volume lies open on its face and as dropped under extreme coercion. Somebody else presently finds it and transfers it, with its air of momentary desolation, to another piece of furniture. Everyone's asking everyone about it all day, and everyone's telling everyone where they put it last. I'm sure it's rather smudgy about the twentieth page. I've a strong impression too that the second volume is lost – has been packed in the bag of some departing guest; and yet everybody has the impression that somebody else has read to the end. You see therefore that the beautiful book plays a great part in our existence. Why should I take the occasion of such distinguished honours to say that I begin to see deeper into Gustave Flaubert's doleful refrain about the hatred of literature? I refer you again to the perverse constitution of man.

'The Princess is a massive lady with the organisation of an athlete and the confusion of tongues of a *valet de place*. She contrives to commit herself extraordinarily little in a great many languages, and is entertained and conversed with in detachments and relays, like an institution which goes on from generation to generation or a big building contracted for under a forfeit. She can't have a personal taste any more than, when her husband succeeds, she can have a personal crown, and her opinion on any matter is rusty and heavy and plain – made, in the night of ages, to last and be transmitted. I feel as if I ought to 'tip' some *custode* for my glimpse of it. She has been told everything in the world and has never perceived anything, and the echoes of her education respond awfully to the rash footfall – I mean the casual remark – in the cold Valhalla of her memory. Mrs Wimbush delights in her wit and says there's nothing so charming as to hear Mr Paraday draw it out. He's perpetually detailed for this job, and he tells me it has a peculiarly exhausting effect. Everyone's beginning – at the end of two days – to sidle obsequiously away from her, and Mrs Wimbush pushes him again and again into the breach. None of the uses I have yet seen him put to infuriate me quite so much. He looks very fagged and has at last confessed to me that his condition makes him uneasy – has even promised me he'll go straight home instead of returning to his final engagements in town. Last night I had some talk with him about going today, cutting his visit short; so sure am I that he'll be better as soon as he's shut up in his lighthouse. He told me that this is what he would like to do; reminding me, however, that the first lesson of his greatness has been precisely that he can't do what he likes. Mrs Wimbush would never forgive him if he should leave her before the Princess has received the last hand. When I hint that a violent rupture with our hostess would be the best thing in the world for him he gives me to understand that if his reason assents to the proposition his courage hangs woefully back. He makes no secret of being mortally afraid of her, and when I ask what harm she can do him that she hasn't already done he simply repeats: 'I'm afraid, I'm afraid! Don't

enquire too closely,' he said last night: 'only believe that I feel
a sort of terror. It's strange, when she's so kind! At any rate,
I'd as soon overturn that piece of priceless Sèvres as tell her I
must go before my date.' It sounds dreadfully weak, but he has
some reason, and he pays for his imagination, which puts him
(I should hate it) in the place of others and makes him feel,
even against himself, their feelings, their appetites, their motives.
It's indeed inveterately against himself that he makes his
imagination act. What a pity he has such a lot of it! He's too
beastly intelligent. Besides, the famous reading's still to come
off, and it has been postponed a day to allow Guy Walsingham
to arrive. It appears this eminent lady's staying at a house a
few miles off, which means of course that Mrs Wimbush has
forcibly annexed her. She's to come over in a day or two –
Mrs Wimbush wants her to hear Mr Paraday.

'Today's wet and cold, and several of the company, at the
invitation of the Duke, have driven over to luncheon at Bigwood. I saw poor Paraday wedge himself, by command, into
the little supplementary seat of a brougham in which the
Princess and our hostess were already ensconced. If the front
glass isn't open on his dear old back perhaps he'll survive.
Bigwood, I believe, is very grand and frigid, all marble and
precedence, and I wish him well out of the adventure. I can't
tell you how much more and more *your* attitude to him, in the
midst of all this, shines out by contrast. I never willingly talk
to these people about him, but see what a comfort I find it to
scribble to you! I appreciate it – it keeps me warm; there are
no fires in the house. Mrs Wimbush goes by the calendar, the
temperature goes by the weather, the weather goes by God
knows what, and the Princess is easily heated. I've nothing but
my acrimony to warm me, and have been out under an
umbrella to restore my circulation. Coming in an hour ago I
found Lady Augusta Minch rummaging about the hall. When
I asked her what she was looking for she said she had mislaid
something that Mr Paraday had lent her. I ascertained in a
moment that the article in question is a manuscript, and I've a
foreboding that it's the noble morsel he read me six weeks ago.
When I expressed my surprise that he should have bandied
about anything so precious (I happen to know it's his only copy
– in the most beautiful hand in all the world) Lady Augusta

confessed to me that she hadn't had it from himself, but from Mrs Wimbush, who had wished to give her a glimpse of it as a salve for her not being able to stay and hear it read.

'"Is that the piece he's to read," I asked, "when Guy Walsingham arrives?"

'"It's not for Guy Walsingham they're waiting now, it's for Dora Forbes," Lady Augusta said. "She's coming, I believe, early tomorrow. Meanwhile Mrs Wimbush has found out about *him*, and is actively wiring to him. She says he also must hear him."

'"You bewilder me a little," I replied; "in the age we live in one gets lost among the genders and the pronouns. The clear thing is that Mrs Wimbush doesn't guard such a treasure so jealously as she might."

'"Poor dear, she has the Princess to guard! Mr Paraday lent her the manuscript to look over."

'"She spoke, you mean, as if it were the morning paper?"

'Lady Augusta stared – my irony was lost on her. "She didn't have time, so she gave me a chance first; because unfortunately I go tomorrow to Bigwood."

'"And your chance has only proved a chance to lose it?"

'"I haven't lost it. I remember now – it was very stupid of me to have forgotten. I told my maid to give it to Lord Dorimont – or at least to his man."

'"And Lord Dorimont went away directly after luncheon."

'"Of course he gave it back to my maid – or else his man did," said Lady Augusta. "I dare say it's all right."

'The conscience of these people is like a summer sea. They haven't time to "look over" a priceless composition; they've only time to kick it about the house. I suggested that the "man", fired with a noble emulation, had perhaps kept the work for his own perusal; and her ladyship wanted to know whether, if the thing shouldn't reappear for the grand occasion appointed by our hostess, the author wouldn't have something else to read that would do just as well. Their questions are too delightful! I declared to Lady Augusta briefly that nothing in the world can ever do so well as the thing that does best; and at this she looked a little disconcerted. But I added that if the manuscript had gone astray our little circle would have the less of an effort of attention to make. The piece in question was very long – it would keep them three hours.

'"Three hours! Oh the Princess will get up!" said Lady Augusta.

'"I thought she was Mr Paraday's greatest admirer."

'"I dare say she is – she's so awfully clever. But what's the use of being a Princess—"

'"If you can't dissemble your love?" I asked as Lady Augusta was vague. She said at any rate that she'd question her maid; and I'm hoping that when I go down to dinner I shall find the manuscript has been recovered.'

# X

'IT has *not* been recovered,' I wrote early the next day, 'and I'm moreover much troubled about our friend. He came back from Bigwood with a chill and, being allowed to have a fire in his room, lay down a while before dinner. I tried to send him to bed and indeed thought I had put him in the way of it; but after I had gone to dress Mrs Wimbush came up to see him, with the inevitable result that when I returned I found him under arms and flushed and feverish, though decorated with the rare flower she had brought him for his button-hole. He came down to dinner, but Lady Augusta Minch was very shy of him. Today he's in great pain, and the advent of *ces dames* – I mean of Guy Walsingham and Dora Forbes – doesn't at all console me. It does Mrs Wimbush, however, for she has consented to his remaining in bed so that he may be all right tomorrow for the listening circle. Guy Walsingham's already on the scene, and the doctor for Paraday also arrived early. I haven't yet seen the author of "Obsessions," but of course I've had a moment by myself with the Doctor. I tried to get him to say that our invalid must go straight home – I mean tomorrow or next day; but he quite refuses to talk about the future. Absolute quiet and warmth and the regular administration of an important remedy are the points he mainly insists on. He returns this afternoon, and I'm to go back to see the patient at one o'clock, when he next takes his medicine. It consoles me a little that he certainly won't be able to read – an exertion he was already more than unfit for. Lady Augusta went off after breakfast, assuring me her first care would be to follow up the lost manuscript. I can see she thinks me a shocking busybody and doesn't understand my alarm, but she'll do what she can, for she's a good-natured woman. "So are they all honourable men." That was precisely what made her give the thing to Lord Dorimont and made Lord Dorimont bag it. What use *he* has for it God only knows. I've the worst forebodings, but somehow I'm strangely without passion – desperately calm. As I consider the unconscious, the well-meaning ravages of our appreciative circle I bow my head in submission to some great natural, some universal accident; I'm rendered almost indifferent in fact quite gay (ha-ha!) by the sense of immitigable fate. Lady Augusta promises me to trace the precious object and let me have it through the post by the time Paraday's well enough to play his part with it. The last evidence is that her maid did give it to his lordship's valet. One would suppose it some thrilling number of *The Family Budget*. Mrs Wimbush, who's aware of the accident, is much less agitated by it than she would doubtless be were she not for the hour inevitably engrossed with Guy Walsingham.'

Later in the day I informed my correspondent, for whom indeed I kept a loose diary of the situation, that I had made the acquaintance of this celebrity and that she was a pretty little girl who wore her hair in what used to be called a crop. She looked so juvenile and so innocent that if, as Mr Morrow had announced, she was resigned to the larger latitude, her superiority to prejudice must have come to her early. I spent most of the day hovering about Neil Paraday's room, but it was communicated to me from below that Guy Walsingham, at Prestidge, was a success. Toward evening I became conscious somehow that her superiority was contagious, and by the time the company separated for the night I was sure the larger latitude had been generally accepted. I thought of Dora Forbes and felt that he had no time to lose. Before dinner I received a telegram from Lady Augusta Minch. 'Lord Dorimont thinks he must have left bundle in train – enquire.' How could I enquire – if I was to take the word as a command? I was too worried and now too alarmed about Neil Paraday. The Doctor came back, and it was an immense satisfaction to me to be sure he was wise and interested. He was proud of being called to so distinguished a patient, but he admitted to me that night that my friend was gravely ill. It was really a relapse, a recrudescence of his old malady. There could be no question of moving him: we must at any rate see first, on the spot, what turn his condition would take. Meanwhile, on the morrow, he was to have a nurse. On the morrow the dear man was easier, and my spirits rose to such cheerfulness that I could almost laugh over Lady Augusta's second telegram: 'Lord Dorimont's servant been to station – nothing found. Push enquiries.' I did laugh, I'm sure, as I remembered this to be the mystic scroll I had scarcely allowed poor Mr Morrow to point his umbrella at. Fool that

I had been: the thirty-seven influential journals wouldn't have destroyed it, they'd only have printed it. Of course I said nothing to Paraday.

When the nurse arrived she turned me out of the room, on which I went downstairs. I should premise that at breakfast the news that our brilliant friend was doing well excited universal complacency, and the Princess graciously remarked that he was only to be commiserated for missing the society of Miss Collop. Mrs Wimbush, whose social gift never shone brighter than in the dry decorum with which she accepted this fizzle in her fireworks, mentioned to me that Guy Walsingham had made a very favourable impression on her Imperial Highness. Indeed I think every one did so, and that, like the money-market or the national honour, her Imperial Highness was constitutionally sensitive. There was a certain gladness, a perceptible bustle in the air, however, which I thought slightly anomalous in a house where a great author lay critically ill. 'Le roy est mort – vive le roy': I was reminded that another great author had already stepped into his shoes. When I came down again after the nurse had taken possession I found a strange gentleman hanging about the hall and pacing to and fro by the closed door of the drawing-room. This personage was florid and bald; he had a big red moustache and wore showy knickerbockers – characteristics all that fitted to my conception of the identity of Dora Forbes. In a moment I saw what had happened: the author of 'The Other Way Round' had just alighted at the portals of Prestidge, but had suffered a scruple to restrain him from penetrating further. I recognised his scruple when, pausing to listen at his gesture of caution, I heard a shrill voice lifted in a sort of rhythmic uncanny chant. The famous reading had begun, only it was the author of 'Obsessions' who now furnished the sacrifice. The new visitor whispered to me that he judged something was going on he oughtn't to interrupt.

'Miss Collop arrived last night,' I smiled, 'and the Princess has a thirst for the *inédit*.'

Dora Forbes raised his bushy brows. 'Miss Collop?'

'Guy Walsingham, your distinguished confrère – or shall I say your formidable rival?'

'Oh!' growled Dora Forbes. Then he added: 'Shall I spoil it if I go in?'

'I should think nothing could spoil it!' I ambiguously laughed.

Dora Forbes evidently felt the dilemma; he gave an irritated crook to his moustache. '*Shall* I go in?' he presently asked.

We looked at each other hard a moment; then I expressed something bitter that was in me, expressed it in an infernal 'Do!' After this I got out into the air, but not so fast as not to hear, when the door of the drawing-room opened, the disconcerted drop of Miss Collop's public manner: she must have been in the midst of the larger latitude. Producing with extreme rapidity, Guy Walsingham has just published a work in which amiable people who are not initiated have been pained to see the genius of a sister-novelist held up to unmistakeable ridicule; so fresh an exhibition does it seem to them of the dreadful way men have always treated women. Dora Forbes, it's true, at the present hour, is immensely pushed by Mrs Wimbush and has sat for his portrait to the young artists she protects, sat for it not only in oils but in monumental alabaster.

What happened at Prestidge later in the day is of course contemporary history. If the interruption I had whimsically sanctioned was almost a scandal, what is to be said of that general scatter of the company which, under the Doctor's rule, began to take place in the evening? His rule was soothing to behold, small comfort as I was to have at the end. He decreed in the interest of his patient an absolutely soundless house and a consequent break-up of the party. Little country practitioner as he was, he literally packed off the Princess. She departed as promptly as if a revolution had broken out, and Guy Walsingham emigrated with her. I was kindly permitted to remain, and this was not denied even to Mrs Wimbush. The privilege was withheld indeed from Dora Forbes; so Mrs Wimbush kept her latest capture temporarily concealed. This was so little, however, her usual way of dealing with her eminent friends that a couple of days of it exhausted her patience and she went up to town with him in great publicity. The sudden turn for the worse her afflicted guest had, after a brief improvement, taken on the third night raised an obstacle to her seeing him before her retreat; a fortunate circumstance doubtless, for she was fundamentally disappointed in him. This was not the kind of performance for which she had invited him to Prestidge, let

alone invited the Princess. I must add that none of the generous
acts marking her patronage of intellectual and other merit have
done so much for her reputation as her lending Neil Paraday
the most beautiful of her numerous homes to die in. He took
advantage to the utmost of the singular favour. Day by day I
saw him sink, and I roamed alone about the empty terraces
and gardens. His wife never came near him, but I scarcely
noticed it: as I paced there with rage in my heart I was too
full of another wrong. In the event of his death it would fall
to me perhaps to bring out in some charming form, with notes,
with the tenderest editorial care, that precious heritage of his
written project. But where *was* that precious heritage, and
were both the author and the book to have been snatched
from us? Lady Augusta wrote me she had done all she could
and that poor Lord Dorimont, who had really been worried to
death, was extremely sorry. I couldn't have the matter out with
Mrs Wimbush, for I didn't want to be taunted by her with
desiring to aggrandise myself by a public connexion with Mr
Paraday's sweepings. She had signified her willingness to meet
the expense of all advertising, as indeed she was always ready
to do. The last night of the horrible series, the night before he
died, I put my ear closer to his pillow.

'That thing I read you that morning, you know.'

'In your garden that dreadful day? Yes!'

'Won't it do as it is?'

'It would have been a glorious book.'

'It *is* a glorious book,' Neil Paraday murmured. 'Print it as
it stands – beautifully.'

'Beautifully!' I passionately promised.

It may be imagined whether, now that he's gone, the promise
seems to me less sacred. I'm convinced that if such pages had
appeared in his lifetime the Abbey would hold him to-day. I've
kept the advertising in my own hands, but the manuscript has
not been recovered. It's impossible, and at any rate intolerable,
to suppose it can have been wantonly destroyed. Perhaps some
hazard of a blind hand, some brutal fatal ignorance has lighted
kitchen-fires with it. Every stupid and hideous accident haunts
my meditations. My undiscourageable search for the lost
treasure would make a long chapter. Fortunately I've a devoted
associate in the person of a young lady who has every day a

fresh indignation and a fresh idea, and who maintains with intensity that the prize will still turn up. Sometimes I believe her, but I've quite ceased to believe myself. The only thing for us at all events is to go on seeking and hoping together, and we should be closely united by this firm tie even were we not at present by another.

# NOTES

(The references are to page and line numbers)

### PREFACES

xxvii. 18. *It was in Florence years ago*: 12 January 1887 is the date of James's Notebook entry for the anecdote he heard from Eugene Lee-Hamilton about Captain Silsbee, 'the Boston art-critic and Shelley-worshipper' (*The Complete Notebooks of Henry James*, see 'Further Reading').

xxx. 2. *In her habit as she lived*: a wittily evocative echo of Hamlet's last words before the disappearance of his father's Ghost – 'My father, in his habit as he lived!' (*Hamlet*, III, iv. 135).

xxxiii. 30. *the general question . . . can't but come up for us again*: it does come up again and is eloquently answered in the Preface that deals with 'The Death of the Lion', where James reproduces 'the whole passion' of his retort to the criticism that the writers his stories imagine (the 'supersubtle fry') have no basis in fact. See pp. xi–xli here.

xxxv. 32. *I proceed*: James has been discussing the tales which precede 'The Private Life' in vol. XVII of the New York Edition, 'The Altar of the Dead', 'The Beast in the Jungle' and 'The Birthplace'.

xxxvi. 13. *A highly distinguished man*: Robert Browning.

xxxvi. 31. *no 'sensitive poor gentleman' he!*: a reference to the central characters of the three preceding tales discussed in this Preface: George Stransom )'The Altar of the Dead'), John Marcher ('The Beast in the Jungle') and Morris Gedge ('The Birthplace'). All are 'sensitive poor gentlemen'.

xxxvii. 30. *that most accomplished of artists*: Frederick, in due course Lord, Leighton (1833–1905), most fashionably successful of Victorian painters. See Adeline Tintner, 'Lord Leighton and His Paintings in "The Private Life"' ('Further Reading').

xxxviii. 10. *the interlunar swoon*: 'interlunar' cannot but recall its most famous precedent in English literature from Samson's great speech in Milton's *Samson Agonistes* – as usual in James, the allusion is glancingly pointed:

> The sun to me is dark
> And silent as the moon,
> When she deserts the night
> Hid in her vacant interlunar cave.

xxxviii. 26. *What I had lately . . .* to say: at the end of the Preface to vol. XV of the New York Edition, James had written of 'The Coxon Fund' that 'it takes its place for me in a series of which the main merit and sign is the effort to do the complicated thing with a strong brevity and lucidity – to arrive, on behalf of the multiplicity, at a certain science of control.'

xxxviii. 33. *some 5550*: this is, curiously, not the case: the count is closer to 7,500 words.

xxxviii. 34. *the exception I shall presently name*: 'The Tree of Knowledge'.

xxxviii. 37. *Some warden of the insane . . . making fast a victim's straitjacket*: the astonishing image is typical of the blend of the sportive and the anguished with which James dramatizes his tussles with the demands of short fiction. The distinction he employs between the more extended *nouvelle* and the more concise 'anecdote' is, as he admits, no simple matter. See Krishna Baldev Vaid, *Technique in the Tales of Henry James* ('Further Reading').

xl. 12. *These pieces*: namely, 'The Death of the Lion', 'The Coxon Fund' and 'The Next Time'. These were the 'three bantlings held by Harland at the baptismal font' – or, in common parlance, published by Henry Harland in *The Yellow Book*.

xli. 5. *I have already mentioned the particular rebuke*: in the Preface to 'The Aspern Papers'; see note to p. xxxiii. 30.


## THE ASPERN PAPERS

1. 4. *She . . . loosed the Gordian knot*: it is true that there is Shakesperian authority for trying to 'unloose' the Gordian knot (*Henry V*. I. i. 46), but the point about Alexander the Great's solution was that he didn't try to loosen it or untie it but severed it with his sword. In 1888 Mrs Prest boldly 'severed' the Gordian knot, but in 1908 she more subtly 'unlooses it'; this is perhaps a less trenchant 'short cut'. The narrator is no Alexander, but might he turn out to be a Napoleon? Leon Edel notes that Aspern in Austria was the scene of Napoleon's first crushing defeat.

2. 21. *a dying fall*: this allusion to the famous opening lines of *Twelfth Night* ('If music be the food of love, play on,') is a haunting revision of the earlier, more prosaic 'a faint reverberation' of 1888. It is balanced by another revision near the end of the tale which alludes to Shakespeare's *other* best-known lines about music from *The Merchant of Venice*. see note to p. 95. It is possible that given the Shelleyan provenance of the tale, the 'dying fall' may here be recalling the Shelley lyric which recalls and in a sense answers the Shakespeare lines. They are very pertinently concerned with memory.

> Music, When soft voices die,
> Vibrates in the memory —
> Odours, when sweet violets sicken,
> Live within the sense they quicken.

3. 2. *Mrs Siddons . . . Queen Caroline . . . Lady Hamilton*: three female celebrities collectively signifying 'the Byronic age'.

6. 5. *quartier perdu*: an elegant way of saying the district is 'out of the way'.

6. 22. *felze*: 'the cabin of a gondola'. It is a matter of small but distinct interest – it would certainly have interested James – that in our own century these *felze* have disappeared. Gondolas can no longer afford the luxury of such privacy; tourists have nothing to hide and they require maximum visibility. One may note that the narrator does not always feel so safe and sound in his *felze* but that he can imagine the gondolier behind him observing his red ears (p. 91. 20).

8. 11. *nom de guerre*: 'pseudonym' – literally, 'war-name'; a witty revision for the plainer 'a name that was not my own' (1888). He conspicuously forgets to tell the reader both his false and true name.

9. 3. *scagliola*: a kind of highly ornamented plaster-work.

14. 7. *louche*: 'suspicious', 'shady'.

15. 3. *a horrible green shade*: Leon Edel has suggested that the portrait of Juliana Bordereau owes something to James's great-aunt Wyckoff who sported just such a green shade. Others have pointed out the unnervingly jocular materialisation of a part of Marvell's famous phrase from his poem 'The Garden' – 'a green thought in a green shade'. This sounds fanciful, but the garden is a prominent feature of the tale, and Juliana is something of a Marvell name; she causes his Mower a lot of distress in a number of poems, including one in which *he* tries to find some shade from the 'scorching beams' of her eyes. Privacy and its violation are as important topics in Marvell as they are in this story, and a reader might well be tempted by the ghostly chuckle of these half-heard echoes. But if one is listening out for ghosts, one might also entertain Byron's Donna Julia, and Shakespeare's Juliet is explicitly referred to. One might even remotely hear a compound of the other Juliet in *Measure for Measure* with Marianna, that reaches out to Tennyson's Mariana and her 'lonely moated grange' – and in 'Mariana in the South' she has 'Old letters, breathing of her worth'. And so on. The lady is certainly literary.

19. 37. *her wasted antiquity*: in his *Autobiography* James describes his great-aunt Wyckoff (see previous note) as 'an image of living antiquity . . . that I was never to see surpassed'; he wrote further – 'It was the Past that one touched in her, the American past of a preponderant unthinkable queerness . . .'.

21. 7. *forestieri*: 'foreigners', 'strangers'.

32. 12. *contadina and pifferaro*: 'peasant-girl' and (literally) 'pipe-player', a sort of 'busker', as we would now say.

32. 23. *When Americans went abroad*: the 'sentimental interest' which the narrator displays in this passage is one to which James often gave eloquent voice in his own person. See for example the opening chapter of

*William Wetmore Story and His Friends* (1903), where James writes of the honour and gratitude due to an earlier generation of passionate American pilgrims to Europe, 'the light skirmishers, the *éclaireurs*': 'Europe, for Americans, has in a word, been *made* easy; . . .'

39. 19. *passeggio*: 'outing'.

39. 24. *Bombicci . . . Altemura*: with their whimsically pertinent suggestions of bombs and high walls these extravagant names might appear ominous to a more suspicious ear than Miss Tina seems to possess.

39. 33. *avvocato*: 'lawyer'; his name announces that he has 'little in the head'.

39. 35. *capo d'anno*; 'new year'.

40. 22. *Goldoni and Casanova*: famous comic dramatist and reminiscing amorist, both associated with eighteenth-century Venice. 'Goldoni', however, is an addition in 1908, perhaps anticipating the important passage near the end of the tale when the narrator is wandering round Venice and sees the place as a theatre with 'members of an endless dramatic troupe' (p. 94).

46. 19. *Sardanapalus*: this allusion is, like several others, a 1908 addition. 'The Death of Sardanapalus' is the subject of a famous painting by Delacroix, but it is more likely that James has in mind a literary allusion to the climax of Byron's play *Sardanapalus* (1821), at which the Assyrian King announces to his ancestors that he will not leave the palace 'To the defilement of usurping bondmen'. He assures them that – 'Your treasure, your abode, your sacred relics / Of arms and records, monuments, and spoils' will go up in smoke along with him and his favourite Greek slave.

47. 22. *I think of great captains*: perhaps he has in mind the Cromwell of Marvell's 'Horatian Ode'.

51. 23. *giro*: 'tour' 'round trip'.

59. 21. *combinare*: 'fix something up'.

60. 11. *a rough way of treading it down*: perhaps a faint echo of Keats's 'No hungry generations tread thee down' in the 'Ode to a Nightingale'.

61. 26. *parti*: 'a match'.

62. 26. *a small oval portrait*: there is a little fable by Edgar Allan Poe entitled 'The Oval Portrait', and Poe has been claimed as a vaguely supportive 'source' for Jeffrey Aspern, the nearest thing to an American Shelley/ Byron. It is scarcely worth pressing a specific allusion here to Poe's tale, but one may note that it figures a number of elements (an abandoned 'Romantic' chateau, a female figure preserved and entombed by the life-in-death of art, an equivocally intrusive and inquisitive male figure who is the reader's representative) that associate it with the diffused set of literary models which James's tale ironically invokes. Tony Tanner suggests that Walt Whitman may have been in James's mind (*Venice Desired*, see 'Further Reading').

78. 26. *the super-subtle inference*: 'super-subtle' in Venice is bound to

recall Iago's 'super-subtle Venetian' (*Othello*, I. iii. 356); the narrator's kinship is of course with the man who coins the phrase rather than with the woman to whom he tries to apply it. It is another 'literary' revision in the 1908 text.

81. 19. *quella vecchia*: 'the old woman' – but with a slightly more disparaging emphasis than the simpler '*la vecchia*' of 1888.

81. 27. *roba da niente – un piccolo passeggio brutto*: 'poor stuff – a rotten little show'; a good deal stronger than the earlier version: 'it was a dull little passeggio'.

84. 6. *the Giorgione at Castelfranco*: the altarpiece Madonna and Child of Giorgione (?1478–1510) in the church of S. Liberale in the town of his birth.

91. 12. *Dove commanda*: 'where to?'

91. 16. *my hat pulled over my brow*: James's revision of 'brow' for the earlier 'face' brings into play an echo of Malcolm's exhortation to Macduff at the news of his family's murder: 'What, man, ne'er pull your hat upon your brows; / Give sorrow words.' (*Macbeth*, IV. iii. 208–9).

91. 21. *tenda*: 'curtain', over the entrance to the *felze* (see note to p. 6).

93. 14. *the triumphant captain*: James's reference to works of art is invariably cunning. Bartolommeo Colleoni (1400–76) was one of the most famous and ruthless of Italian Renaissance mercenaries, and his lucrative violence is commemorated in Verrocchio's bronze statue in Venice. It is probably to the narrator's credit that he fails to find instruction from this 'triumphant captain' whose emblem was a pair of *coglioni* (testicles). Marcus Aurelius, Stoic Roman Emperor and author of the *Meditations*, would surely have been a better bet for an 'oracle'. But one should note that, although the narrator now finds himself able to invoke the figure of this probably more auspicious mentor, he does so not to seek instruction, but rather to impress the reader with his capacity for nice aesthetic judgements. This is one of those important moments in the tale when the narrator makes a distinction between the 'now' of writing and the 'then' of experience. But the reader will look in vain for any admission that he has learned from his experience; indeed his manner is that of a man who would be suprised by any suggestion that he *ought* to have done so.

94. 8. *fondamentas*: 'quays'.

95. 9. *stratagems and spoils*: a 1908 revision replacing 'my literary concupiscence' and alluding to the wonderful passage about music in *The Merchant of Venice* (v. i. 83–8). The lines are painfully pertinent – though whether the narrator is conscious of this and thereby obliquely passing a judgement on himself, it is impossible to say. (Compare note to p. 2).

> The man that hath not music in himself,
> Nor is not moved with concord of sweet sounds,
> Is fit for treasons, stratagems, and spoils;
> The motions of his spirit are dull as night,

And his affections dark as Erebus:
Let no such man be trusted.

For Philip Horne's argument that it *is* possible to say, see *James and Revision* ('Further Reading').


### THE PRIVATE LIFE

99. 17. *the fleur des pois*: 'pink of fashion', 'best society'.

107. 1. *a finer grain*: a favoured phrase of James's – *The Finer Grain* is the title of the last collection of tales published in his lifetime in 1910.

108. 6. *a high régal*: 'treat'.

109. 2. *débit*: 'a good delivery'.

114. [*chapter opening*]: the 1893 text is not divided in two in this way. But there is a slight oddity in the New York Edition, in that while the second part of the tale is here announced by a 'II' there is no corresponding 'I' to precede it at the start. (This 'error' is rectified in the 1922 Macmillan text.) There is a very remote possibility that this is a weird typographical joke mirroring the tale's concern with ones and twos. Compare the much more plausible joke in the 'I' which heads 'The Middle Years' – to which there is no subsequent 'II' (see note to p. 135 below).

116. 5. *Où voulez-vous en venir?*: 'What are you driving at?' The use of italics for foreign words and phrases is slightly inconsistent in the New York Edition.

130. 17. *Manfred*: the hero of Byron's stormy and Alpine dramatic poem, *Manfred* (1817).


### THE MIDDLE YEARS

135. [*chapter-opening*]: there is no Part II to 'The Middle Years', yet both the 1895 and 1909 texts are headed by a 'I' (the 1893 magazine version is not, however). Robert L. Gale suggests that this is a witty allusion to the writer's discovery within the story that 'There never was to be but one' – that there is for him no second chance (*Explicator*, 22 (Nov. 1962), Item 22). Compare note to 'The Private Life', p. 114.

135. 14. *the Island*: the Isle of Wight.

135. 18. *The infinite of life was gone*: there is a faint late-Shakespearean ring to a number of phrases in the tale, perhaps assisted by the associations of the cliff and the sea. Here, for instance, one might hear a diffused echo of *Antony and Cleopatra*'s 'the nobleness of life', 'nature's infinite book', 'infinite variety', and 'The crown o' th' earth'. But the likeness seems as much to do with rhythm as diction. Compare: 'The infinite of life was gone, and what remained of the dose . . .', and some of Cleopatra's words at Antony's death: 'the odds is gone, / And there is nothing left remarkable / Beneath the visiting moon' (IV. xiv. 66–8). A few pages later there is a

similarly fugitive kinship between 'leaving scarce a superstition behind' and *The Tempest*'s 'leave not a rack behind'. Dencombe shares with Prospero 'the sense of ebbing time', and although the phrase is James's it could, as it were, be Shakespeare's. *The Tempest* contains Shakespeare's only two uses of 'ebbing'.

137. 6. *the very odour of sanctity*: a witty appropriation of the phrase denoting the sweet odour supposedly exhaled by the bodies of saints at their death.

138. 15. *diligence vincit omnia*: James twists another well-known phrase, for it is not usually 'diligence' that is supposed to conquer everything but 'love', The phrase *Omnia vincit amor* comes from Virgil, *Eclogues*, x. 69.

## THE DEATH OF THE LION

161. 34. *the revealing and reverberating sketch*: *The Reverberator* in the short satirical novel of the same name (1888) is the newspaper which employs the outrageous journalist, George Flack.

163. 36. *passe encore*: 'well and good'.

191. 30. *So are they all honourable men*: this line from Antony's funeral speech in *Julius Caesar* (III. ii. 83) suggests that the narrator is trying to dignify his role in the whole affair by identifying himself with Antony's righteous indignation – and moral opportunism.

193. 35. *the inédit*: 'unpublished work' and, figuratively, 'novelty'.

See Philip Horne's illuminating study, *Henry James and Revision* ('Further Reading'), which includes a chapter on *The Aspern Papers*.

# VARIANT READINGS

THE following pages offer a brief analysis and a select list of the most significant changes between the texts first published in book form and the texts of the New York Edition. See Philip Horne's illuminating study, *Henry James and Revision* ('Further Reading'), which includes a chapter on *The Aspern Papers*.

## I. THE ASPERN PAPERS

Like the writer Dencombe in 'The Middle Years', James was 'a passionate corrector, a fingerer of style', and a close comparison of the 1888 text with the revised New York Edition text of 1908 makes an absorbing study. One notable change involves the alteration of a single letter, of 'Miss Tita' to 'Miss Tina'. Not every reader will be as confident as William Bysshe Stein that her name suggests that 'she is a feminine Christ'. The more obvious effect of a change from 'Tita' to 'Tina' is to shrink and feminise her name ('Tita' sounds comparatively statuesque, even imperial), and it allows the narrator the chance of a more pointedly demeaning gibe about the incongruity between name and person. She is not 'tiny' at all, but as he revealingly calls her a 'high tremulous spinster'. Indeed many of the most delicate and intricate revisions are concerned with the narrator's apprehension of Miss Tina. He is much more wary of her in 1908, more prompt to intercept the feelings she might arouse in him. He is made to seem more threatened both by Juliana (who looks at him with 'great attention' in 1888 and with 'great penetration' in 1908) and by Miss Tina (who in 1888 in the penultimate proposal scene between them merely 'faces' him, but in 1908 is 'up at' him). But if he is generally more apprehensive, he is also more resolute or more candid about his resolutions and he watches himself with no less vigilance than he does others. His more subtly troubled intelligence is reflected in the closing sentence which in revision makes him recognise that his 'loss' might be thought to consist of more than 'the precious papers'. The earlier text reads: 'my chagrin at the loss of the letters becomes almost intolerable.' The later: 'I can scarcely bear my loss – I mean of the precious papers.' The general trend of the revisions, in short, is towards a more nuanced and more vivid drama of a teller and his tale.

This list is a selection of the most interesting changes.

| Page | New York Edition (1908) | First edition (1888) |
|---|---|---|
| 2. 26 | I saw how my eagerness amused her and that she found my interest in my possible spoil a fine case of monomania. | I could see that she was amused by my infatuation, the way my interest in the papers had become a fixed idea. |
| 4. 9 | 'Orpheus and the Mænads!' had been of course my foreseen judgement | 'Orpheus and the Mænads!' was the exclamation that rose to my lips |
| 5. 9 | our promulgations | our publishings |
| 6. 33 | I might get what I wanted | I might obtain the documents |
| 6. 38 | her relics and tokens | the documents |
| 7. 2 | my spoils | the papers |
| 7. 5 | there's no baseness I wouldn't commit for Jeffrey Aspern's sake. | for Jeffrey Aspern's sake I would do worse still. |
| 9. 17 | with my resolve to be genial from the threshold at any price | I was so determined to be genial |
| 9. 29 | I felt my foot in the citadel and promised myself ever so firmly to keep it there. | I felt that I had a foot in the citadel. |
| 11. 6 | a wan vague smile | a shy, melancholy smile |
| 11. 13 | I went on with as sociable a smile as I could risk. | I went on, smiling. |
| 11. 16 | letting her weak wonder deal – helplessly enough, as I felt – with my strangeness. | letting her embarrassed eyes wander all over my strangeness. |
| 11. 36 | a small quaver of sound | a queer little sigh |
| 11. 38 | she gasped | she observed |
| 12. 9 | so lost in her blankness and gentleness | so lost in staring at me |
| 12. 25 | I feel again my thrill at this close identification of Juliana; in spite of which, however, I kept my head. 'Only one other…!' | 'Only one other…!' |
| 12. 29 | almost as for the rich unwonted joy to her of spoken words. | in the same dazed way. |
| 13. 13 | rather pleasingly incalculable and interesting. | an odd and affecting person. |
| 15. 14 | I could pounce on her possessions and ransack her drawers. | I could seize her papers. |

20. 29 she struck me as more deeply futile, because her inefficiency was inward

she struck me as still more helpless, because her inefficiency was spiritual

25. 33 with a promptitude that prevented my seeing her aunt.

so that I did not see her aunt.

27. 40 the sense of playing with my opportunity was much greater after all than any sense of being played with.

the sense of holding my opportunity was much greater than the sense of losing it.

30. 7 I possessed my soul

So I composed myself

33. 7 what I had prized him for

what I had loved him for

35. 40 I escaped this ordeal

she did nothing of the kind

36. 23 I felt it make for irritation.

I was considerably irritated.

38. 24 she pronounced poor Miss Tina 'a worry, a bore and a source of aggravation'.

she said her niece irritated her, made her nervous.

38. 29 This sad personage

Miss Tita

41. 24 a perfectly artless and a considerably witless woman.

a completely innocent woman.

42. 34 'She said he was a god.'... their sound might have been the light rustle of an old unfolded love-letter.

'She said he was a god.'... it seemed such a direct testimony.

47. 30 it was so I first heard the strange sound of her laugh, which was as if the faint 'walking' ghost of her old-time tone had suddenly cut a caper.

it was the first time I had heard her laugh.

50. 11 you've never seen an agreeable woman. What do you people know about good society?' she cried; but before I could tell her,

you have never seen an agreeable woman.

53. 19 She didn't speak, sunk in the sense of opportunities, for ever lost,

She became silent, as if she were thinking with a secret sadness of opportunities, for ever lost,

56. 19 this frail creature

that faithful domestic

59. 24 as from the mouth of her cave.

in her barricaded way.

62. 27 with fingers of which I could only hope that they didn't betray the intensity of their clutch,

with a hand of which I could only hope that she did not perceive the tremor,

68. 33 I fear that in my heart

I grant that in my heart

70. 5 an appetite well-nigh indecent

a preoccupation that was almost profane

75. 3 I grinned, I fear, to admit.

I conceded, smiling.

| | | |
|---|---|---|
| 76. 8 | she seemed to bethink herself of some propriety of showing me more rigour. | she appeared to become aware of the necessity of being a little more rigid. |
| 77. 37 | at the hour of freedom and safety, nearer to the source of my hopes | at the hour of temptation and secrecy, nearer to the tormenting treasure |
| 79. 1 | They glared at me; they were like the sudden drench, for a caught burglar, of a flood of gaslight; they made me horribly ashamed. | They glared at me, they made me horribly ashamed. |
| 80. 14 | I had had to gulp down a bitter draught and couldn't get rid of the taste. | there was too strong a taste of the disagreeable in my life. |
| 80. 19 | My humiliation galled me, but I had to make the best of it, had, in writing to Miss Tina, to minimise it, as well as account for the posture in which I had been discovered. | In writing to Miss Tita I attempted to minimise these irregularities; |
| 82. 24 | she had none of the airs or graces of grief, | she had none of the formalism or the self-consciousness of grief, |
| 82. 36 | this poor lady's dull face ceased to be dull, almost ceased to be plain, as she turned it gladly to her late aunt's lodger. | Tita Bordereau's countenance expressed unqualified pleasure in seeing her late aunt's lodger. |
| 85. 19 | it turned to comfort for me that I hadn't played even to that mild extent on her sensibility. | it became a satisfaction to me that I had not indulged in that rather tender joke. |
| 88. 20 | only lost in the queerness of her case. | full of her dolefulness. |
| 95. 14 | This trick of her expression, this magic of her spirit, transfigured her, | This optical trick gave her a sort of phantasmagoric brightness, |
| 95. 40 | 'Destroyed them?' I wailed. | 'Destroyed them?' I faltered. |
| 96. 23 | When I look at it I can scarcely bear my loss – I mean of the precious papers. | When I look at it, my chagrin at the loss of the letters becomes almost intolerable. |

## II.   THE PRIVATE LIFE

One of the most important kinds of revision in this tale is to do with Blanche Adney and the narrator's relationship with her. Instead of 'the actress' and 'Mrs Adney' she becomes 'Blanche' and 'my friend', and their relationship is made generally more intimate and flirtatious. This strengthening of their alliance heightens the effect of her 'betrayal' when she pairs off with the 'real' Vawdrey and leaves the narrator morosely attached to the public deputy. Perhaps the single most striking adjustment to our view of the narrator and his neediness occurs near the end when he is closeted with the 'public' Vawdrey in the hillside cabin. 'I suppose I wanted him to make an exception for *me*' – and then James adds the following words in the later revised version, which suddenly extend our sense of his longing for admission to a real intimacy – 'for me all alone, and all handsomely and tenderly, in the vast horde of the dull.' It is also noticeable that James takes some pains in revision to characterise more closely the quality of Lord Mellifont's disappearing trick.

| Page | New York Edition (1909) | First edition (1983) |
|---|---|---|
| 99. 30 | chalk-marked for recognition by signs from the same alphabet. | we participated in the same miscellaneous publicity. |
| 101. 21 | I used to wail to myself over | I used to feel a despair at |
| 103. 2 | with loosened hair and the gait of a wood-nymph, | with loosened hair, |
| 106. 36 | made her melancholy more arch than her mirth. | made her sadness even sweeter than her laughter. |
| 113. 3 | I took in at every pore his identity. | I was conscious that I was in no sort of error about his identity. |
| 116. 9 | her eyes had a sheen | her eyes had an expression |
| 117. 12 | I could have hugged her – and perhaps I did. 'That's what makes you such a comfort to talk to...' | 'That's what makes you such a comfort to talk to...' |
| 118. 25 | 'That's what makes *you* a comfort.' She didn't, alas, hug me, but she promptly went on. 'Did you ever...' | 'That's what makes *you* a comfort. Did you ever...' |
| 118. 32 | She glared at me | Blanche Adney glanced at me |
| 120. 19 | but how utter a blank mustn't it take to repair such a plenitude of presence! – how intense an *entr'acte* to make possible more such performances! | but what form of rest could repair such a plenitude of presence? |
| 120. 32 | his remarkable tact never more remarkable, his one conceivable *raison d'être*, the | his remarkable tact had never been more remarkable. |

absolute singleness of his
identity, never more attested.

122. 22   a pretty one, a lucky one like      marriage is ruinous.
      ours, is ruinous.

122. 39   velvet gorge                    grassy valley

124. 30   Ah Blanche had quite      'Oh, it's a fine shade...'
      mastered it! 'It's a fine
      shade...'

125. 13   'He was too absent, too      'He was too utterly
      utterly gone, as gone as a      gone,...'
      candle blown out;...'

126. 34   ... till Lord Mellifont's sketch     ...till Lord Mellifont's
      should be finished. All nature    sketch should be finished.
      deferred to him and the very
      elements waited.

130. 10   we could see the show, watch    we could watch the splendid
      the grand rage of nature.       spectacle of the tempest.

130. 35   I suppose I wanted him to     I suppose I wanted him to
      make an exception for *me*      make an exception for *me*.
      — for me all alone, and all hand-
      somely and tenderly, in the
      vast horde of the dull.

131. 37   I quite wailed.                I exclaimed ruefully.

## III.   THE MIDDLE YEARS

The revisions to this tale are relatively light, and the most notable
consist of slight adjustments to Dencombe's reactions and responses.
After his fainting-attack on the cliff, for instance, he is characterised
as a good deal more resigned; instead of being 'disappointed,
disgusted', he becomes more temperately 'rueful and sore'. There
is a striking recurrence in the way James makes Dencombe in the
revision 'wail' near the end of the story. In the revisions of both
'The Aspern Papers' and 'The Private Life' the narrators are
similarly made to 'wail' near the end, at a moment of forfeiture.
It is a strangely unplaceable sound, hovering between grievous
pain and histrionic pathos. In this story, however, unlike the
other two, the 'wailer' is not the man who has had to renounce
a prospect but his sympathetic auditor. Doctor Hugh seems quite
cheerful in the face of the Countess's curse.

Page    *New York Edition* (1909)      *First edition* (1895)

135. 8    he was thankful now for the    now he was reconciled to
      commonest conveniences.       the prosaic.

135. 12   a bench he had already      a convenient bench that he
      haunted                     knew of

137. 39   He dived once more         He lived once more

| | | |
|---|---|---|
| 138. 19 | the process had been painful enough. | the process had been manful enough. |
| 140. 25 | a gage of earnest return | a sign that he would return |
| 142. 34 | Dencombe ... rejoiced more inwardly than ever | Dencombe . . . felicitated himself more than ever |
| 144. 33 | he was rueful and sore. | he was disappointed, disgusted. |
| 146. 4 | Dencombe felt his own face pressing. | Dencombe looked at him with a calculating earnestness. |
| 148. 30 | to find a richer sense between its covers. | to find a deeper meaning in its pages. |
| 148. 34 | the diffused massive weight that could be thrown into the missing of an intention. | the fine, full way with which an intention could be missed. |
| 149. 33 | a wondrous explanatory hour. | a wonderful explanatory hour. |
| 150. 16 | our poor friend | Dencombe |
| 151. 22 | his racked nerves | his humming nerves |
| 152. 22 | two dismal days | two atrocious days |
| 153. 27 | 'Cursed you?' Dencombe wailed. | 'Cursed you?' Dencombe murmured. |

## IV.   THE DEATH OF THE LION

The revisions to this tale are not extensive; the most important trends are towards a broadening of the comedy, particularly surrounding Mr Morrow in chapter IV, and a coarsening of Fanny Hurter's role, particularly in the pivotal chapter VII. The narrator is made both slightly more self-important and slightly more conscious of his own ineffectuality in the face of 'society's' impervious boorishness.

| Page | New York Edition (1909) | First edition (1895) |
|---|---|---|
| 160. 21 | the rude motions of the jig were set to music. | the dance was set to music. |
| 161. 10 | trying to fob off on him such stuff. | sending him such stuff. |
| 162. 2 | my great man | Neil Paraday |
| 167. 24 | a mere pseudonym – rather pretty, isn't it? – and convenient, | a mere pseudonym; but convenient, |
| 168. 18 | a more fatherly pat. | a more motherly pat. |
| 168. 39 | in his acting on that idea – which is clever, isn't it? – | in this assumption |
| 176. 17 | I could only disclose my dread of it. 'Most people apply . . .' | 'Most people apply . . .' |

| | | |
|---|---|---|
| 177. 5 | if it will make me more seduc- tive | if it will make me more appealing |
| 178. 17 | no author about whom I'm in such a state as I'm in about | no author about whom I feel as I do about |
| 178. 32 | I wailed | I exclaimed |
| 179. 27 | she despairingly breathed. | she softly wailed. |
| 179. 34 | – she suppressed a shriek for it. | she pathetically gasped. |
| 181. 20 | 'Read him, read him – *that* will be an education in decency,' | 'Read him, read him,' |
| 181. 21 | seeking him in his works even as God in nature, | seeking him in his works, |
| 184. 18 | his the impressions and the harvest. | his the impressions and the anecdotes. |
| 187. 24 | infuriate me | irritate me |
| 189. 37 | she looked a little dis- concerted. | she looked a little confused and scared. |